God's Trailblazer of Contextual Theology

First Published in 2020 by

Christian World Imprints
Christian Publishing & Books from India
C-3, Wazirpur Industrial Area, **Delhi-110052**
cwidelhi2017@gmail.com
www.ChristianWorldImprints.com
Phone: +91 11 41526079

ISBN: 978-93-5148-424-0 (HB)
ISBN: 978-93-5148-425-7 (PB)

Printed in India.

Samanvayam *Contextual Theology Series - 9*

God's Trailblazer of Contextual Theology

Fr. Louis Malieckal CMI

Editor:
Cyril Kuttiyanikkal

Christian World Imprints

Contents

Introduction

Fr. Louis Malieckal CMI has broken new ground in Indian contextual theological thinking, especially in the contextual theological formation. His life unravels the story of a theological and experiential search, responding dynamically to the challenge of a constant dialogue with the religions and cultures of India. When Indian church was dominated by the western attitudes and modes of thought, Fr. Louis found ways to express the Christian faith in authentically Indian ways and categories. He was able to lead a life of *samanvayam*, i.e., integration of the best of East and West, of Hindu and Christian, of vison and life and of *bhakti, jnana* and *karma*.

It is said that a man is not dead while his name is still spoken. Fr. Louis Malieckal's name is spoken of frequently, since he has walked into the lives of many people and left his footprints deep and long. His life, legacy and contributions to Indian theology, particularly to contextual theology has made him shine like a morning star. He was a pioneer in the process of inspiring and initiating others to contextual theological thinking. The legacy and pioneering contributions of his creative mind will continue to inspire generations to come.

He was a hard worker who was willing to take up any challenge. Even in his retired life, he was passionately engaged in academic activities. He was engaged in writing articles and giving courses. Never had you to remind him about the deadline for completing any academic work. He was well ahead in submitting them. He had often pointed out the dictum from Bhagavad Gita, *karmanye vaadikaraste, ma phaleshu kadanchana,* i.e., you are entitled to doing work, but never to its fruits. Although, his unpublished articles were ready for publication in a book in January 2019 (and eventually published in March 2019), he had already written two more before he breathed his last in February 2019. We have included them in this book.

The present volume is a humble effort to keep burning the fire of the zeal lit by Fr. Louis. This book has been envisaged in five parts. All the articles in this commemorative volume is written by people who are closely associated with Fr. Louis. Although, there are many who wanted to pen down their appreciation and affection, we have selected only a few as we could not reach others in time.

Part one of this book is dedicated mostly to the tributes and messages from the animators of the CMI congregation, Archdiocese of Bhopal and his family members. We also present here his life story and his contributions in brief. His younger brother Francis fondly narrates his childhood memories and the early life of Fr. Louis, while his niece Annie gives a brief note on his paternal and maternal love. Besides the narratives by the family members and messages from his superiors, we have included in this part the account of his seminary life by Fr. Paul Kalluveettil and his life and contributions by Cyril Kuttiyanikkal.

Part two gathers together the relevance and importance of his contributions in the field of contextualization and inculturation particularly in liturgy and theology. This part gives some insiders' view of the great efforts Fr. Louis undertook to implement the vision of the Second Vatican Council. All the three articles in this section take us to travels, efforts, trails, enthusiasm, achievements, disappointments and success of the pioneering efforts for the realization of an Indian church especially an Indian Liturgy. His co-workers recall the fond memories of the past when they travelled with him through the untrodden paths. With Fr. Louis as mentor, leader and colleague they ventured into the unchartered territory. Dr. Augustine recollects their journey in the early 1970s through various ashrams of India in their efforts to compose an Indian Eucharist. In their travel as 'Vallbhan', he was their guide and guru. Dr. Augustine qualifies Father Malieckal as *Paramahamsa*, which is the highest form of Indian *sannyasa*. Similarly according to Dr. Augustine, Fr. Louis lived and moved in the world; but stood above all mundane things; he used the things of this earth, but was able to discern things and accept only the things that are meaningful, useful and beneficial to his spiritual growth. Dr. Issac takes stoke of the effort they took under his leadership to interpret the mystery of Christ, the Incarnation of the Word of God and the redemptive action of Jesus in the limelight of our Indian ethos and its cultural and artistic expression, which was essential for the Christian existence in the missions at that point of time. Dr. James Gurudas finds Fr. Louis neither too progressive nor too conservative but steadily balanced and realistic. He bloomed immensely wherever he was planted, displaying his charming beauty and spreading his sweet fragrance. Dr. Gurudas recalls how as a lover of Indian culture Fr. Louis would miss no opportunity to familiarize the seminarians with Indian Philosophy and Hindu rituals and customs. At the same time, although Fr. Louis was deeply interested and involved in the Vedic heritage, he never lost sight of the tribal values and their identity, and the Dalits and their problems.

Part three sheds light on the contextual theological contribution of Fr. Louis. It includes his significant contribution in contextual theology, contextual theological formation and evangelization. Majority of the articles in this section are written by his students, co-workers and conferrers. These articles clearly show the methodological shift he has brought into the contextual theological education and discussion. Written by scholars who have known him personally and closely, the articles point out why we consider him as one of the pioneers of contextual theological education, formation and thinking. Dr. Sebastian Elavathingal shows how Fr. Louis envisaged and implemented a formation of blending of theoretical learning with practical field experiences in such a way as to activate in each student a personal reflection on theological questions. Dr. Elavathingal shows under the leadership of Fr. Louis how different social and pastoral sensitization programmes were arranged for the students to make them attentive to the problems of the poor and the socially marginalized people. Dr. Amarnad looks at how Fr. Louis was a mentor to the youth and salutes him for his contributions in scripting new chapters in inculturation and theological formation of priests and religious. According to Dr. Amarnad the success of Fr. Louis lie in his simple life style as well as his openness and gentleness to understand the young people from their perspective. Dr. Davis points out how the style of formation which had earlier focused on uniformity was transformed by Fr. Louis into a creative, positive and open atmosphere, for practicing the contextual theological method. Fr. Louis thus worked hard to move away from the heavily centralized system of formation to a decentralized system of formation. It was done by the kind of formation he had imparted, which Dr. Joshy Pazhukathara has termed as the "Loui-Way" of formation. According to Dr. Pazhukathara, Fr. Louis made sure that seminaries are not remedy centers, but places where they discern and decide for oneself, what, why, and how. Instead of being a course corrector, Fr. Louis showed how he forms himself. Dr. Benny Thettayil looks at the unique way in which Fr. Louis formulated his theology. He calls Fr. Louis essentially a religious priest from whose prayer and meditations emerged his theology. Dr. Thettayil notes that Fr. Louis mined the resources of scripture and tradition for a fuller understanding of a God who, rather than being remote is found "in the midst" the suffering of God's people. Therefore Fr. Louis was able to show us the importance of taking the context seriously in conversation with the Christian 'text' for all authentic theologizing.

Fr. Louis was a complete package of sensitive and intellectual qualities. His administrative style and his approach to community life and evangelization made him different from others. Therefore, part four of this book focuses on a different aspect of his personality. This section is written by the members of St. Paul Province Bhopal, where he was elected provincial two terms consecutively. He had brought a fresh lease of life to the province. He left his distinctive mark in administration and community building. Several dioceses and congregations sought his inspiration and counsel to tide over crisis situations to peace and reconciliation. This section presents the kind of leadership he gave and the kind of management skills he was endowed with. Dr. Jacob Peenikaparambil gives an overview of his leadership skills and human management styles, while Shepherd Thelappilly gives a bird's eye view of his vision for community life and Dr. Johnson Vadakkumchery gives a broad picture of how he animated the province.

Practically, his whole life was spent in formation houses and his contribution to the field of formation is remarkable. He had a vision for contextual priestly and missionary formation, particularly for contextual theological education. He has published several books and articles. Even with his advancing years he did not stop writing. His latest two articles were not published due to his untimely and sad demise. In part five, we are publishing two of his last articles on theological formation in Dharmaram College and Samanvaya Theological College.

We hope these articles in the present volume shall inspire to keep the light of contextual theological enquiry burning in the hearts and works of us, his students, conferrers and colleagues.

Dr. Cyril Kuttiyanikkal

PART I

LIFE AND CONTRIBUTIONS OF FR. LOUIS MALIECKAL CMI

Truly a Model and Patron for Formators

Fr. Paul Achandy CMI, Prior General

CMI Congregation proudly presented to Rev. Fr. Louis Malieckal CMI posthumously the CMI Award 2020 in connection with the founder's day and feast of St. Kuriakose Elias Chavara in the sesquicentennial jubilee of his death. The entire community applauded the decision of the Award Committee. For contextual theology, he becomes a symbol and synonym in India. There is no better name or reference point for contextualized formation.

Even before Pope John Paul II scripted Pastores Dabo Vobis in March 1992, Rev. Fr. Louis created a legacy of human formation. He challenged the status quo of rigidity and ritualism in the formative context to freedom with responsibility. More than exteriors and external disciplines, he disciplined on discipleship and freedom of the children of God. He showed the model for any seminarian or seeker of truth, the model of Jesus – the complete man. Every seminarian was asked to grow like Jesus as He grew in stature and wisdom and in favour with God and man (Luke 2:52). The smell of the sheep formative pedagogy was practised by Rev. Fr. Louis before Pope Francis kept on asserting its impact in seminary formation and priestly ministry. He was prophetic in thinking and action as he was convinced of his call to choose the road less travelled by and to set a legacy for future formators.

"He, who sings, prays twice." (St. Augustine) Being a rare musician with innate gift of composing and tuning, he knew the power of music in the liturgy. On year before his death, he sent me a set of hymns and tunes to help me for meditation and concentration. His life has been a saga of music. He had his perfect melody, harmony and rhythm and he translated it into his life and his life too has been musical. He has been truly a harp of the Holy Spirit like St. Ephrem. The harmony hc found in music found a place in the formation and he called it Samanvaya, integration. His voice, his tone, tempo and articulation had its vibration. When life provides the rhythm and beauty of the music, the presence of such people itself becomes edifying to others. I have seen so much engrossed in music and in the same way, I have found him getting lost in the presence of the Lord in prayer.

He was my liturgy professor and he was all the more a liberated liturgical theologian. Despite the schools of thought and its complexities, he found in liturgy a liberative dimension rising above its rigid ritualism. He had the audacity to research, experiment and innovate the liturgy reading the signs of the time and the cultural context of the people. He found the Eucharist as the summit of Christian life and the ritual of sacrifice for him was only a preface to the real sacrifice, daily life. He could dialogue with different schools of thought in the liturgy and he was open and generous enough to take the best for the public worship feeling with the mind of the Church. He could find the symphony of the East and the West and Indian and the Syrian and for people of integrity, integration becomes the mantra.

The final question asked by Jesus to Peter was his norm in life. "Simon son of John, do you love me more than these?" (John 21:15). His formative principle was the same. He loved the disciples. Love was his pedagogy and his accompanying presence inspired the young for lifetime. He transformed the students through his life of love and friendship. "I have called you friends, for everything that I learned from my Father I have made known to you." (John 15: 15) Rev. Fr. Louis has been a rare friend to me and more than a teacher, he has been trustworthy friend who encouraged me during my life in CMI family. This is the same legacy handed over by St. Kuriakose Elias Chavara. We are called to be members of a loving family and all shall live together as children of the same mother in its real sense.

The first apostolic endeavor taken up by the CMI founding fathers was seminary formation in Mannanam in 1833. St. Kuriakose Elias Chavara, Malpan Thomas Palackal and Malpan Thomas Porukara believed that the church needed right leadership and they focused on quality priests and established seminary and reinvented priestly formation in seminary from the existing malpanate system. Rev. Fr. Louis followed the same legacy of founding fathers and he reinvented the seminary formation from a static model to a dynamic model. With enough exposure to the context of the people, multi religious traditions of India and the pastoral and social situations of the people, the disciples moved with the masters as the first disciples accompanied Jesus in various contexts from Cana to Calavary. Samanvya would have not been a reality without Rev. Fr. Louis and we salute this patron of formators and we imbibe his dynamic and open approach and attitude to make the right discernment. He fully believed in the providence of God that the formators are only instruments in the hands of God and the Holy Spirit is the formator. All the more he had deep trust in the promise of the Lord. "I will give you shepherds after my own heart, who will lead you with knowledge and understanding" (Jeremiah 3:15).

When the Catholic Church experiences a credibility crisis, we need exemplary models like Rev. Fr. Louis to be the light and to enlighten others. "Be sure that you first preach by the way you live. If you do not, people will notice that you say one thing, but live otherwise, and your words will bring only cynical laughter and a derisive shake of the head." This was the advice of St. Charles Borromeo to his priests to live an authentic life. It is a fact that to form quality priest after the model of Jesus, they must be formed in the image of Christ by priests modeling that virtue in their own lives

Congratulations to Rev. Fr. Cyril Kuttianickal CMI who took the pain and effort to edit this work *God's Trailblazer of Contextual Theology* on Rev. Fr. Louis Malieckal CMI, the illustrious son of CMI family. I salute all who have contributed to this book to keep the legacy and memory of Rev. Fr. Louis. "Where, O death, is your victory? Where, O death, is your sting?" (1 Corinthians 15:55) "Everyone who lives in me and believes in me will never ever die." (John 11:26) Truly we believe, today you are with Him in paradise." (Luke 23:43). Dear Rev. Fr. Louis, Remember and Pray for us.

Fr. Louis Malieckal a Pathfinder

Fr. Justin Akkara CMI, Provincial, St. Pauls Province, Bhopal

Fr. Louis Malieckal is a nationally known theologian and formator who contributed considerably to Indian Christian Theology and theological formation of students. His theological thinking is something originated from his own life experiences, self-reflections and a deep sense of being part of the Universal Family. He was always in search of unifying elements which connects different cultures and religions. He was never a man in search of unique identities of one's own belief and existence but in contrast he was a seeker who was in pursuit of unifying factors of human existence.

It is also the reason why he was successful as a great formator of students. No matter what the differences or divergences of a student are, he could find positive elements which he nurtured and allowed to bloom. Many of the priests of the Dioceses and congregations working in central India are living witnesses to the unique capacity of Fr. Louis to mentor students in difficult situations.

The reason why he was able to create a unique style of theological formation catering to the needs of North India, integrating the context of the living faith, is that he could experience these unifying factors among the diverse cultural and religious elements, social and political expressions, and economic and educational status of the people around us.

The Universal Church, Indian Church, CMI Congregation and St. Paul Province, Bhopal are indebted to this great soul who made a difference in the way we experience and interpret God in our lives. May God bless this unique soul who lived among us. May his ideals be a beacon, guiding us in these times of divisions and identities created in the name of religion, political ideologies and cultural differences.

Fr. Louis a Timely Blessing

Fr. Peter Kochalumkal, Rector, Samanvaya

Pleasant memories of Fr. Louis Malieckal CMI is firmly imprinted in my mind as an eminent theologian, cynosure and intelligent formator and spiritual animator who profoundly contributed in nurturing and nourishing the Samanvaya Theologate.

My mind is surfeit with his affectionate memories and the golden moments of friendship and guidance I had experienced when he was at Samanvaya Theologate, Bhopal and Rishikesh. The very appearance of him vividly reminds me of a true stalwart who had the saturation of realization of life as a religious priest and made everyone gain from his prolific and priestly presence on earth. I personally had experienced a sort of eminent and ethereal empathy during my interactions with him.

He was an inspiration for all of us who have had the opportunity to be with him. He had a detached mind at the end of his life notwithstanding his community activities till the day of his sad demise on 25th February, 2019. Detachment is one of the rare characteristics of a fulfilled personality. It is not with the things earned but the satisfaction one derived through contributing to society that matters and gives fulfilment. Fr. Louis had the voice and behaviour of a matured approach to everything and everybody. I can emphatically confirm that he obviously and genuinely relished and savoured the religious trail, fully experienced the depth and breadth of religious life and community life and fulfilled his duty as an evangelizer par excellence in the church.

Fr. Louis Malieckal was a man well known for his contributions to the Church, society, and to the religious and priestly communities of North Indian Missions, especially to those in Madhya Pradesh. He served the Church in versatile capacities, e.g., through the offices and ministries assigned to him: as religious superior, priestly and religious formator, professor of theology and liturgy, as an academician, writer etc. I admire his spirit, intellectual ability and passion in taking up initiatives for transforming the Church in India to become truly Indian in her theology and liturgy, and in her spirituality and lifestyle.

In the book of Genesis, we see the sevenfold covenant promised to Abraham by God when He appeared to Abraham who is known as the father of Faith. God said to Abraham that 'you will be a blessing". Every religious is called to be a blessing, but blessing to whom - The answer and response are with the concerned person. If we look at the life of Fr. Louis, we see he was a trailblazer… a true blessing to humanity, the universal Church and his congregation and to many people.

When we think of him, the contribution he has given to the CMI congregation and the church in India is that he lived for a particular cause that is to interpret the Gospel for India and particularly using Indian ethos and terms. As a whole if we evaluate his contributions it may not be a success compared with its value because of many external and internal impediments and constraints. He proved that adversity cannot stop those who are committed to succeed. There is a new start at every bend in the road. If you can dream big and wish to grow, no one can ever stop you. A major portion of his time was spent in seminaries. He is known for his contextual theological formation to seminarians. He developed in them aptitude for contextual theological thinking.

We can pacify ourselves with saying that all prophets had gone through such setbacks in their life but still they proved themselves to be pacesetters and role models for all of us to emulate. Fr. Louis, though well aware of the consequences of his writings, always stood for what the Vatican Council II envisaged and he imbibed from the teaching of the church. An Indian liturgical renovation he viewed but it was, in fact, an abortive attempt. He always thought with the spirit of Vatican council II and stood for the good and growth of the Church. He, staunchly believed in 'I will make you a great nation' (Genesis 12:2) when he engaged with some seemingly 'fruitless' attempts to do justice to go with a new way of approaching theology with Indian mind. The intention of the Vatican council II was giving a direction mainly to Christians to widen their creative and Gospel-value-based entrance to whole world and show the face of God's love for humanity though it is not remarkably implemented from the Church side. Fr. Louis' contributions complementing and synchronizing to the thought pattern of the Vatican council II and in particular liturgical renovation which means he is part of the 'great nation' in Genesis.

Fr. Louis was blessed by the Lord as the founding Rector of Samanvaya Mission Theologate. The General council of CMI congregation believed it was easy for him to start and sustain Samanvaya Theologate with the experience of the Khrist Premalaya, Ashta, in Madhya Pradesh where he was the Rector for a decade. It was very assiduous task for him to form Samanvaya but with the help of other fathers with him, he could do justice to his responsibility the congregation assigned to him. He often mentioned that it was possible only because of hope in the promise of God and he believed and proved the writing of Genesis 12:2, "I will make you into a great nation, and I will bless you; I will make your name great, and you will be a blessing."

He was keen to do things without compromising the great traditions and patrimony. He was positively paradoxical in the patterns of his insight-filled-thoughts and challenging style of living. Sometimes he gave us a feeling that he is very liberal in thinking, especially with liturgy; but in fact, those who know him closely know that he was very genuine and sincere in following the teachings of the Church. He never diverged from the track that was shown by the Church. He is an accepted, well-known, and well-discussed theologian in the national and international theological circles. At the same time, he was a humble and simple teacher for the students of theology and the burgeoning theologians. He had a very tolerant approach towards others, but never was hesitant in highlighting, instructing Church's position to those who approached him; he showed meticulous care in faithfully upholding the truth and was upright in following the teachings of the church. He was a senior-most priest among the seniors, he was a middle-aged man among the middle aged, a youthful energetic youngster among the youngsters, and a lovely little one among the little ones. He was highly interested in games and sports, but he did not let them distract his intellectual pursuits. He was a man of great comprehension, was one who could advice and encourage those who approach him for spiritual direction, especially so, to the priests, religious and seminarians. But his soft, pliable mood never permitted them to be lazy or irresponsible.

Genuinely and hopefully he guided and directed religious and priests in their spiritual journey. There is no exaggeration if I reiterate that he was always a highly sought-after spiritual guide and instructor. He insisted for a new prayer culture that is to be cultivated in the line of the great traditions of India. Yet he was ever a faithful son of the Catholic Church. This was the beauty of the marvelous life he lived.

Samanvaya theologate has been a blessing to the priests, religious and people of God for the last twenty-five years. Its humble beginning and simple living are the signature of Rev. Fr. Louis Malieckal CMI. Now more than 260 priests are in the field to proclaim the word of God from Samanvaya. Samanvaya is a blessing to the Church especially church in North India. Samanvaya is publishing a book commemorating Fr. Louis and acknowledging his contributions to the people of good will. I congratulate Rev. Fr. Cyril Kuttiyanikkal CMI, the superior of the house and the master of the scholastics at Rishikesh where Fr. Louis was the member when he went for heavenly abode for taking interest to collect, edit and publish this book *God's Trailblazer of*

Contextual Theology as Samanvaya staff and the community have proposed. With folded hands and utmost reverence, I acknowledge that Fr. Louis Malieckal was a blessing; may the blessing continue to enlighten the Church in the way of proclaiming the Lord's message through his contributions.

Trust in the Lord and do good;
dwell in the land and enjoy safe pasture.
Take delight in the Lord,
and He will give you the desires of your heart. (Psalm 37:3-4)

1

A Tribute to Dr. Fr. Louis Malieckal CMI

Fr. V. C. Mathew, Vicar General, Archdiocese of Bhopal

I am not sure whether it is fate or destiny that has brought me here. Because, on this day, at this time, someone else, whom I revered, admired and looked upon as my guide and mentor, was scheduled to express his thoughts on a topic that was very dear to him. But here I am to pay our tribute to him, highlighting in the process his contributions in contextualizing theology.

The task of theology, I believe, is to articulate the divine revelation in given a context using its language, symbols and idea of the divine so that the revelation could be better communicated and understood, and it could become experiential for others. The efforts at contextualization of revelation depend on one's understanding of one's call and mission. In other words, one commits oneself to a cause, whatever it might be, due to certain convictions, which come about only if only one is in communion with the Divine who as a result reveals not only of himself but also one's purpose in life.

I wish to look at the life of Rev. Fr. Louis Malieckal from these aspects of communion, conviction, and commitment. What one could notice in him, above everything else, was his sense commitment to whatever was assigned to him. One can have such a commitment only when one has experienced personally one's source of strength and trust, who in turn convinces him/her of whatever one attempts to do. So, we find Fr. Louis writing with contentment in his Golden Jubilee memento, 'The Lord is my shepherd, I have everything I need'.

Hence, with ease he could follow the Lord as he led him on. As a teacher of Mathematics, that too in a prestigious institute, he soon realized that his call as a priest was not in solving mathematical problems within the confines of classrooms but in helping people to experience God and so he chose Liturgy as he saw in it an effective means of relating oneself to God. As a liturgist, instead of falling into the trap of traditionalism and legalism, he wanted liturgy to be a means of God realization. So, we find him interpreting the essentials of Christian worship in and through the language and symbols of the context as he deemed it necessity to make it relevant for people, for evangelization. In doing so he had an unparalleled inner freedom as he was convinced that liturgy was for humans and not vice versa. So, he emphasized to his students and to others the need and importance of learning the scriptures of other religions and interacting with the people of other religions. It soon took a concrete shape in the form of '*sarva dharma maîtree samiti*' in Ashta, his first karmabhumi, which often experienced communal riots. He always saw to it that he and all those who were entrusted to his care involved actively in the prayer meetings of the *Samiti*. Providentially, this *samiti* could play great role in bringing people of different religions together and ensured peace and harmony in Ashta township on several occasions. Similarly, with equal force he stressed the importance of learning the language of the people as it was a necessary condition to insert oneself into a particular context.

As he himself had expressed to us a couple of times, his assignment to M.P. Regional Theologate after the completion of his studies in Liturgy was not something that he looked forward to as he had intended to proceed to Dharmaram College. He realised soon that God was leading him to a new promised land where he would be the new Moses. Committing himself to the vision and objectives of the new venture of MP Bishops, the Khrist Premalaya Theologate, we find him not only giving to it flesh and life, but spearheading a new student-centred, people-oriented method of priestly formation with its unique methodology of 'action-reflection-action'. This new methodology was the test ground for many of the traditional theology subjects. Soon new subjects that were more relevant to the context were added to the syllabi while several of the so called important traditional subjects lost their prominence in the curriculum as his purpose was to form well equipped missionaries to suit the need of the time.

In the process of such experimentation there emerged a new formator in the person of Fr. Louis, after the model of Jesus, the formator par excellence. The effectiveness of a formator depends on to the extent he/she embodies the attitudes and style of Jesus, and follows the logic of incarnation by being with them, by probing them with relevant questions, by confronting them with the ideal, by affirming their talents and contributions, by respecting their boundaries and limitations, by giving them enough freedom to grow into maturity, and by loving them dearly.

His regular presence in the prayers in the chapel just like one of us and his encouragement to us to be innovative and creative in conducting prayers, and even in the Eucharist, was the result of his conviction that 'God is spirit, and those who worship him must worship in spirit and truth'. This inner freedom led him to install, to the surprise and even annoyance, of many, an image of resurrected Jesus in *nataraja* style, instead of a Crucifix, in the sanctuary of the Seminary chapel.

His vision of 'doing theology' rather than 'learning it' found its expression when he encouraged us to stay in the villages in order to experience poverty and lack of most of the basic facilities of people there and come to seminary only for the classes. Well aware of the challenges and risks involved in such experimentation, often he himself used to take time to be with them to encourage and to help them to discover for themselves in the process the relevance or irrelevance of a formation that was imparted in the seminaries.

His regularity in conducting community meetings where various aspects of community life were discussed and decisions were arrived at was another feature of his method of formation. He was of the view that formation was dialogical and it necessarily involves a community which should evolve by the interactive participation of its every member. So he could state that, 'by imposing order and discipline in the community, no inner transformation and growth of the members would take place. Externally everything may appear fine and smooth sailing to the satisfaction of the formator concerned. But, in reality the spirit within would be getting rotten; and deformation, instead of transformation, would be the end result.'[1] Hence he suggested that, "the only way to ensure inner growth and transformation is to infuse trust and confidence in the members about the person, words and actions of the formator. This of course requires self-emptying and sacrifice on the part of the formator, coupled with integrity and transparency in all that he does."[2] In other words, what he envisaged in the priests who come out of formation houses was not robots after the model of a formator, but fully convinced disciples of Jesus who would even be willing to lay down their lives for the Lord and his Kingdom.

His lectures were aimed at not just communicating the knowledge of the subject alone, but also were a means to probe the students with relevant questions and to confront them with the ideal. This dialogical approach prompted every student to be a participant to get personally involve in the subjects discussed and taught. Moreover, for him one did theology not for grades in the report cards but to form oneself after the Master who has called him to share his priesthood.

---

1 Louis Maliecka, *The Diary of Fr. Louis Malieckal on the lessons he learned as a formator.*

2 *Ibid.*

Yet another feature of Fr. Louis as well was his contribution to theology was his attempt to make theology and those who did theology, as harbingers of reconciliation and integration. Experiencing his Master and Shepherd as a great reconciler between God and humans, and between humans, becoming a reconciler himself was for him, being true to his call to be a disciple. Whenever a situation of difference or discord or tension arose in the community his basic approach was to look at the issues from the perspective of the other. For he believed that, 'through dialogue, discussion and sitting together, we can find solutions to the problems and find ways to live and work together. There is always a way forward.'[3] When, we in the Archdiocese had certain issues a couple of years ago, it was to him that we turned to and he could find, with much effort, a way out of the deadlock. The fact that he was a much sought-after spiritual guide and confessor to many showed his quality of bringing reconciliation with God as well. For him, revelation of God was primarily and basically message of reconciliation – between God and humans, and between humans, and theology being the articulation of this revelation, its task is to bring about this reconciliation, leading thereby to an integration of whole humanity under the fatherhood of God. Perhaps, that is the dream he has left behind for us to realise. He has laid the foundation; we are to build upon it and complete the edifice. That I feel would be a fitting tribute to this great son of the Church, of the Carmelite Order, of our time.

I take great pride in stating that he was my teacher, guide, support and a role model. May he continue to be source of inspiration to each of us to realise his dream of a total samanvayam of the whole creation.

Let me conclude by quoting a few lines from Frances Coelho's poem - *God Saw You Getting Tired*

> God saw you getting tired, and a cure was not to be
> So he put His arms around you, and whispered Come to me.
>
> With tearful eyes we watched you, as you slowly slipped away
> And though we loved you dearly, we couldn't make you stay.
> Your golden heart stopped beating; your tired hands put to rest
> God broke our hearts to prove to us, He only takes the best.
>
> Thank you. May God bless all of you.

3 *Ibid.*

2

Immortal Memories

Francis Malieckal

It is almost one year since Fr. Louis Malieckal CMI who was a man of real religious identity and integrity left us for his eternal goal. Fr. Louis was born on 27th July, 1936 at Vellangallur then, belonging to the diocese of Thrissur, from the parents Ouseph and Mariam genuinely God believing and loving couple. He was the sixth child of the ten children of the parents and the third child died at the very early childhood itself in an accident and the only sister Thresea died in Bombay in the year I978. Being a big family of ten children the home itself was a so called little school where the teachers father and mother though had little knowledge in letters could guide their 'students' in and through the godly path from the heavenly light they got from above. Little Louis learned from the parents the significance and depth of indomitable spirit of higher values like god fearing, sharing, compromise, adjustment, forgetting and forgiving and so on.

Fr. Louis did his primary education at Govt. Primary school at Kalparamba and he impressed very much his teachers as an exemplary student both in studies and in character. After the completion of his primary education, he was moved to his mother's house at Chittissery near Thalore and joined St. Teresa's' UP school at Thalore, a reputed school run by C.M.I fathers of the Devamata Province, Thrissur. It deserves special mention that Fr. Louis got inspiration to became a CMI priest during his stay and study at Thalore from our mother's sister Rosa, unmarried and very saintly woman and Fr. Louis was deeply grateful to her till the last moment of his life for the advice and the support she had given him to single out the path of priesthood. Needless to say the late C.M.I fathers Alypius and Leander who were his teachers at UP School Thalore at that time also had played a great role for his religious vocation. I still recall a comment made by a teacher of the UP School Thalore when I joined the school for studies after the departure Fr. Louis from there "I know you are the brother of Louis, very good. Louis was an asset to this school outstanding at studies and excellently incomparable in character, so try to follow suit." Realizing this comment has become a liability for me. I tried to the best of my ability to follow suit though it was not that easy for me.

After the completion of his upper primary studies at Thalore he was taken to St. Aloysius aspirants' house at Elthuruth and started his high school studies there. As in the other schools here also he kept the graph of excellence in studies and character ever upward, coming out with flying colours, with distinction in the SSLC examination, really extraordinary students could achieve at that time and there after he was sent to Varandarappilly where from he started his real journey for his priesthood and perfection. After the Latin course at Varandarappilly he was sent Christ College Irinjalakuda for PUC and thereafter to Ampazhakad for novitiate. He made his religious profession in 1958. He was then sent to Dharmaram College, Bangalore for philosophy course after which he did his B.Sc in Statistics at St. Thomas College in Thrissur and M.Sc at St. Thomas College Pala and thereafter coming back to Dharmaram College, he did his studies in theology and got ordained on 22nd April 1969. After a long journey of 83 years of life, fulfilling a lot of dreams and duties for the good of the people and C.M.I congregation, the almighty had entrusted upon him he left for his eternal abode to be ever with God on 25th February 2019.

Imbibing the real spirit and message of Holy Bible, Mahatma Gandhi once wrote "Man becomes great exactly in the degree in which he works for the wellbeing of his fellow men" and that statement was quite applicable with the life of Fr. Louis also. He very well knew the meaning of heavenly immortality and made his journey of life accordingly to achieve it fully realizing that earthly immortality also is an integral part of the above as if one cannot be separated from the other. The excellence award a man has to receive after death is the laudable comment. "He was good at heart and indeed" and this is what earthly immortality means. Doubtless to say Fr. Louis is an award winner in this regard. Everybody who knew him personally would say in one accord that he was a man of simplicity and humility to the core and he knew to live with the bare minimum. He was a consoler, moderator and great visionary spiritual leader, he had a large circle of friends of different caste and creed, people of different walks of life who had had some kind of help from him in one way or other. And intimate friend of him Dr. Professor Gopalankutty in U.S.A has instituted an endowment of a substantial sum to perpetuate his memory for the best student in the S.S.L.C Examination at the Deepthi High School, Thalore which he was very much related with. This goodwill of Mr. Gopalankutty is enough to substantiate how much people loved him. His option to work as a missionary in North India itself was a vivid manifestation for his interest and desire to work and live for the poor and needy. Whenever we, invited him to participate in any function connected with the family members or relatives without any excuse or hesitation he accepted our requests and reached before time at Sagar Bhavan where from he was picked up by our youngest brother Vincent to the venue. Vincent being the youngest had a close attachment with him and vice versa. He travelled from a long way from Bhopal to Kerala even without any reservation in the train as an ordinary traveler at his old age even. I have seen him collecting old newspapers and putting them into the bag before going back to Bhopal for the purpose of spreading on the floor in the train to sleep at night. This kind of living lessons of simplicity to live with bare minimum was an eye opener for us to be contented with what we have and to adjust ourselves according to the situations. His concern for the old especially the sick and bed ridden was very deep and sensational. He never forgot to call on his old friends and relatives who were at sick bed before leaving for Bhopal from Kerala. The patients whom he visited used to say his visit was very therapeutic indeed.

The message he gave last to the parishioners during the Holy mass of the Jubilee celebrations still recalls in my ears that in this precarious situation of the dwindling doom of vocation to priesthood the parents have grave responsibility of encouraging their children to hear the call of God to priesthood by exemplary life rooted in Christian faith and beliefs. As he had a heavenly revelation he also said to the faithful that "I don't think I will be much longer with you". Though Fr. Louis was very hectic with different activities during his life he was always truly guided by the real meaning of death only. He was fully aware and conscious of the fact packed statement of the great German theologian Karl Rahner, "We cannot make sense out of life until we make sense out of death".

We will ever be very grateful to God the Almighty for letting us celebrate the golden jubilee of his priestly ordination in a befitting manner at his own parish, Vellangallur and to participate also in the celebration of the 50th wedding anniversary of his younger brother David at St. Thomas Cathedral Church, Irinjalakuda on the previous day of the above. How cheerful and jubilant he was in these days with a heavenly glittering face.

We have no words to say how much we miss him. His words and presence were always an enduring inspiration and unending encouragement for us to move smoothly in the path of life, but we realize his intercession from above will ever guide us giving unfading light. Finally a word of heartfelt thanks and gratitude from the Malieckal family to the CMI, Congregation in general and

St. Paul's Province Bhopal, in particular, for giving him never failing support and encouragement for becoming an ideal knowledgeable priest of people of god who could ever leave immortal memories behind.

3

Like a Father and a Mother

Ms. Annie Varghese

Our life is like a chapter of a book. It can really become more transparent and meaningful in the way we live. A life which lived and passed from our midst after the golden jubilee celebration of the priesthood in the CMI congregation, Bhopal. This is no one else but Fr. Louis Malieckal.

Those who had close interaction with him could understand his touching mind and golden heart. Fr. Louis Malieckal was an open person willing to live a sacrificial life as per the vows of poverty, chastity and obedience taken on his first profession to priesthood life. A true follower of Jesus Christ living up to the mark. He was an admiring person wherever he was called for.

Fr. Louis Malieckal, had a personal taste for books, the knowledge that he had received never failed to share with others. A man of great vision always implemented into practice. Every event or stories of his life get embedded into the culture they become master narratives as blue prints for people to follow. He was filled with kindness, courtesy, humility, patience and forgiving. He was a man of disciplined living of the commandments of God.

My contribution as a niece of Fr. Louis Malieckal, was a great support and help in times of need, even if every hands failed to come to my help. He was a chosen person of God to come to my help. He came as a help and support to my life not as my maternal uncle but as my dad and sometimes he consoled me as a mother consoles and takes care of her children.

My final touching to this book; "If we are to follow the example of Christ and walk in his footsteps, we must seek to do the same things after the pattern he set."

4

Reminiscence of an Authentic Indian Christian Religious

Paul Kalluveettil CMI

Before the memory of beloved Fr. Louis Maliekal CMI (henceforth LM) I bow my knees. He was a friend of mine, a man of gentleness and tenderness, one who has imbibed the Indian spirituality, and tried to live its spirit in the mission and formation fields. Below I try to give articulation to some of my reminiscences about this noble soul.

1. At Varantharappilly

LM was a year senior to me at Varantharappilly Aspirants House. He was a very intelligent student who topped in the examinations. While some of his classmates used to get up early in order to study the portions and memorize the pertinent parts, LM did not exert himself, and slept quietly till the bell for rising rang. He was not particular to get the first rank. Still he was often first in most of the examinations. LM was a man of few words, and it seems that he had kept his ideas and ideals to himself. This may be the reason why LM was not appointed or elected to the important posts coveted by most of the aspirants.

2. At Ambazhakad

After finishing the studies at Varantharappilly, LM was chosen as one of the five brothers who were sent to Irinjalakuda for College studies (one year). Thus at Ambazhakad Novitiate he became a novice of my batch. During the canonical year of the Novitiate at which everyone strived to attain perfection, there was no time to cultivate intimate relationships. LM was rather silent and prayerful during that period. At the time of Juniorate, I remember, that he was appointed as choir master, and to my surprise he chose me as a member of the choir, since I was not a good singer. I think that LM had noticed that I sang with my heart and soul. That may be the reason that he made me a choir member. Here I find a special trait of his character. He wanted to encourage others so that they could develop their talents, even though limited ones.

3. At Dharmaram

Since I was chosen to study Philosophy at Pontifical Athenaeum, Pune, I went only during vacation days to Dharmaram Collage, Bangalore. In one batch of Philosophy there were about sixty-sixty five students, it was not easy to meet all the brothers. Thus, I do not have any memory concerning my contact with LM during the period of Philosophy. Even at that time he as very much interested in Indian Christian Liturgy, and seems to have made personal studies on that topic. After Philosophy he was sent for graduate studies to Christ Collage Irinjalakuda. Without interruption I continued my Theological study at Pune.

4. A Champion of Indian Liturgy

It seems that LM had not much interest to study MSc statistics. As he graduated without obtaining rank, he was not appointed to the teaching staff of Christ Collage, Irinjalakuda. During his Theological studies at Dharmaram Collage, he got more and more involved in the Liturgical matters, and took leadership in celebrating Holy Mass in Indian style, by assuming the posture of sitting and offering *arathi* and chanting Christian *bhajans*.

5. Studies at Louvain

While LM was at Louvain, he visited me once in Germany where I was spending my holidays. He came to me with another confrere from a long distance. In that act I find his spirit of fraternal love and concern for others. From the University of Louvain he took STD degree by presenting the dissertation, *Yagna and Eucharist*, an interreligious approach to the Theology of Sacrifice, which was published from Dharmaram Publications, Bangalore 1989. At Dharmaram the presentation of his thesis, together with a discussion was conducted. I raised an objection in making comparison of *Yagna* with Eucharist, since LM has depended on the secondary meaning of *Yagna* in his study. An scientific comparative study should be based on the primary meaning of the term. Of course, LM would have been perturbed by my criticism, but he calmly tried to avoid my objection by saying that it was a mere observation.

6. Dean and Rector at *Ashta*

After returning from Louvain LM was appointed first as dean, and later as Rector at *Khrist Premalaya Regional Theologate,* Ashta, Bhopal (1986-1994). I was invited to teach the themes, Prophets in the Old Testament, and Pentateuch. The staff used to concelebrate the Holy Mass in Hindi by sitting; and I was asked to give a short sermon on the Gospel reading. As I exposed the biblical perspective of the text, LM used to hasten to complement it from Hindu Scriptures. I was not always happy, since his exposition seemed to me often a little farfetched. Here we find LM's passionate 'addiction' to the Indian Scriptures.

7. Rector at *Samanvaya*, Bhopal

This erudite and sympathetic person won the heart of the students. Hence, he was appointed as Rector of Samanvaya Theological Collage, Bhopal 1994-2000). With all humility I want to say that it was the brainchild of mine.

While I was the Provincial of Mar Thomas Province of Chanda, I was convinced of the importence of giving theological formation based on Indian context and traditions for the future missionaries of North India. Therefore I convened a meeting of the Major Superiors of the mission regions and discussed with them about the proposed venture. All of them wholeheartedly supported me. Later I spoke about my plan in the Provincial Synaxis of Chanda. Enthusiastically all of us resolved to appeal to the forthcoming General Synaxis of CMI Congregation.

At the first session of the General Synaxis the idea of a Mission Theologate was accepted, and a committee was elected to make concrete proposals at the next session of the Synaxis, myself being the convener. I studied how the Jesuit Regional Theologates were working, with the positive and negative results. Some CMIs were doing mission work at Maharashtra, Jagadalpur, Sagar and Rajkot, a programme was envisaged, which later came to be known as "Theology on Wheels". These proposals were presented and approved at the second session of the General Synaxis.

Although I was asked to undertake rectorship I declined the offer, since I was mainly an academic person. I suggested the name of LM who belonged to Sagar Province. This was how he was appointed as the first Rector of the *Samanvaya.*

8. A Man of Vision

LM served two terms as pioneer Rector of the first CMI Mission Theologate at Bhopal. It was his able leadership and unfaltering vision that helped the Theologate to pass through its infancy period. The CMI Congregation owes to him a great indebtedness for this.

Some of LM's creative contributions of the Mission Theologate: afternoons the students are left free to go to the neighboring villages to earn a firsthand experience of the life of the people; evening meditation by chanting *bhajans* or using similar methods; Saturdays were meant to spend the whole day with villagers, etc. Such innovative practices would help sincere students to foster genuine love for the missions and to prepare effectively for their future missionary life.

9. A Philanthropic Person

The benign and benevolent character of LM had very beneficial results. He inculcated the spirit in many of the students to develop a love for the poor and the marginalized of the society that inspired many of them to opt for working in rural areas or among *Dalits* and the tribals. He tried to live the ideal of *Samanvaya* to integrate and harmonizaise the different cultural and cultic ideas and ideals. His all-embracing mind and heart welcomed everybody and everything good and humane. I feel little uneasy that some students would have taken profit of his generous and liberal attitude. Also I could not assert with certainty whether LM had been always giving the youngsters a fully religious and divine formation. I may be wrong, and ask pardon from this humble and noble person.

10. Air Reservation

Every new experiment will not be perfect from the beginning. One has to evaluate sincerely and critically the merits and demerits of it. That means one has to be open to criticism from the students as well as others who are one way or other related to the new venture. Unfortunately I got the impression that LM did not give the students full freedom to expose these reservations. He used to censure the news sent to be published in *Carmelasandesam*, the official periodical of the CMI Congregation. It may be due to his zeal for *Samanvaya* to make every effort to grow into a full-fledged seminary. Thus outsiders did not get an objective picture of the Mission Theologate.

11. A Devoted *Chēla* (disciple)

Let me conclude by citing another instance which shows the filial reverence that LM had for his professors. I was forced to publish a booklet refuting the position of an eminent historian who belittled the part played by St. Kuriakose Elias Chavara in founding the first indigenous Religious Congregation of India. Even his devotees and the members of his Province could not find fault with my arguments, and congratulated me. When I casually met LM he was not happy about the booklet. He gently told me that I would not have written the booklet, out of respect for the veteran Church historian, even though what I had exposed was the truth. Here I appreciate the differential attitude that

LM had maintained for his teachers. In this case, however the professor was one who totally supported these attempts of LM in propagating the Indian Christian Liturgy.

5

Life, Legacy and Contributions of Fr. Louis Malieckal CMI

Cyril Kuttiyanikkal CMI

The childhood and early life of Fr. Louis Malieckal at family and school and his various studies seminary life until priesthood are already described by Mr. Francis Malieckal, the younger brother of Fr. Louis and Fr. Paul Kalluveetil. I would like to present his life and activities after his priestly ordination that too mainly focusing on his contribution to the North Indian Church and society.

1. Teaching Career at Christ College Bangalore

Immediately after his ordination in 1969, he was sent to Bangalore. He taught at Christ College (presently Christ Deemed to be University) from 1975 to 1975. During this time he also co-authored a textbook on Mathematics for B.Sc students, which was published by the Bangalore University in 1976. Although, his task was primarily in the college, he was also the director of Liturgical centre at Dharmaram, Bangalore, besides being the lecturer-cum Bursar in Christ College Bangalore. He also animated pastoral and liturgical inculturation programme at Dharmaram College, in the wake of Second Vatican Council, producing together with some other fathers a new inculturated text on Christian worship in 1974.

Thereafter he was sent to Louvain University, Belgium for his higher studies. He gained both his L.Th and his Ph.D in Liturgy & Systematic Theology from the same university. His L.Th was in Liturgy defending a dissertation in Oriental Liturgies with the title *The Liturgical Homilies of Narsai the Doctor of Nisibis* in 1977. He came back to Dharmaram and taught for one year at the Faculty of Theology while working on his Doctoral programme. He defended his doctoral dissertation titled *Yajna and Eucharist: An inter-religious Approach to the Theology of Sacrifice,* published in the year 1989. He had mentally prepared to resume his teaching carrier at Bangalore. But, something else was in store for him.

2. Life at Khrist Premalaya, Ashta

In 1983, when Fr. Louis returned to India, he was appointed initially as the Dean of Studies and Vice rector of Khrist Premalaya, Regional Theologate (KPRT), at Ashta, where Fr. Eustace Thottan CMI was the first Rector until 1986. Fr. Louis took over as the Rector of KPRT from 1986 to 1994. This budding MP Regional Theologate, Ashta was completely different from other theological institutions. This was a pioneering venture in the field of priestly formation as decided by the then undivided MP Bishops' conference led by the metropolitan archbishop Eugene D'Souza, after a series of thinking, consultations and decision-making at different levels in the spirit of the II Vatican Council's call for contextualized priestly formation.

In the year 1971 the CBCI had produced a provisional draft with the title *Programme of Priestly Formation in India* (PPFI), which was prepared in the light of the Second Vatican Council's teaching on the issue and following the recommendations of the *Ratio Fundamentalis* issued by the Congregation of Catholic Education in 1969. The document PPFI was further revised and updated to suit the context of the Hindi-belt in the next meetings of the Bishops in Ranchi in 1979 and in Patna in 1980. The final draft contained several recommendations proposed by the Rectors of the Hindi-region emphasizing "missionary formation" of priest-candidates of the major seminaries. It is largely in the light of these recommendations that KPRT, Ashta was started in the year 1982-83.

3. The Enterprise of Establishing KPRT, Ashta, M.P.

When the MP Bishops decided to start a Regional Theologate under the name Khrist Premalaya, in the spirit of the Council and the particular vision articulated by the regional consultation called Priestly Formation in North India (PFNI), the question of who could be entrusted with the task of effectively running the seminary appeared to them unanswerable for quite some time. Archbishop Eugene D'Souza of Bhopal, after having failed to elicit any positive response from other religious orders and congregations working in MP and elsewhere in North India, sought the help of the CMIs to take up the task of running the proposed regional major seminary in the context of the undivided MP state, responding to the clarion call of Vatican II. It was the year 1982/83, when Dharmaram College, 25 years after its establishment in 1957 had grown mature enough in the field of theological education and priestly formation in tune with the vision of the Council. Naturally the Prior General Fr. Thomas Aykara of the CMIs must have looked hopefully towards Dharmaram College before taking a decision in this regard with the consent of his team of counsellors. Finally he "as a successful religious leader"[4] took the bold step of committing to the challenge thrown up by the Archbishop Eugene. Surely in doing so, he must have tried to foresee the consequences and implications of the steps forward in terms of the required CMI personnel, competent and resourceful in matters of academics, formation and administration of this new Major Seminary for the whole of the undivided Madhya Pradesh Church. Accordingly Fr. Prior General sent a core team there. After its formal opening in July 1982 in Arera colony Bhopal with just six students and three CMI staff-members,[5] KPRT was shifted within 10 months to the rural context of the township called Ashta in the spirit of the original vision of the seminary and was housed in the existing simple structures of country-tiled roofing in the midst of a cluster of villages, Fr. Louis was sent to this seminary in May 1983, making the strength of the staff to four.

As one can imagine, the running of this seminary from out of nothing was not an easy task. And Fr. Louis had not expected this turn of events. He was sent abroad from Dharmaram College and had mentally prepared to continue the teaching carrier back in Dharmaram. However as an obedient religious, he accepted the proposal and came to Ashta. He was not at all happy with what he found there. The situation is described in his own words; "When I had joined the initial team of the seminary in Ashta in 1983, a few months after its formal launching in Bhopal, I found myself in a totally disappointing and hopeless situation for the following reasons":

1. Lack of necessary infra-structure facilities
2. Lack of sufficient number of members on the staff
3. Lack of a sizable number of students on the rolls
4. For me a kind of 'cultural shock', because I had landed there straight from Europe after my doctoral studies, obeying the order of my religious superior, without any preparations fitting to the context.

He had to work out his own solution. Instead of losing heart, he accepted the challenge. He says "It took several months for me to come to terms with the 'reality of this village seminary." The process began by asking myself a few questions like:

---

4 Maliecka Louis, "Profile of a Successful Religious Leader", in Thomas Kollamparampil etal Eds. *Power of Positive Presence (Festschrift in Honour of Prof. Dr. Thomas Aykara CMI), Dharmaram Publications: Bangalore pp. 111-128.*

5 Fr. Eustace Thottan CMI (Rector), Fr. Raymond Mancheril, CMI (Administrator) and Fr. Prasad Puthukulangara, CMI (Spiritual Director) were the original staff-members.

1. What could be the purpose of starting this seminary in this unknown country-side, far away from the city of Bhopal?
2. What must be the vision behind this humble seminary housed by a cluster of simple buildings in the midst of number of small villages near a humble township like Ashta?
3. What is the task assigned to me by Providence in this particular context?

He believed the words of Jesus who promised, 'seek you will find, knock and the door will be opened'. He was committed to find out the reasons for this new venture and to put them into practice. He says "the following 11 years (1983-94), until the CMI congregation handed over charge of the seminary in April 1994 to the Pallotine fathers, my whole life was focused on studying the vision and objectives on the one hand, and chalking out and implementing the necessary action plan towards that vision of a new style of priestly formation on the other, as dreamed by the MP bishops in the spirit of the Council. And I am happy to note that my committed efforts with the cooperation of the team members produced good results". Fr. Louis thus tried to find out why was he sent there and what was expected of him by the Church at that moment of time. His sincere search and committed effort found its good result. The result was not just a successful seminary but a model, a methodology of formation was born. He says "The name of Ashta seminary led by the CMIs offered a paradigm shift in the field of formation and it gradually got wide currency in the whole of north India, especially in the undivided MP state. The positive CMI-influence on the students was mainly due to the unity, simplicity and integrity of the staff-members and their solidarity with the formees as well as the people of the locality." Thus, he notes the sacrifice and exemplary life of all staff members as a reason for the success of formation.

On the one hand Fr. Louis had to cope up with the 'hopeless situation' on the other had to learn the art of forming the young minds. He recollects how he had to change his style of formation. He says, "Initially… I was bit strict with the seminarians. I would observe them closely and try to give corrections and guidance accordingly. Soon I realized that this was being taken negatively by the students; a kind of unrest and tension began to mount among them. Gradually I felt that something was lacking somewhere in the community, that my approach at least at the theology stage of formation would not hold water."

So he looked for a solution to what was to be done. He looked at the church and its leaders for inspiration. He found it in the person of Pope John XXIII. He says "It was then that I came to know a little more about the late Pope John XXIII and his way of handling similar situations: In one of his allocutions/audiences to Rectors/Major Superiors/Formators, he seems to have observed in this way: You shall see all things that happen in the community;

shall look at closely some of them; but correct only a few key mistakes. **I liked this trilogy**: **See everything**; **look at some of them**, **and correct only a few** as a general principle of my approach to formation. And I have been practicing it ever since, all through my offices of authority and have found it very effective both in keeping peace of mind, and peace and progress in the community."

One of the innovative programmes at Ashta was establishment of a Centre for Religious Dialogue (SARVA-DHARMA-SAMITI) as early 1988, getting the cooperation of the religious heads of Hinduism, Jainism, Sikhhism, Islam of Ashta and Christianity, at a time when there used to be communal disharmony and even violence during major festivals of Hindus and Muslims. And this centre has produced very good results of religious harmony and mutual appreciation. Considering this great contribution to the society, Fr. Louis was specially remembered and honoured for it on the occasions of 15th anniversary of this Centre by the Ashta public and that of the 25th year of the opening of the seminary by the seminary authorities.

Another important contribution in the pastoral field was the publication of a book of homilies on Sundays and special occasions in Hindi (PREM PRAVACHAN) with the cooperation of a few students (Deacons) of the Ashta seminary. It was first of its kind in Hindi and two volumes were published in 1993 and 94. Publication of these volumes certainly contributed towards boosting the good name of the CMIs and the seminary especially among the Hindi-speaking Catholics.

One can say in the hindsight that the positive 'Ashta CMI-image' played a major role in boosting the CMI mission image in the North among the dioceses and religious congregations whose candidates were students of Ashta under the CMIs during the years 1980s and 1990s. The overall success of KPRT was the result of the leadership provided by Fr. Louis in implementing the vision of the MP Bishops as remarked by Archbishop Emeritus Paschal Topno:

> The vision of the bishops of Madhya Pradesh after Vatican II was realized by Fr. Louis and his devoted team of CMI professors in what is known as the action-reflection programme of theological training based on the living experience of the seminarians in villages and other life-situations. The results of this theological education are very encouraging. Many priests coming out of this Theologate personally opt for working in rural areas or among Dalits, Tribals and slum dwellers. They develop a missionary spirit and love for the poor and the marginalized. Certainly Fr. Malieckal as the first Rector of Samanvaya has also inculcated the same spirit in this great institution.......[6]

6 Most Rev. Paschal Topno, S.J. "A Tribute to Fr. Louis Malieckal, CMI", in Davis Varayilan Ed. *Theology on Wheels: A Movement for Contextualized Theological Education (Festschrift in Honour Dr. Louis Malieckal CMI), ISPCK: Delhi, 2011, p. 328.*

4. The Enterprise of Establishing Samanvaya Mission Theologate

From 1994 to 1999 he was the first Rector of Samanvaya, first at Jagdalpur and then at Bhopal. Already during the last years of our presence at Ashta, the idea of a prospective CMI mission Theologate was in the air for which the experience of Ashta had been a catalyst. And when the question of withdrawal within a fixed time frame was finally decided by the Prior General in Council, steps for launching the Mission Theologate began to gather momentum. Fr. Thomas Mampra, the then Prior General assigned to Fr. Louis a hard double task: one, the challenge of handing over charge of Ashta seminary to the Pallotine fathers with all its assets and liabilities through a fully transparent statement of accounts before April 1994, and the other, that of taking immediate steps to open the proposed mission seminary in July the same year. Fr. Louis speaks about its completion with lots of satisfaction, "I am happy to say that this twofold challenging task, owing to God's grace and full support of the team members of both Ashta and of the would-be seminary, was accomplished to the satisfaction of all concerned".

Already during the late 1980s and the early 1990s the CMI Congregation became increasingly aware of the need and relevance of the kind of new theological education and formation of its priest-candidates due to various factors in the field – the successful KPRT, Ashta experience, challenges of the mission context of North India in which hundreds of CMI priests, including half a dozen bishops began to be engaged in a big way, examples of other agencies like the Society of Jesus with their meaningful RTC theological formation. The CMIs had already shifted their philosophical training for the missions from Bangalore to Wardha. There were also several small attempts at starting mission theologate.

A slow but intense deliberation, discernment and multi-stage preparation at least since 1989 preceded the launching of this Theological College, "SAMANVAY", at Jagdalpur in 1994, the same year of CMI withdrawal from Ashta. Samanvaya form of training is not just it is content but its methodology. Fr. Louis notes, "What is characteristic of its theological education is its vision, method of learning and teaching as well as life-style. Of course all these still remain as unfulfilled ideals but sought after with more or less diligence by the communities concerned".

The spirit of this theological experience and enterprise may be said to have been captured by the name of the institute given by Fr. Louis-Samanvaya or ***"Samanvayam"*** (Integration/harmony/wholeness). *Samanvayena sakshatkarah,* says Bhagvat Gita. Only through an experience of wholeness and harmony within oneself and with creation can one attain God-realization. Theological education must lead a person to a holistic and harmonious experience of personal integration in which knowing, loving and doing (*jnana-bhakti-karma*) are united. The theological programmes and life-activities of Samanvaya are accordingly organized in view of attaining this goal. Hence, the shifting of location of formation, starting with Jagdalpur, through Rishikesh, and Bangalore to Bhopal with in the four years of theology, in order to familiarize the students well with the Tribal context (socio-economical marginalization), authentic Hindu religious context (religio-cultural pluralism), modern cosmopolitan city context Bangalore and towards an experience of integration in the Bhopal Centre of Samanvaya.[7] Being a programme of contextualized theological formation, Samanvaya offers direct exposure of students to concrete life situations, and this is an essential aspect of the method of theological formation. This method gives importance to the ability of students to raise questions, emerging from the contextual experience, which is considered to be the starting point of Post-Vatican II 'doing theology'. Thus academic inputs are not to be limited to giving ready-made answers to possible questions, but must take into consideration the questions emerging from the contexts. Thus learning and teaching become participatory, following a 'question-answer' method.[8]

5. Provincial of St. Paul's Province Bhopal

After leading Samanvaya successfully in and through its infancy and initial growth, he was elected the provincial of St. Paul's Province Bhopal for two consecutive terms from 1999 to 2005. What he did as provincial was also remarkable. He says, "When I look back on the growth of St. Paul Province, Bhopal, my tenure of the office of provincial may be seen as one of restoration of peace and a process of building confidence of the members in their self-worth and resourcefulness. Luckily for me, I took seriously the recommendations of the Mission Audit made by Fr. Sebasti Raj S.J., which had been undertaken by the out-going ministry under Fr. Werner Chakkalakal, provincial (1996-99)". He resisted the temptation of beginning new mission stations or new ministries. Instead what he focused was the development of human resources. His endeavor was to assure the personal fulfillment of members rather than undertaking new projects. He says "I tried in all sincerity to find the best assignment for every member of the province most fitting to his aptitude, character and temperament".

As a provincial he animated the community well and took several steps to improve the quality of community life and spiritual life of its members. Some of the steps he took became milestones in the history of the Province

---

7 For a detailed presentation of these points see Sebastian Elavathingal, "Samanvaya Theological College" in Davis Varayilan Ed. *Theology on Wheels: A Movement for Contextualized Theological Education (Festschrift in Honour Dr. Louis Malieckal CMI), ISPCK: Delhi, 2011, p. 312-318.*

8 *Ibid.*

and the Congregation. Many provinces also adopted those measures. Some of the prominent measures to improve the mutual understanding and appreciation of members, and to build up fellowship and community consciousness are the following:

1. Annual Province Gathering with suitable programmes of evaluation and relaxation, including a financial statement of accounts for discussion and suggestions
2. Division of the Province into different zones, appointment of Zonal Superiors to conduct occasional zonal gatherings with monthly recollections
3. Appointment of a Province-Level Formation Coordinator to help the Provincial to look into various aspects of formation of our candidates.
4. Signing of a contract between the Province and the bishop of Port-Elizabeth (SA) extending our mission commitment beyond our Motherland.
5. Introduction of a Province-Level Statutes in the tenor of General Resolutions of GS 34, 1996, no. 3, incorporating the necessary structures and institutions in order to cope with the mission context and challenges of the province

So, the first term of his office as provincial was as a time of investing in the human resources of the Province. His methodology of guiding the province was already learned during his long stay at seminary. He says, "By imposing order and discipline in the community, no inner transformation and growth of the members would take place. Externally everything may appear fine and smooth sailing to the satisfaction of the Superior/Rector/Formator concerned. But, in reality the spirit within would be getting rotten; and deformation, instead of transformation would be the end result. The only way to ensure inner growth and transformation is to infuse trust and confidence in the members about the person, words and actions of the Superior/Formator. This of course requires self-emptying and sacrifice on the part of the Superior/Formator, coupled with integrity and transparency in all that he does. He would thus become a person of 'authority' for the members who would look up to him as a source of inspiration, leading to willing and faith-full acceptance of his words and deeds."

During the second term of office as Provincial (2002-2005), he carried forward those same policies with renewed vigour and insistence on the one hand, and also initiated some new ventures for the structural growth of the province. Thus the following activities are put in place:

1. In the annual province-gathering, chances of the fathers' coming to know and mixing with the scholastics in the different activities were made more effective and meaningful.

2. The system of "central pooling" of finances, which was just started towards the end of the first term of office, was made more effective and systematic in the tenor of GS 35, resolutions no. 48, by insisting on presenting realistic annual budgets of every units in the province to be examined by a budget committee and approved by the Provincial Council taking into account the recommendation of the committee. On account of this system a more equitable distribution of the financial resources among the houses and for the different apostolates of the province was made possible.
3. Accepting the invitation of Most Rev. Archbishop Abraham Viruthakulangara of Nagapur, and after getting the no-objection letter from the Provincial of Mar Thoma Province, Chanda, the St. Paul Province Bhopal made the maiden entry on to the Chindwarha district and took charge of the Barkui parish. This mission under the banner Parasia mission has developed and made considerable progress.
4. For the structural development of the province, some constructions and land purchases were also made, for example, shifting of the provincial house from Padariya to Govind Garden, purchasing a land and building; extending the campus of St. Paul School by purchasing the adjacent plot of land; putting an additional building flanked by a beautiful chapel in the campus of Sagar Bhavan, Thrissur, for the stay and medical treatment of the members; construction of houses for the CMC and OSF sisters at Kheri and Kareli school campus, respectively, as well as Chavra Bhavan house for CMI fathers at Kheri – all due to good contributions from abroad. In the Silwani area, apart from offering all possible support, supplying necessary personnel and help to get projects sanctioned for RDSS in its much strained relation with the local ordinary, special funds were made available for the development of Tada mission under Fr. Jose Pariadan.

6. Formation Coordinator

After the second term as Provincial he wanted to work in the province as an ordinary member since he had never worked in the province before becoming Provincial. Therefore he requested the then Prior General Antony Kariyil not to reserve him for service under Prior General. He was made the rector of college going CMI scholastics at Jabalpur as well as the provincial formation coordinator for one term from 2005 until 2008. This was the occasion when he had the opportunity to meet his former students from Ashta, now as priests working under different capacities in the diocese. From his association and interaction with them, he got the confirmation of the appreciation they had about the kind of formation they received at KPRT, Ashta. Besides being the Rector of the scholastics, he also served the diocese, as spiritual director-confessor of sisters, preaching monthly recollection and Sunday/Feast day sermons etc. With the whole hearted cooperation of the scholastics put up an innovative Christmas program, first of its kind, for the public of the Jabalpur city which was appreciated by many priests and the bishop in year 2008.

From 2005 to 2009, as the provincial formation coordinator Fr. Louis assisted the Provincials Frs. George Thanchan and Jose Paul in the tenor of Provincial statues no. 70 in organizing formative programmes at different stages for the vocation promotion and formation of CMI candidates. This system of continuing the Formation coordinator's office one more year till the new provincial gets elected and matters in the province get settled, was introduced in the statutes during his 2nd term of office as provincial so that no matters with regards to the formation of the students need to suffer during the interim-period of the election in the province.

7. Formator Par Excellence

Thereafter he came back to Samanvaya as master of students at Bhopal until 2014 while serving as the **general formation coordinator** for the CMI congregation from 2008 to 2014. Simultaneously, from 2008 onwards he was coordinating the formation in the congregation from the stage of vocation promotion and pre-novitiate formation to post-ordination stage, conducting meetings and seminars for the formators of different stages. What he intended was to have at least a common minimum programme for the formation of our candidates of different stages in all our provinces.

Back in Samanvaya after a gap of nine years he had a different challenge now. He says, "Much water had flowed under the bridge since 1999 and Samanvaya has now crossed its capricious adolescence over to vibrant youthfulness with its own demands and problems of growth. I am trying to see eye to eye with the authorities of the present administration, cooperating for its further growth so that it may not be skewed or one-sided but genuine and integral keeping its original vision".

For one year he was sent to Samanvaya, Rishikesh as the Master and Prefect. And in 2016 he was brought back to Bhopal Samanvaya as the Spiritual director. Later he was again appointed as the spiritual director at Samanvaya Rishikesh in 2017 which proved to be his last appointment. In Rishikesh he was very happy with the atmosphere of tranquility, peace and prayer both inside and outside the campus. Rishikesh was the preferred place for the Hindu devotees who reach a certain age of maturity and enter the *vanaprastha* stage of life. He also had now renounced all his attractions to this world and entered into a blissful happy life of *vairagya*. He spent most of his time in reading, writing, reflecting and praying. He wrote down on the souvenir of his Golden

Jubilee memento the part of the original psalm changing a bit to make it his own. He wrote, "The Lord is my shepherd, I have everything I need" instead of 'the Lord is my shepherd, there is nothing I shall want.' He lived a happy and contented life. No one ever heard him criticize or speak ill of anyone. He was a *sthitaprajna*-one who was satisfied in himself and by himself, because he lived his motto, 'the Lord is my shepherd, I have everything I need'. As the culmination of a happy and contended priestly life he celebrated the Golden Jubilee of his priestly ordination at several places. The last phase of the celebration was in Bhopal and he had reserved the train ticket to return to Rishikesh on 1st March. But, the Lord invited him for his eternal reward on 25th February 2019.

8. Special Honour or Awards Received

1. Founder of *Sarvadharma Samiti*, Ashta in 1988, award on its 12th anniversary.
2. The Commemorative Volume ***Theology on Wheels: A Movement for Contextualized Theological Training*** (A Festschrift in honor of Dr. Louis Malieckal, CMI, edited by Davis Varayilaan) 2008, by Samanvaya on 70th birthday and Golden Jubilee of religious profession.
3. The Golden Jubilee of priestly Ordination celebrated on 18/11/2018 at Samanvaya Vidya Dham Rishikesh.
4. Left for Eternal Reward on 25/02/2019, at Devamatha Hospital, Bhopal.
5. His articles were collected and published in the volume ***Interface of Cult and Culture*** and released during Samanvaya Jubilee celebrations 26/03/2019.
6. CMI Excellence Award in Contextual Theological Formation posthumously given on 3rd January 2020.

PART II

THEOLOGY LITURGY AND INCULTURATION

6

Reminiscences About Revered Louis Malieckal, CMI (1936-2019) Champion and Crusader of Inculturation

Augustine Thottakara CMI

Part I: Louis Malieckal, CMI

1. Prologue

Let me begin my deliberations with an incident that happened in my relation with Father Louis Malieckal. After my ordination in 1971, I was at Dharmaram for two years learning German language, and preparing myself for my higher studies in Europe. At that time, we three, that is, Father Louis Malieckal (in the circle of his friends he was known as 'Vallabhan'), Father Isaac Chackalaparambil (popularly known as 'Gunavan'), and I formed a gang. In the summer holidays of 1972 we decided to undertake a South Indian tour. Our plan was to visit the Aurobindo Asram and Auroville at Pondicherry; Sri Ramana-maharsi's Asram at Thiruvannamalai; Swami Bede Griffith's Asram at Kulithalai, Tiruchirappalli; the temple town Srirangam; and Minaksi Temple at Madurai. From Bangalore we took the bus to Pondicherry. Unfortunately, the bus broke down on the way, and we reached in Pondicherry at around 11.30 p.m. There was no soul in the streets; an eerie feeling of angst and anxiety pervaded us. We walked aimlessly, hoping to meet somebody to ask our way. At some point a gentleman started walking behind us. Sensing that we lost our way, he came up to us and said: 'You look as educated people; what are you looking for here in this night?' We said that we are from Bangalore, and we have heard that the Aurobindo Asram has a place where travellers and tourists can spend the night free of cost. He said: 'It is true; but that place is invaded by street urchins, hooligans, gangsters and anti-social elements. I would advise you not to go there.' He continued, 'I will find some place for you to sleep this night; tomorrow I will find a hotel for you'. He took us to a huge building, and showed its outside corridor, and said: 'This night you have to sleep here. Get out of this place before the people start coming to offices'. Father Louis was our leader and spokesperson. He went around and found out a tap with running water, and a toilette, the stench and sight of which will make you unconscious instantly! Father Louis told us to use the bags as pillows, and sleep; he will keep watch while we sleep; but eventually, he also went into sound slumber!

The gentleman turned up next day morning; and took us to a hotel. We were famished; have not consumed anything for almost a day and a night. We literally devoured the breakfast, and had sound sleep till afternoon. The gentleman has arranged our trip to Auroville. He asked for our names. We did not want to disclose our real names. Our names were Vallabhan, Gunavan and Agastyan! We grew suspicious of this man; why is he helping us? Father Louis thanked him profusely, and asked him bluntly who he was. He happened to be a member of the Aurobindo Asram. Asram has two types of members: (i) Those who lived in the Asram; (ii) Members from all walks of life. They engage in their works, as officers, merchants, teachers, advocates, etc. But, their pay/remuneration will go to the Asram. Asram will take care of all their needs, like dress, travel, medicine, stationery, postage, toilet articles, etc. Once in a week all these members come together and they have common prayers and practice of Yoga.

2. Indian Liturgy

To my mind the greatest contribution of Father Louis is the formation of the Indian Mass; the inculturated Holy Eucharist of the Syro-Malabar Church. To create this wonderful liturgy, he travelled all over India, visited all the Hindu and Christian asrams, personally met great Hindu and Christian leaders and sannyasins, like Abhishiktananda, Bede Griffiths, Vandana Mataji, Nitya Caitanya Yati, Nataraja Guru, Monks of Sivananda Asram in Rishikesh, Monks of Ramakrishna Mission in Belur, Asram of Nitya Chaitanya Yati, etc. Those who collaborated with him to compose the Indian Mass were Fathers Francis Vineeth Vadakethala, Prasanna Bhai Kapiarmala, Thomas Manickam, and John Peter Muringathery. Fathers Thomas Kochumuttom, Franco Malieckal and I were in the second line of co-workers.

The composition of this Indian Liturgy needed great *tapasya* and one-pointed concentration *(ekagrata)*. The hymns of this liturgy are exquisite both in melody and in content. Of course, being the Indian Liturgy, it uses prudently Indian symbols, vocabulary and style. Indian thought is more experiential than experimental, more subjective than objective, more synthetical than analytical, more a search than a research, more immanent than transcendent and more intuitive than logical. These senses and sensibilities are brilliantly incorporated in the Indian Mass. The Holy Eucharist is celebrated sitting on the ground (squatting) on a low altar. Purification of the sanctuary with water, offering of flowers to the altar, *arati* with flower, light and incense, etc., were parts of this liturgy. Superiors examined the text of the Holy Mass and permitted Father Louis to celebrate it privately with officially selected concelebrants on an experimental basis.

Cardinal Joseph Parecattil was an enthusiast of this Liturgy, and he once celebrated this Indian Liturgy in a public function at Ernakulam, Kerala.

I was a regular con-celebrant of this beautiful Liturgy at Dharmaram. Unfortunately, there were voices of dissent about this Liturgy in Dharmaram Community, particularly from the Oriental protagonists. Complaints and criticisms were sent to the CMI General Council. Ultimately, the then CMI Prior General Father Theobald Pothanikkad asked us to stop the celebration of this Holy Mass. That was the end of the Indian Mass for the CMI. But, it survived in the Asram of Kurisumala in Vagamon. Francis Acarya, the Abbot of this Asram, liked the Indian Holy Mass, and started to celebrate it occasionally. I presume, it is still in use in that Asram.

3. An Authentic *Sannyasin*

I have always considered Father Louis Malieckal as a genuine Christian *sannyasin* in the right and strict sense of the term. The word "*sannyasa*", as it is often explained, is a combination of two words, namely, the prefix "sam", which stands for *samyag,* meaning perfectly, beautifully, completely, well, etc., and the noun "nyasa", meaning placing, surrendering, putting, leaving, renouncing, throwing away, etc. *Sannyasa*, therefore, can mean two things:

The verbal form of *nyasa* is *nyasati*. Negatively the verb "nyasati" means to throw away, and applied to spiritual theology and spiritual life, it would mean renouncing everything, throwing away everything material, leaving back goods, fortunes and dear ones, etc. It is also a renunciation of the way of life and view of life to embrace a totally different one. It is basically a *nivrtti-marga*, a means to liberation through not-doing. One becomes a total, radical renouncer, *sannyasin.*

Positively the word "nysasa" means to surrender oneself to God, to submit one's body, sense, mind, consciousness and self, one's actions, words and thoughts completely and absolutely to the divine providence. Some sects like the Srivaisnavites believe that in this *Kaliyuga* a seeker is not capable of treading the difficult classical spiritual paths, namely, the paths of knowledge, devotion and disinterested action *(jnana-bhakti-karma-margas).* The only *sadhana* opened to humans for liberation from the bondage of embodied life and from the exigencies of existence caused by the inexorable law of *karma*, is the path or Yoga of self-surrender, the *prapatti-marga,* or *saranagati-marga,* or, *nyasa-vidya.* The spiritual seeker realizes that left to himself/herself he/she is incapable of working out his/her salvation. He/she understands that God is capable of leading him/her out of the mire of sinful existence and that God is accessible and approachable to all genuine seekers. Therefore, he/she totally surrenders himself/herself, his/her life, activities, results of actions and the responsibility of his/her salvation to this loving and caring God.[9]

Louisan spirituality, spirituality of all religious for that matter, is a harmonious combination of these two aspects. Renunciation of world and mundane things and surrendering oneself totally and radically to the divine power. These two aspects are two sides of the same coin. Renunciation without surrender to the ultimate cause and ground of all existence is meaningless; surrender to this divine being is impossible without renunciation of ego and things that nourish this ego.

I would very much like to qualify Father Malieckal as *Paramahamsa,* which is the highest form of Indian *sannyasa.* The Indian Law Codes speak of four types of *sannyasins,* namely, *Kuticaka, Bahudaka, Hamsa* and *Paramahamsa.* It seems that this division is based on the intensity of detachment and renunciation in an ascending scale culminating in *Paramahamsa*, whose renunciation is complete and most intensive, and hose holiness is exalted and high in the scale of sanctity. This division among the renouncers was first mentioned in *Mahabharata:* "There are indeed four types of mendicants: *Kuticaka, Bahudaka, Hamsa* and *Paramahamsa.* Of these the last one is the noblest."[10] (i) *Kuticaka* or *Kuticara* is a renouncer who lives in a hut *(kuti)* outside the village and takes alms from his own son. (ii) *Bahudakas* are mendicants who take alms in holy places, especially bathing places of holy rivers. (iii) *Hamsa* is a permanent pilgrim on the earth, always on the move. He begs his food and always lives in the presence of God. (iv) *Paramahamsa* is the highest form of *sannyasa.* He has completely controlled his body, senses, mind and thought and always lives totally detached from this ephemeral world. He is fully engrossed in abstract meditation.

Hamsa is a legendary divine bird. Two important characteristics are attributed to it, which the other ordinary birds do not possess. Firstly, it flies very high, above and over all mundane things. A *sannyasin* should be like that. He lives and moves in the world, but should be able to stand above the world, should be able to transcend body, matter and world. The second characteristic of *Hamsa* is its power of discernment *(viveka)*. Pure milk is supposed to be its

9 Some sections of this article are taken from an essay I wrote before.

10 *caturtha bhiksavas tu syuh kuticara-bahudakau/hamsah paramahamsas ca yo yah pascāt sa uttamah // (Mahabharata* XIII. 64.78.).

only food. If we offer it milk diluted with water or any other liquid, it has the ability to draw and consume only the milk element from the mixed liquid. The adulterating liquid will stay back in the bowl. The *sannyasin* Louis was like that. He lived and moved in the world; but stood above all mundane things; he used the things of this earth, but was able to discern things and accept only the things that are meaningful, useful and beneficial to his spiritual growth.

4. A Guru Par Excellence

Father Louis was an eminent Guru. All throughout his priestly life, Father Maleickal was with students, first in Christ College with college students, then in Ashta, Bhopal and *Samanvaya* with seminarians. A Guru is one who destroys the ignorance of his disciples; who shows them right path to the other shore of existence; who accompanies them in the pilgrimage to perfection. A Sanskrit verse is relevant here: *Ajnana-timirandhsya jnananjana-salakyaya / caksur unmilitam yena tasmai sri-gurave namah //* 'I salute my teacher, who, with collirium stick of knowledge, has opened my eyes, which were blind with the cataract of ignorance.' Indian spiritual tradition, especially as it is demonstrated in the Upanisadic body of literature, is very emphatic and clear on the need of the help of a Guru in the pilgrimage of the spiritual seeker to perfection and liberation. "This Atman can never be comprehended if taught by an inferior person. Unless it is taught by a competent person, there is no way to it" (*Katha Up.* II.8). "The knowledge directly learnt from one's own teacher becomes most beneficial" *(Chandogya Up.* IV.9.3). Guru Nanak says: "If a hundred moons went up, and a thousand suns arose, even in such enormous light, intense darkness will prevail without a Guru."[11] Listen to what Vivekananda has to say in this regard:

> You cannot conquer the world by your own efforts. The ego is a very powerful elephant, which cannot be brought under control by any other creatures less powerful than a Guru, whose very looks make the elephant-like-ego tremble and die. You will know in due course that your glory lies where you cease to exist. In order to gain that state, you should surrender yourself. Then the master sees that you are in a fit state to receive guidance and he guides you.[12]

The following Upanisadic sentences depict succinctly but clearly the nature and role of a Guru, and the character and duty of a disciple.

> After having carefully examined the worlds gained by deeds, an intelligent seeker should become indifferent to them, because deeds, which are

11 Guru Nanak quoted in S. S. Uban, *The Gurus of India*, New Delhi: Motilal Banarsidass, 1970, p. 130.

12 Vivekananda quoted in T. N. Venkataraman, *Maharshi's Gospel,* Madras: Ramakrishna Math, 1969, p. 37.

> transient, cannot win the Supreme Being, who is unoriginated. Therefore, to know that Being, let him, with sacrificial fuel in hand, approach a Guru, who is well-versed in the scriptures and already established in Brahman. To such a disciple, whose mind is tranquil and senses are controlled, and who approaches the Guru in the proper manner, let the wise teacher impart the science of Brahman in its very essence – the science by which one knows the true, imperishable Being *(Mundaka Up.* I.2.12-13).

This text in a way eminently enunciates the Upanisadic vision of a real Guru and a genuine disciple. A Guru should be a wise man with the great power of discernment *(vidvan)*; he should be a knower of the sacred texts *(srotriya)*, which embody the eternal truths about God, soul and matter; and he should live in constant union with God, that is, should be already established in Brahman *(brahma-nista)*. The text also indirectly declares that a Guru should be accessible and approachable to a genuine seeker. Based on this text, Sankaracarya in his famous work *Viveka-cudamaṇi* ("The Crest-Jewel of Discrimination") elaborates the specific characteristics of a real Guru: "He is a man well-versed in the sacred scriptures and is straightforward, who is not tormented by desires, who is the best among the knowers of Brahman, who has taken refuge in Brahman only, who is calm, and is like the fire which has consumed all its fuel, who is an ocean of unconditional mercy, and who is like a close relative to those who take refuge in him" (verse 33).

In the same text Sankara declares that there are three noble and rare things that can happen to a migrating self, namely, 'birth as a human being, the genuine desire for liberation in that birth, and the possibility of taking refuge in the care of a perfected person (Guru) *(mahapuruṣa-samsrayah)'* (v.3).

Kularnava Tantra, a Saiva Agama text, enumerates some auspicious and common sense qualities of a Guru: 'He is clean and modest in dress, charming, endowed with auspicious signs, knower of the truths of Agama literature, pleasing in appearance, happy-faced, easily accessible to students, clean in body, destroyer of illusion and doubt, seer of external things with an inner eye, all-knowing, compassionate to all creatures, who has controlled the cravings of the senses, and who is dear to devotees.'[13]

Needless to say that these beautiful descriptions of a Guru are fully and entirely applicable to the savant Father Malieckal Louis.

5. A Genuine CMI

Having depicted Father Louis as a perfect Indian *Sannyasin,* an eminent Guru, now I do want to portray him as a perfect CMI, a genuine Carmelite of Mary Immaculate. The spirit of the CMI Congregation is based on three basic

13 Cf. *Kularnava Tantra* XIII. 38-50; XIII. 69-81: *śuddha-veşa, manohara, sarvalakşaṇa-smpanna, priyadarśana, sumukha, sulabha, śauca, bhrama-samśaya-nāśaka, antarlakşya-bahirdṛşṭi, sarvajña, sarvajīva-dayāpara, svādhīnendriya-samcāra, bhaktapriya /.*

spiritual traditions, what we call the 'Triple Root', namely, the Oriental, Indian and Carmelite.

> Faithful to the East Syrian Tradition of St. Thomas Christians and the example and teachings of the eastern fathers, we must constantly endeavour to realize and celebrate the joy of Christ's resurrection, and his personal presence in the community of our brethren. With the prophetic spirit of Carmel, we must pursue a life of inner solitude and sacrifice, reaching out towards the mystical union with God so masterfully explained by the great mystics like St. Theresa and St. John of the Cross and at the same time combine it with the burning zeal of Elias for God's Kingdom on earth. Looking with sincere respect (NA 2) upon the holy 'seers' *(rishis)* and upon the age old tradition in India, we must seek God in the cave of the heart and strive to establish the rule of the Spirit in our material environment and in the world (*CMI Constitutions*, C.4 #2).

Our Oriental tradition distinguishes us from other Churches through our particular way of liturgical worship and liturgical spirituality, and through the Eastern theological understanding of Christ, Church, history of salvation, etc. The Indian root demands from us greater interiority and inner experience of the Divine *(anubhava)*. Carmelite tradition demands from an intense prayer culture, dedicated community life and observance of monastic rules.[14]

Father Louis Malieckal encountered these three roots creatively and responded to them on two levels. Firstly, he gained a thorough knowledge and intuitive insights of these three religious-spiritual traditions; his enlightened awareness of these roots is evident from his writings. Secondly, he interiorized the spirit of these trends and made them guiding principles of his day-to-day activities, part of his spiritual life, objects of his meditation and subjects of his preaching. He had a deep spiritual rapport to these foundational components and constituent concepts of the Congregation.

Part II: Inculturation

The title of this essay mentions that Father Louis Malieckal, CMI is a champion and crusader of inculturation. The Indian Liturgy/Indian Mass that he created is a superb example of his consciousness, knowledge and action

---

14 *The Constitutions and Directory of Carmelites of Mary Immaculate* (Revised Edition), Ernakulam-Kochi: Prior General's House, 2003.

General Synaxis Secretariat-Prior General's House, *In Search of CMI Charism and Identity*, Vol. I, Bangalore: Dharmaram Publications, 2003.

General Synaxis Secretariat, *CMI Charism on the Path of Growth*, Vol. II, Kochi: Prior General's House, 2006.

CMI Generalate, *CMI Spiritual Pilgrimage to Perfect Love, Formation Programme: Principles and Norms (Ratio Fundamentalis Institutionis)*, Kochi: Prior General's House, 2004.

plan of inculturation.[15] His doctoral dissertation is a study of Vedic Sacrifice and Christian Holy Eucharist. He tried to interpret the elements of the Holy Eucharist in the light of the *Yajna* of the Vedas.

1. Culture

Christopher Dawson defines culture as, "an organized way of life which is based on common traditions and conditioned by common environment. It is the sum-total of a nation's thinking and living, transmitted for a long period of time so as to form a tradition capable of influencing society."[16] Culture is evolved from the communitarian life, attitudes and activities of a people. It encompasses all aspects of life like rules of societal life, patterns of behaviour, food habits, folklores, art forms, celebrations, customs and traditions. Culture and religion are two separate realities and have distinct identities of their own. But, they are not opposed to each other. They influence, enrich and transform each other.

2. What is Inculturation

Inculturation is defined and described by Prof. A. Crollius in the following manner:

> (It is) the integration of the Christian experience of the local Church into the culture of its people, in such a way that this experience not only expresses itself in elements of this culture, but becomes a force that animates, orientates and innovates this culture so as to create a new unity and communion, not only in the culture in question but also as an enrichment of the Church universal.[17]

So, inculturation process aims at assimilating and integrating the local culture by the local Church to use it as an important medium of living and expressing the Christian faith. Inculturation, in effect, is a form of living dialogue by which both the partners of dialogue, namely, the local Church and its cultural *milieu* are mutually influenced, enriched and enlightened.

3. Need and Relevance of Inculturation: Theological Reflections

Nobody doubts the need and relevance of inculturation. Father Malieckal understood the process of inculturation as a basic and unquestionable principle of the life of faith in the Church. And it started right from the beginning of Christianity. The very fact that there exist four Gospels of the one Lord Jesus Christ is a great example of the need and urge the early Church felt to

---

15 This section on Inculturation is an edited and updated version of an article I wrote on Inculturation.

16 C. Dawson, *Religion and Culture*, London: 1948, p. 47.

17 A. R. Crollius, "What is New about Inculturation? A Concept and its Implications", *Gregorianum* 59 (1979), p. 735.

inculturate the message of Christ into the particular cultural context in which it was being preached. Revelation of God, the response of man to this revelation, the expression of this response in worship, in daily life through symbols, art forms, patterns of behaviour, etc., are all intimately related to the particular culture in which these things happen. St. Paul says: "God wanted all things to be reconciled through him and for him, when he made peace by his death on the cross." (Col.1: 20). Christ, the Word of God, is present in the whole of creation, and reveals his presence in all the cultures in various ways.

Father Malieckal says that the theological basis for inculturation is the Incarnation of Jesus Christ. The incarnation of the Word is the final, decisive and unique covenant of God with humanity. He sees Christ's incarnation as a very radical act of inculturation. The eternal Word of God takes flesh and shape in space and time. The humanity of Christ is the enfleshment of God's self-gift. This humanity in the person of Jesus of Nazareth took birth and lived in a particular time, place and culture. Humanity of Christ was the instrument and agency for the salvation of the world.

Incarnation is a very dynamic reality and process. The union of two natures, divine and human, in one person is not a static existence side by side, but is the most dynamic expression of God's word and a very powerful act of God's intervention in human history. This is the most personal and concrete encounter of God with humanity. This encounter and intervention happened in a specific socio-cultural context, in a particular space-time milieu and in a special point of the history of human existence. This dynamic and personal God-man encounter in incarnation, and in the death and resurrection of this incarnated Word Jesus Christ, set in motion a living process of change and transformation in the history and cosmos. The incarnation event caused wholeness in human beings, communion among peoples and harmony in the whole creation. The process of inculturation has to follow the example of the incarnated Word.

The Church's being and doing have to be incarnational. The incarnational procedure is possible only through inculturation. Just as Jesus, the cosmic *Purusa,* manifested the power of God through words, deeds and signs in a particular time, space and culture, so too the Church should manifest the message of Jesus in its own particular cultural and time-space context. That means Church needs concretization and visibilization. The living Gospel has to be lived by the Church in its living cultural context. So, Father Malieckal opines that there can be no preaching of the Gospel without inculturation. There is no authentic local Church without inculturation. It is not an option. It belongs to the very nature of the Church.

> The Gospel, and therefore evangelization, are certainly not identical with culture, and they are independent in regard to all culture. Nevertheless, the Kingdom, which the Gospel proclaims, is lived by men who are

> profoundly linked to a culture, and the building up of the Kingdom cannot avoid borrowing elements of human culture or cultures. Though independent of culture, the Gospel and evangelization are nor necessarily incompatible with them; rather they are capable of permeating them all without becoming subject to any one of them.[18]

Prof. Amalorpavadass, a noted Indian theologian, says:

> So, in a theological perspective, indigenization is a logical consequence of the nature of the Church and the Incarnation of the Word. It is indissolubly connected with the very nature of the Church, and is an indispensable dimension and activity of its mission. If so, the choice is not between indigenization and non-indigenization, but between being an authentic Church of Christ and not being a Church at all.[19]

The II Vatican Council was deeply concerned with the local Churches and their interactions with the respective cultures. The Council says:

> In order to be able to offer all of them the mystery of salvation and the life brought by God, the Church must become part of all these groups for the same motive which led Christ to bind Himself, in virtue of His Incarnation, to the definite social and cultural conditions of those human beings among whom He dwelt ...
>
> Let them share in cultural and social life by the various exchanges and enterprises of human living. Let them be familiar with their national and religious traditions, gladly and reverently laying bare the seeds of the Word which lie hidden in them.[20]

This concern is more clearly formulated in the Synod of the Bishops in 1977 on Evangelization. Its document says: "The Christian message must find its roots in human cultures and must also transform these cultures. In this sense we can say that catechesis is an instrument of 'inculturation.'"[21] (This is the first time that a Church document, addressed to the universal Church, uses the word "inculturation").

India is vastly a Hindu country. 79% of the total population of India are Hindus. And therefore, we will be speaking here on the inculturation efforts of the Indian Church in relation to the Hindu culture. Hinduism, however, is not just one religion or one culture. It comprises many religions, many

---

18 Pope Paul VI, *Evangelium Nuntiandi,* No. 20.

19 D.S. Amalorpavadass, *Gospel and Culture, Evangelization and Inculturation*, Mission Theology For Our Times Series No.11, Bangalore: NBCLC, 1985, p. 30.

20 Documents of Vatican II, *Ad Gentes (AD)*, A. P. Flannery (ed.), Michigan: W. B. Eerdmans Publishing Co., 1975, Nos 10b, 11b.

21 "Message of the Synod of Bishops to the People of God" *L'Osservatore Romano*, English edition, 3 November 1977.

cultures, many spiritualties and many philosophies. And therefore, we cannot prescribe uniform norms for the whole of India. But, there are some general characteristics that are valid for the whole of India. We base our deliberations here on these general characteristics of the Indian culture.

Father Louis says that the political freedom gave a new self-awareness and new identity-consciousness to the developing countries, particularly to India. They experienced a renaissance, a resuscitation and re-establishment of their cultural heritage and patrimony. The II Vatican Council helped the local Churches to become conscious of their false cultural identity and gave an immense boost for inculturation or re-culturation. The Federation of the Asian Bishops' Conferences in its first assembly expressed the urgent need of inculturation and stated:

> (The Church has to be) a Church incarnate in a people, a Church indigenous and inculturated. And this means concretely a Church in continuous, humble and loving dialogue with the living traditions, the cultures, the religions - in brief, with all the life-realities of the people in whose midst it has sunk its roots deeply and whose history and life it gladly makes its own. It seeks to share in whatever truly belongs to that people: its meanings and its values, its inspirations, its thought and its language, its songs and its artistry - ; Even its frailties and failings it assumes, so that they too may be healed. For so did God's son assume the totality of our fallen human condition (save only for sin) so that He might make it truly His own, and redeem it in His paschal mystery.[22]

> We accept them (the great religions of Asia) as significant and positive elements in the economy of God's design of salvation ... over many centuries they have been the treasury of the religious experience of our ancestors, from which our contemporaries do not cease to draw light and strength ... And how can we not acknowledge that God has drawn our peoples to Himself through them.[23]

With these few introductory remarks, let me now try to delineate some aspects of the efforts that the Indian Churches have carried out in the past, and also that are being done now.

---

22 *Texts, Documents and other Papers from the Federations of the Asian Bishops' Conferences (FABC) in Connection with the Third General Synod of Bishops, Rome.* 1974, book 2, Taipei, Digna C. Dacanay (ed.), Manila: Cardinal Bea Institute, 1976, p. 332.

23 FABC, "Statement of the Plenary Assembly of the Federation of Asian Bishop's Conference," Taipei: 1974.

4. Inculturation in India

4.1. Attempts of Inculturation in India before the II Vatican Council

Long before the II Vatican Council, the Church in India had made earnest attempts in the line of inculturation. I would like to call your attention to the following examples.

Inculturation and Indianization of the Thomas Christians: India has a very long tradition of Christianity. It goes back to the apostle Thomas, who is supposed to have come to India in the year 52 and preached the Gospel in Kerala and its neighbourhoods. The faithful of this Apostolic Church, right from the beginning, adopted in socio-cultural matters, the life-style of their co-countrymen. St. Thomas Christians found no contradiction between their faith and the socio-cultural customs they inherited from their forefathers. As the high caste Hindus, the Thomas Christians were vegetarians. In external appearance, a Thomas-Christian did not differ from a high caste Hindu. Men, also priests, used to wear the sacred thread and the tuft of hair in the crown of the head. However, the Christians used to insert a metal cross in the tuft of hair. Married woman, following the Hindu custom, wore in the sacred chain (*tali*) which her husband tied around her neck during the matrimonial rite, a small golden medal with a cross in the middle. This custom is kept up even to this day. The Church architecture was much the same as the Hindu temple, but the Church definitely had its distinguishing marks, like the huge stone cross in the front of the Church in the place of the stone mast before the Hindu temples. The Church properties were administered by the 'Church-assembly' (*palliyogam*), which was an imitation of the mode of the temple administration. The candidate for priesthood were selected by the faithful and, according to the Hindu custom, was sent to a guru (*malpan*) for instruction and formation. In the religious life too they adopted many of the family and sacramental rites (*samskara*) of the high caste Hindus with necessary adaptation. Thus they used to observe the rites like the name-giving ceremony (*namakarana*), the ritual of giving the child solid food for the first time (*annaprasana*), the ceremony to mark the beginning of education (*vidyarambha*), the initiation to the sacred scriptures (*upanayana*), matrimonial and funeral rites, and the solemn commemoration of the dead (*sraddha*). Even in the holy Eucharist, which was celebrated only on Sundays and on special occasions, they introduced local customs of worship. Thus, it is believed that in the celebration of the Eucharist the faithful carried freshly baked bread in a lotus leaf to the priest for offertory. It is to be noted here that in this process of indianization and inculturation the St. Thomas Christians also accepted the caste system that was prevalent in India at that time, and were respected in the society as members of a high cast, which was against Christian principle of charity.

It is however, a matter of great regret that this ancient Church did not hand down to the succeeding generations any notable literary or artistic work on its life and spirituality.

But, unfortunately the arrival of the Portuguese missionaries and their authoritarian and unnecessary interventions in the affairs of this Church in the sixteenth century not only blocked many of these meaningful, at any rate harmless, adaptations, but also imposed on them western style of living and worshipping. The rule of the Portuguese over the St. Thomas Christians of Kerala was beneficial in many respects, but as regards inculturation was concerned, it was also a sad and dark period of its long history. The Syro-Malabar Church of the St. Thomas Christians is now seriously engaged in the restoration of its heritage and renewal of the life of the Church.

The theology, spirituality and way of life of Father Louis Malieckal were influenced in one way or other by some great protagonists and their works of Inculturation and adaption of the Indian Church.

4.2. Roberto de Nobili

One of the great pioneers of inculturation of the Indian Church was Roberto de Nobili, a Roman Jesuit, who came to India and settled down in Madurai in Tamil Nadu in the year 1606. He immediately understood that the methods employed by the western missionaries are entirely wrong. The Hindus despised the missionaries and avoided all contacts with them, because they were meat-eaters and drank alcohol. The missionaries and the Christians were addressed by the Hindus with the deprecatory name *parangis*. De Nobili perceived that one has to become an Indian in appearance, life style and in thinking to attract the Hindus. So, he started to live like a high caste Hindu *sannyasin*. He wore saffron clothes, ate only vegetarian meals cooked by a Brahmin and behaved like a high caste Hindu. (His father was a General of the Army of the Pope. So he considered himself to be a *Ksatriya*). He learned Sanskrit and started to study the Vedas and Vedanta in Sanskrit. He wanted to present Christianity to the Hindus in the language of the Vedas and Vedanta. De Nobili is first European to master Sanskrit, the sacred language of the Hindus, in which all their scriptures are written. He learned also Tamil. De Nobili wrote many works on Christian doctrines in Sanskrit and in Tamil, among which the summary of the Christian doctrine in hundred Sanskrit verses and the catechism in Tamil in five volumes deserve special mention. He understood also the need of training priests in the Indian style and traditions and planned to open a training centre for Indian priests which, however was not materialized. It is amazing to note that De Nobili even asked permission from Rome to use Sanskrit as the liturgical language instead of Latin! And that was three and half centuries before the II. Vat. Council! Many high caste and low caste Hindus were attracted to the Christian faith. He founded a new order of *sannyasins* known as *pandarasvamins*. They were, as it is in Hinduism, allowed to look after the spiritual needs of also low caste converts.[24]

It is, however, to be remembered here about the accusations that the succeeding generations have levelled against him. His attempts, it was pointed out, were wrongly conceived and incorrectly carried out. De Nobilian attempts in inculturation perpetuated the caste system and caste discrimination within the Church of Tamil Nadu.

4.3. Brahmabandhab Upadhyaya

Father Malieckal was particularly fond of the thoughts of the great theologian Brahmabadhav Upadyay. He was born in a Bengal Brahmin family in 1861. His Hindu name was Bavani Charan Banerjee. In 1891 he received baptism and became an Anglican. In the same year he was received in the Catholic Church and received the name Theophilus, the translation of which is Brahmabadhav (Friend of God). He believed that Christian faith should be presented to India in the language of Vedanta, just as Greek philosophy was used to interpret Christianity in Europe. He said:

> In our humble opinion it is the foreign clothes of the Catholic faith that have chiefly prevented our countrymen from perceiving its universal nature. Catholicism has donned the European garb in India. Our Hindu brethren cannot see the subtlety and sanctity of our Divine religion because of its hard coating of Europeanism.[25]

He was convinced that only Catholic mendicants (*sannaysins*) in the life style of Hindu *sannyasins* could preach the Gospel using the Vedantic philosophy. For this purpose he founded a Catholic *asram* on the banks of Narmada near Jabalpur. About this *asram* he said:

> In this hermitage will the words of the Eternal Word be strung in the hymns of Eastern melody; in this Holy place will the transcendent Catholic devotions be clothed in Hindu garb. Here, on the banks of the classic river, will the children of India sit at the feet of the Angelic and the Seraphic Doctors to drink deep of the Divine Science; here will the Vedanta philosophy be assimilated to the universal truth.[26]

But he had to close down the *asram* because of ecclesiastical objections. His greatest contribution is perhaps the fact that he tried to initiate an Indian Christian theology. He tried to explain the Trinity with the Vedantic concept of *saccidananda (sat-cit-ananda)*. He interpreted creation with the Hindu

---

24 Cf. R. Boyd, *An Introduction to Indian Christian Theology*, Madras: The Christian Literature Society, 1979, pp. 11 ff.

25 B. Animananda, *The Blade: Life and Work of Brahmabandhav Upadhay*, Calcutta: Roy & Son, 1947, pp. 74-75.

26 B. Animananda, *The Blade*, p. 79.

concept of *maya*. However, he had to face strong objections from the part of the official Church.

4.4. *Jule Monchanin (Swami Parama Arupi Anandam) and Henri le Saux (Swami Abhishiktananda)*

Father Louis had direct contacts with these two great souls. They were two French Catholic priests, the latter a Benedictine monk. Monchanin came to India in 1938 and Le Saux in 1947. They together founded an *asram* at Kulithalai on the banks of river Kaveri in 1950 and dedicated it to the worship of the holy Trinity. They named it *Saccidananda Asram. Saccidananda* is the Sanskrit term used to designate the Trinity. Monchanin died in 1957. Then Abhishiktananda entrusted the *asram* to Fr. Bede Griffiths and went to the Himalayas, where he spent the rest of his life in prayer, contemplation and writing books. He died in 1973. The greatest contribution of these two great priests to the Indian Church and to the process of the inculturation in India, is that they discovered the contemplative dimension of Indian spirituality and presented it to the Church. Both of them wanted to encounter Hinduism and engage in fruitful dialogue with it at the deepest level, namely, at the level of prayer and contemplation.[27]

These are some examples of the attempts of inculturation in the Catholic Church before the II Vatican Council. The non-Catholic Churches have also given serious thought to the issue of inculturation. Scholars and teachers like Kesahb Chandra Sen (1838-1884), Nehemiah Goreh (Nilakantha Sastri Goreh) (1825-1895), Sadhu Sundar Singh (1889-1929), Aiyadurai Jesudasan Appasamy (born in 1891), Panipeddi Chenchiah (1886-1959), V. Chakkarai (1880-1958) and Dr. Paul David Devanandan (1901-1962) had done great services in the fields of Hindu-Christian dialogue, inculturation and Indian Christian theology.

4.5. *Inculturation in India after the II Vatican Council*

The II Vatican Council unleashed fervent and concerted activities in the Indian Church. The Catholic Bishops Conference of India (CBCI) lost no time to set to work to implement the suggestions of the Council. In its general meeting at Delhi in 1966 (13-20 October), CBCI drew up its plan of action, especially in the field of inculturation. The question that faced the Indian Church, as Amalorpavadass puts it, is:

> We are Indians and Christians. Hence we are heirs to both Indian Culture and Christian Faith. Now the question is: How to interact and integrate both into a living and dynamic synthesis? And how to live in all aspects and

27 Three other Christian missionaries who honestly tried for inculturation in India are: Joseph Constantius Beschi (came to India in 1710), Ziegelbalg (1682-1719) and William Carey (1716-1834).

> areas of life authentically and fully as Indians and authentically and fully as Christians?[28]

Following the CBCI meeting, many national seminars and conferences were organized in different parts of India to discuss this issue. The Bombay International Theological Seminar in 1969, the historic All-India Seminar on the "Church in India Today" in Bangalore in 1969, The Nagapur International Theological Conference on "Evangelization, Dialogue and Development" in 1971, The Patna All-India Consultation on Evangelization in 1973, The Research Seminar on "Non-Biblical Scriptures" in Bangalore in 1974, The Research Seminar on "Pastoral Consultation on Ministries in India" in Bangalore in 1976, The Poona All-India Seminar on the "Indian Church in the Struggle for a New Society" in 1981, The All-India Research Seminar on "Sharing Worship - *Communicatio in Sacris*" in Bangalore in 1988, The Annual Seminars of the Indian Theological Association since 1974, The Meetings of the Conferences of Religious in India (CRI) since 1964, etc., tried to answer this question. The three main concepts around which the deliberations of these assemblies revolved were: dialogue, inculturation and evangelization. Many institutions came forward to experiment and express an inculturated Christian life. The CBCI set up a the "National Biblical, Catechetical and Liturgical Centre" in 1967 precisely to fulfil this objective. Dialogue Centres like the "Chavara Cultural Centre Cochin", "Samiksa" in Kalady, "Vidyajyoti" in New Delhi, "Centre for the Study of World Religions" (CSWR) in Bangalore, "Divyodaya" in Coimbatore, "Asirvad" in Bangalore, "Isvani" in Poona, etc., were established by different religious congregations to carry on the task of adaptation and dialogue. A few journals are published to articulate the ideas of the Indian theologians on these matters. *Vidyajyoti, Journal of Dharma, Word and Worship, Indian Theological Studies, Jeevadhara,* etc., deserve special mention.

The admonitions of the II Vatican Council and spirit of the Gospel message guided the efforts of inculturation. The following words of the Council inspired the Indian Church in its fruitful encounter with the Indian culture:

> The Church learned in its history to express the Christian message in the concepts and language of different peoples and tried to clarify it in the light of the wisdom of their philosophers: it was an attempt to adapt the Gospel to the understanding of all men and the requirements of the learned, in so far as this could be done. Indeed, this kind of adaptation and preaching of the revealed Word must ever be the law of all evangelization. In this way it is possible to create in every country the possibility of expressing the message

28 D. S. Amalorpavadass, *Gospel and Culture: Evangelization and Inculturation*, p. 17.

of Christ in suitable terms and to foster vital contact and exchange between the Church and different cultures.[29]

5. Areas of Inculturation in India

Inculturation should cover all aspects of Christian life in India. But, especially the areas of liturgy, theology, spirituality, art and architecture, formation of priests and religious and language demand immediate attention.[30] I would like to call your attention to the efforts that are being carried out to inculturate the Christian faith in India in three areas, namely, Liturgy, Theology and Spirituality.

5.1. Inculturation of Liturgy

Needless to say that the main concern of Father Louis Malieckal was the inculturation of the Liturgy. We have already seen above his strenuous efforts in this direction. The greatest proponent of liturgical inculturaion was Father Amalorpavadass. Father Louis was a great admirer and follower of this theologian. For the faithful *aggiornamento* of the Church often means only the changes in the liturgy. For them the importance of the II Vatican Council is that it brought out adaptations in the holy Eucharist. The Council promulgated its Constitution on the Sacred Liturgy, the *Sacrosanctum Concilium* on the 4th of December 1963. The Catholic Bishops' Conference of India in its general meeting at Delhi in 1966 decided to implement the liturgical renewal envisaged by the Council. It set up an Episcopal Commission for Liturgy, it decided to set up a liturgical centre at Bangalore, and it gave the necessary guidelines for liturgical renewal, namely, all attempts of renewal should be in tune with the norms given by the II Vat. Council, there should be a deep respect for Christian message and cult, intense research should be done in the non-Christian rituals and forms of worship in India, all experimentations should be carried out with the clear permission of the local ordinary, texts should be carefully selected and prepared from the non-Christian sacred scriptures of India for para-liturgical services, etc.

The Liturgical Commission drew up a programme for liturgical indigenization in two stages. The first stage consisted in the introduction of minor adaptations with a view of creating an Indian atmosphere of worship, like Indian postures (sitting or standing), gestures (like form of kissing objects), objects and elements (oil lamp, tray, etc.), vestments, decorations, forms of homage and veneration (like *anjali hasta, pancanga pranama*), etc. These items

29 Vatican Council II, *AG* 62.

30 Cf. Amalorpavadass, *Gospel and Culture*, pp. 27-28. He points out sixteen areas for inculturation.

were later codified in twelve points and became famous as the *Twelve Points*.[31] The Congregation for Sacred Liturgy of Vatican approved these twelve points for experimentation in 1969.

The second stage envisaged the following essential adaptations: (i) Original compositions of prayer formulae and spontaneity in expression; (ii) Inclusion of a reading from non-Christian religions and the use of chants inspired from such literature in the liturgy of the Word; (iii) composition of an Indian *Anaphora* (Eucharistic prayer) which would proclaim the marvels done by God not only in Israel but also in India and in the whole world. This is to be composed in a language and way of praying specific to India; (iv) adaptation of Indian initiation ceremonies in the baptismal rite; (v) integration of the rite of matrimony with local marriage customs and ceremonies; (vi) Christian funeral rite with the funeral customs of the society, region and religion and (vii) Christian celebration of Indian festivals, whether national, social or religious.

---

31 The Twelve Points are:

(i) The posture during the Mass, both for the priests and the faithful, may be adapted to local usage, that is, sitting on the floor, standing and the like; footwear may be removed also.

(ii) Genuflections may be replaced by the profound bow with the *anjali hasta.*

(iii) A *pancanga pranam* by both priests and faithful can take place before the liturgy of the Word, as part of the Penitential rite, and at the conclusion of the *Anaphora.*

(iv) Kissing objects may be adapted to local custom, that is, touching the object with one's fingers or palm of one's hand and bringing the hands to one's eyes or forehead.

(v) The kiss of peace could be given by the exchange of the *anjali hasta* and/or the placing of the hands of the giver between the hands of the recipient.

(vi) More use of incense could be made in liturgical services. The receptacle could be the simple incense bowl with handle.

(vii) The vestments could be simplified. A single tunic-type chasuble with a stole (*angavastra*) could replace the traditional vestments of the Roman rite.

(viii) The corporal could be replaced by a tray (*thali* or *thambula thattu*) of fitting material.

(ix) Oil lamps could be used instead of candles.

(x) The preparatory rite of the Mass may include:

   a. The presentation of gifts.

   b. The welcome of the celebrant in an Indian way, e.g. with a single *arati*, washing of hands, etc.

   c. The lighting of the lamp.

   d. The greeting of peace among the faithful in sign of mutual reconciliation.

(xi) In the "Oratio Fidelium" some spontaneity may be permitted both with regard to its structure and the formulation of the intentions. The universal aspect of the Church however should not be left in oblivion.

(xii) In the Offertory rite and at the conclusion of the *Anaphora* the Indian form of worship may be integrated, that is, double or triple "arati" of flowers, and/or incense, and/or light.

Incorporating the twelve points of the first stage, the text of the Mass was formulated and was celebrated at the National Seminar on *Church in India Today* at Bangalore in 1969. Many religious communities, seminaries, *asrams,* etc., started the renewal of the liturgy using these guidelines.[32] But, there was great oppositions to the 'Indian Mass' from the part of some lay people and some priests. Much has been written in the Indian press for and against this Mass. In 1975 Rome asked to stop all liturgical experimentations. The 'Indian Mass' is still used privately in some *asrams* or small communities. But, it is no longer celebrated publicly. However, it is to be noted that these twelve points are not revoked by Rome. So, in future, when the time is ripe these points may be again introduced.

5.2. Indian Christian Theology

In the field of formulating Indian Christian Theology or theologies, the Protestant Churches of India were much ahead of the Catholics. But in recent years an enormous amount of literature on Indian theology has been produced by many eminent Catholic theologians. The names of Raymond Panikkar, Abhishiktananda, Bede Griffiths, Amalorpavadass, Amaladoss, J. B. Chethimattom, Paul Puthanangady, Sr. Sara Grant, V. F. Vineeth, Sr. Vandana, *et alia* are to be recalled here. I would like to analyse shortly the ideas of the Indian theology of two theologians, namely, Fr. Raymond Panikkar and Father Bede Griffiths.

Professor Raymond Panikkar: He was born (in 1918) of a Hindu father and a Spanish Roman Catholic mother and was brought up in these two traditions. He mastered both the Hindu Vedanta and the Christian Bible. His first important work is *The Unknown Christ of Hinduism*, published in 1964. Since then he has revised his concepts of Hindu-Christian dialogue and Indian Christian theology. He has published numerous works in English, German, Spanish, French and Italian. *Trinity and World Religions; The Vedic Experience. Mantramanjari; The Intrareligious Dialogue; Myth, Faith and Hermeneutics* - these works are important. The revised and enlarged edition of his *The Unknown Christ of Hinduism: Towards an Ecumenical Christophany* came out in 1981. Basically he states that Christ is already present in Hinduism and that the Hindus can be saved through Christ who is hidden in Hinduism. Mission then means making this hidden Christ known. His important contribution however, is to the Indian Christology. Employing Upanisadic concept of Brahman, the non-dualistic concept of *Isvara* (*Saguna-brahman)* and the God of the theistic systems, he tried to explain God, Christ and world. Evidently his attempt to equate Christ with Isvara is not without problems. Yet

32 Archbishop D. S. Lourdusamy, Chairman of the Liturgical Commission of the CBCI, also celebrated this 'Indian Mass' before the officials of the Congregation for Sacred Liturgy in Rome.

he gives a new dimension to the understanding of Christ and his mission in the world.

Swami Bede Griffiths: Bede Griffiths is a Benedictine monk from England who came to India in 1955, and since then lived and died in India, adopting a Hindu-Christian sannyasic life. Since 1968 he is the guru of the *Saccidananda Asram* (which is known also as *Santivanam Asram*) at Kulithalai in Tamil Nadu. He contributed much to the development of *asram* spirituality. But, he is also one of the important Indian Christian theologian. He tried to incorporate the ideals of Indian *sannyasa* with Christian monasticism. One of his constant themes of writings is that the western consciousness should constructively encounter the eastern interiority in order to realize a new healthy world order, and in order to realize the Reality fully. The titles of his works like *Return to the Centre; Vedanta and Christian Faith; The Marriage of East and West; The Cosmic Revelation: the Hindu Way to God*; *River of Compassion* which is his interpretation of the *Bhagavadgita* and *A New Vision of Reality: Western Science, Eastern Mysticism and Christian Faith* reveal the theological concerns he has in the context of India. Father Malieckal has personal contacts with Swami Bede Griffiths. Fathers Malieckal, Chackapalaparambil and I had opportunity to stay in the Asram of Bede for a few days.

5.3. Indian Christian Spirituality

Inculturation in the field of spirituality has, as it is evident, covers many areas, like the Christian *asram* movement, Christian *yoga*, Christian *bhakti*, prayer and meditation, etc. I would like to say few words about the *asram* spirituality.

(i) The *asram* movement wants to re-introduce the life style and spirituality of the ancient India's life of renunciation and mendicancy. This was an important stage of life in the social set-up of the classical India. Probably all the sacred scriptures of Hinduism were produced by the sages and saints in the *asram*.

(ii) The *asram* spirituality is a going back to the nature; it is a nature-bound spirituality. The *asrams* are normally in the forest or on the mountains or on the banks of river.

(iii) Life in the *asram* is centred around the person of the guru, the charismatic and spiritual head of the *asram*. There is no *asram* without this central figure of the guru. A flourishing *asram* may cease to exist as an *asram* if the guru disappears from the scene.

(iv) An *asram* is an open place. All are welcome there without any distinction of caste, creed, class or sex. In this sense *asram* is a place of effective inter-religious dialogue, dialogue at the deepest level, an existential and experiential form of dialogue.

(v) An *asram* is definitely a place of peaceful silence, solitude, prayer and meditation and also of physical labour.

(vi) The food, habit and habitation of the asramites are extremely simple, like those of the *sannyasins* of India.

(vii) Compassion to all living beings is an important characteristic of the *asram*. The Christian *asrams* normally try to cater to the spiritual and material needs of the poor of their surroundings.

There were Catholic *asrams* even before the II Vatican Council. But, after the Council the *asram* movement has picked up momentum. There are more than hundred Christian *asrams* in India today, many among them are Catholic. The names of the *Santivanam asram, Kurisumala asram,* etc., are known all over the world.

5.4. Some Objections against Inculturation in India

The local Churches, especially of the developing countries, in their efforts to inculturate its life and activities, had to confront a new situation. Although, on the whole the local Churches wanted to adapt its life-style, worship and theology to its cultural patrimony, there was also great opposition to this process. A section of the people who clung to their accustomed western culture and mode of worship did not wish to change. They saw in the process of inculturation dilution of Christian faith, loss of Christian identity, falsification of Christianity, Hinduisation, betrayal of the Gospel, etc. So, they viewed the attempts for inculturation with caution, suspicion, fear and enmity. They were not open to new ideas, were not generous to their own culture, were still slaves of the colonial culture and thinking, and wanted to keep the status quo.

5.4.1. Inculturation is Hinduisation

This is a common criticism levelled against the attempts of inculturation in India. As I mentioned earlier, the Indian culture is predominantly Hindu culture. But, Indian culture has been formed by taking in many influences. Vatican Council says: "The young Churches in imitation of the plan of Incarnation rooted in Christ take to themselves, in a wonderful exchange, all the riches of the nations which were given to Christ as an inheritance." Again the Council exhorts us "to learn by sincere and patient dialogue what treasures a bountiful God has distributed among the nations of the earth" (AG.11d.). So inculturation includes other religious tradition as part of God's plan for the local Church. But, as Amalorpavadass points out, the efforts of inculturation:

> should be subjected to Christian scrutiny and interpretation. Any authentic inculturation will reject false doctrines, superstitions, all forms of sin and evil and whatever cannot be christianized. Nothing can be integrated into our theology, liturgy, spirituality, unless they have values in them, unless

> they can survive a prophetic critique, unless they acquire a Christian meaning through a Christian interpretation, unless they are oriented towards a Christian goal, under the guidance of the Spirit. This is an important and indispensable condition for inculturation.[33]

5.4.2. Inculturation and Syncretism

The problem of syncretism arises when one tried to bring a symbol that has a function in a special religious and cultural *milieu* into one's own religious tradition and allow it to function in the way of the other religion and culture. An amount of syncretism is unavoidable in all religious traditions. We have to find a positive meaning and interpretation to the concept of syncretism. M. M. Thomas, a noted theologian of India, says:

> Earlier in my writing I kept the distinction between religious syncretism and cultural syncretism, considering the former wrong and the latter right. But I have found the negative connotation of the word syncretism remains a continuing hindrance for the Christian to enter into dialogue with other world religions. ... Now I have come to accept a neutral definition of syncretism from the history of religious traditions: to denote any interpenetration between religions and between cultures, then to distinguish between wrong and right kind of syncretism; the Christian's goal would then be Christ-centred syncretism.[34]

5.4.3. Inculturation **vis-a-vis** *Modernization*

Many think that India is being westernized and modernized. Indians, especially the youth, are not very much concerned with cultural heritage and values they have, and do not, in the present context of history, see the need of living in the past. Why should the Church try to inculturate the things that the Indians are leaving back now? India lives in her villages. More than 85% of the total population live in villages. These villages and their people still hold on to the traditional values and cultures. Even the urban population in India remain 'Indian' in the heart, though it has integrated and absorbed certain values of the West in social life.

5.4.4. Inculturation Causes Confusion and Sense of Insecurity

People are happy and content with the present form of living Christian faith. They have been used to it for centuries. Now why should we create confusion among the faithful by demands for inculturation, which they really do not want? The colonizers have left India long ago. But, even today the colonized cling to

---

33 D. S. Amalorpavadass, *Gospel and Culture*, p. 49.

34 M. M. Thomas, "The Absoluteness of Jesus Christ and Christ-centred Syncretism", *Ecumenical Review*.

the values of the colonial era more tenaciously than the colonizers themselves! With acceptance of Christianity, the faithful had also to accept the culture of the missionaries and their Churches. They became alienated from the mainstream of national life. Christians were considered West-oriented second-rate citizens of India. They became a foreign body in the country. Now the question is: Should we continue in this isolation and alienation? Should we keep up this false identity? Shaking off these things means some initial pain and tension, some confusion and confrontations. But thereby our true identity will emerge, namely, an Indian-Christian![35]

6. Epilogue

A personal note about Prof. Dr. Louis Malieckal, CMI, who was my friend, well-wisher, confrere and fellow-priest. He is no more with us. His unexpected demise and unannounced journey to the other shore caused immense pain and also awful consternation to his friends, confreres and relatives. Many, particularly his colleagues and students, feel desolate and forlorn at the thought that he is no more with them. They would painfully miss his encouraging presence, suave words, gracious comportment, unqualified love for fellow men, and God-oriented simple life-style. I consider him as a sagacious Guru, a compassionate priest, an eminent scholar, a servant of the people, a prominent spiritual master, above all a gentle and benign human being, who had great faith in the goodness of others. His presence exuded calmness and peace. These factors give his dealings, words and thoughts an extra vibrancy, dynamism and spiritual nuance. Grow where you are planted, and let others also grow, seems to be his style of functioning. Eighty-three years of his earthly sojourn were uncompromisingly dedicated to give glory to God, to work for the well-being of the fellowmen, to safeguard the nature around him and to earnestly endeavour for self-sanctification. May God grant him home and resting place in the eternal abode and be compassionate and empathetic to him. God bless his soul!

---

35 S. Rayan, "Flesh of India's Flesh", *Jeevadhara* 6, No. 3 (1976). Cf. also J. Masson, "Objectives and Obligations of Dialogue of Religions", *Journal of Dharma* I (1975), p. 68 ff.; J.B. Chethimattom, "Man's Dialogical Nature and the Dialogue of Religions", *Journal of Dharma*, I (1976), pp.10-29; T. Balasuriya, "Some Thoughts on Evangelization and Dialogue", *Journal of Dharma 2,* No. 10 (1972), p. 337 ff.; M. Amaladoss, "The Christian Creativity", *Jeevadhara* No. 9 (1972), p. 250 ff.; M. Amaladoss, "Symbol and Mystery", *Journal of Dharma* II (Oct. 1977), p. 383 ff.; M. Amaladoss, "Religious Rite as Symbol", *Jeevadhara* No. 29 (1975), p. 325 ff.; M. Amaladoss, "Symbols in Life and Worship", *Jeevadhara* No. 106 (1988), pp. 254-255; Jyoti Sahi, "Indian Symbols of the Holy Spirit", *Jeevadhara* No. 45 (1978), p. 243 ff.; K. Knnumpuram, "Inculturation in Vat. II", *Jeevadhara* 6 No. 33 (1976), pp. 283-292; M. Amaladoss, *Becoming Indian. The Process of Inculturation,* Bangalore: Dharmaram Publications and Rome: CIIS, 1992.

7

A Dedicated Champion Who Understood the need of Evangelizing India Through Inculturation

Dr. Isaac Chakkalaparambil CMI

Our dear Fr. Louis Malieckal was a young CMI Scholastic when St. Pope John XXIII decided in 1962 to open up the windows of our Church of Christ in order to let in fresh air. The saintly Pope John wanted to make this light, the Church, the bride of Christ, shine brightly before the whole world. He wanted the Church of Jesus Christ ever relevant and appealing to the enlightened modern generation of its followers. The Second Vatican Council was convened boldly by St. Pope John XXIII in the year 1962 and continued through St. Pope Paul VI to its conclusion in 1965. Sixteen studied and solid documents were produced as a result, and were promulgated to make the bride of Christ, the Church to shine, as she has to, in the setting of today's modern world. Of course, the conservatives in the institution were alarmed and did not want to let go the ease and comfort they have been privileged to. They were innocently ignorant and unwilling to expose to any challenging newness that was thoughtfully envisaged by the Vatican II for whole world.

Fr. Louis Malieckal and some of us his admirers and friends were starting our Theological program of studies in 1966 onwards at Dharmaram Pontifical Institute of Theology and Philosophy. Rev. Dr. Mathias Mundadan, the eminent Historian and professor, who had fully absorbed the spirit of Vatican II, happened to be our mentor as our section master. His convictions about an Indian Theology (Ref. Paths of Indian Theology, 1998) and our, his students', dreams for an 'Indianized' Catholic Church, in all aspects of worship, liturgy, art and culture, captivated our younger minds to discuss and start worshiping Jesus Christ, our Master ('Guru') in a way our Indian mind can understand and absorb. Enlightened minds, in particular Cardinal Joseph Parekattil of Ernakulam, Dr. Jonas Thaliath (later bishop of Rajkot), Dr. Werner Chackakalackal, Fr. Vineeth Vadakkethala, Cyriac Kanichai and other professors at Dharmaram were all supportive and appreciative of these ideas of presenting the bride of Christ, our Church, to a welcoming mind of our homeland, India.

In the Latin hierarchy of India also this enthusiasm in adapting worship and Liturgy in Indian cultural patterns were getting promoted and going on with great enthusiasm. A glaring example in these efforts was the initiatives of an eminent Indian Theologian, Dr. Amalorpavadass of NBCLC, in Bangalore.

With Fr. Louis Malieckal at the lead, there occurred earnest efforts in "inculturation" experiments at Dharmaram College. It was an effort to interpret the mystery of Christ, the Incarnation of the Word of God and the redemptive action of our Lord and saviour in the limelight of our Indian ethos and its cultural and artistic expression. It was also the time when the CMIs were invited to open up mission areas in North India. Our Christian existence in the mission needed this welcome inculturation. Christian understanding of creation, redemptive action, Christian sacraments and all other worship patterns have to be made acceptable and appealing in a living and vibrant cultural milieu. So, the inculturation experiments were started and progressed with great appreciation and support of our CMI major superiors and section masters.

Genuine "inculturation" efforts envisaged by Vatican II was heartily followed in our study house during our theology-training years. Meaningful and heart-touching "bhajans" and music were composed and sung with devotion. Holy Eucharistic Liturgy in Syro-Malabar Rite was beautifully adapted and celebrated in genuine Indian way. Sanskrit scholars like Fr. Thomas Kochumuttom and Fr. Augustine Thottakara and others enriched these process of genuine Indian inculturation going forward. Our experimental Indian Liturgy texts were in demand at other centers for practice and celebration.

Although, official approval from Rome was granted for inculturation experiments in Liturgy and Worship, (By the Vatican Directive Prot. N. 802/69 of April 25, 1969.), opposition to this inculturation experiments was also surging up from conservative quarters, both from the Syro-Malabar and Roman rite sides. Eventually, forces opposed to the Indian inculturation experiments prevailed upon Rome so much so that the whole process of revival of Catholicism in India through such inculturation efforts had to be shelved and discontinued. Now probably vestiges of such indianized worship practices are only extant in some pocket centers here and there like "Kurishumala Ashram" in Kerala or in some IMS Society Ashrams and centers elsewhere.

Fr. Louis Malieckal and all of us were unhappy at the turn of events. But as an obedient CMI, Fr. Louis, although found it sour and disappointing, drank that cup of set-back with courage. Fr. Louis was a happy man all through his life. He was serving as a professor of statistics at Christ College when these developments occurred in the Indian Church. Thereafter Fr. Louis went for theological studies in Louvain and was serving in North Indian Regional seminary at Ashta, and later in our CMI mission seminary in Bhopal all through his life, teaching his students about the needs of inculturation in Indian missionary efforts.

We, eleven out of 16 priests ordained in 1969, gathered together to celebrate our 50th year of Ordination in 2019 at Chavara Hills, reminiscing all the beautiful things happened in our lives together. But Jesus, the great 'Guru' needed him in heaven and so he went to his eternal reward on February 25, 2019. May this great soul Rest in Peace and inspire the Indian Church to shine and flourish with the ideals for which Fr. Louis always stood with dedication and pride.

Note:

In fact permissions for such liturgical adaptation and experimentation was granted from Rome in 1969. *(By the Vatican Directive Prot. N. 802/69 of April 25, 1969, 12 points of adaptation were permitted in India.) But there was mounting opposition from conservative side in the Church, both from Roman Rite and Syro Malabar Rite. Major opposition to the approval of the 12 points which the then CBCI sent to Rome for approval and got approved was a technical mistake: that instead of a 2/3 majority there needed there were only 34 bishops out of 71 members voted yes to this). Eventually the conservative position prevailed and the Liturgical experimentation had to be discontinued.*

The 12 points are:

1. The posture during the mass, both for the priests and the faithful may be adapted to the local usage; that is sitting on the floor (called squatting mass), standing and the like - footwear may be removed also.
2. Genuflections may be replaced by the añjalī hastā (a profound bow of the head with joined hands on the forehead).
3. A pañcāṅg praṇām (homage of 5 organs of the body) by both priest and faithful can take place before the liturgy of the word, as part of the penitential rite, and at the conclusion of the anaphora.

4. The kissing of the objects may be adapted to local custom, that is, touching the object with one's hand and bringing the hands to one's eyes or forehead.
5. The kiss of peace could be given by the exchange of the añjali hastā or by the placing of hands of the giver between the hands of the recipient.
6. Incense could be used more often in liturgical services. The receptacle could be the simple incense bowl with handle.
7. The vestments could be simplified. A single tunic-type chasuble with a stole (aṅgavastrā) could replace the traditional vestments of the Roman rite.
8. The corporal could be replaced by a tray (thālī or thambūla thattu) of fitting material.
9. Oil lamps could be used instead of candles.
10. The preparatory rite of the Mass may include:
    a. the presentation of gifts
    b. the welcome of the celebrant in an Indian way, e.g., with a single ārtī (the waving of light or incense), washing of hands, etc.
    c. the lighting of the lamp
    d. the greeting of peace among the faithful as a sign of reconciliation.
11. In the *Oratio fidelium* some spontaneity may be permitted with regard to both its structure and the formulation of the intentions. However, care should be taken to maintain the universal aspect of the Church.
12. In the offertory rite and at the conclusion of the anaphora the Indian form of worship may be integrated, that is, double or triple 'ārtī' of flowers, incense, and or light.

8

Footprints Engraved on the Marble of Time
Tribute to Dr. Fr. Louis Malieckal CMI
A Prophet of Inculturation

Dr. Fr. James Gurudas

Introduction

It is certainly worthwhile and praiseworthy to publish a book to eternalize the memory of Fr. Louis Malieckal. No monument is as lasting as a book. Statues and Buildings may crumble; they may be devoured and disappear by earthquakes and volcanoes; they may be destroyed by enemies and idiots, as it happened to the beautiful Buddhist statues at Bamyan in Afganistan. Those ravishing structures were considered as world-heritage and respected and preserved as valuable treasures of humankind by all the thinking humans in the world; but they were rubbish and dangerous to the fools and blockheads.

When the organizers of the would-be publication requested me to contribute to it with a long article on Fr. Louis, I expressed my reluctance, because by nature I am not for personality cult. But, they put me in mind that I am the one who lived the longest time, six years, with him in Kristupremalaya Seminary Ashta. Their reminder brought about a metanoia, change of mind in me and I agreed to write an article but not as long as they desired. Undoubtedly, Fr. Louis deserves to be remembered for all time, and I am only happy to donate at least a small amount for the construction of the planned literary monument in honour of this great visionary and missionary.

1. Fr. Louis: The Person I Know

According to the incomprehensible and unintelligible plan of God the Incomprehensible Absolute Fr. Louis was planted in Khristupremalaya Seminary Ashta, though he would have preferred to be planted in Dharmaram College Bangalore. But, he bloomed immensely for nine years where he was planted, displaying his charming beauty and spreading his sweet fragrance. His God-given talents enabled him to become a superb rector of the seminary. His language capacity was admirable – equally fluent in English and Hindi, with perfect and pleasing phonetics and eloquence. His clarity of thought and articulation was literally marvelous. With his sermons, talks and discussions he has carved indelible marks in the minds of the students. His ideas, ideals and actions were neither too liberal nor puritan. He was neither too progressive nor too conservative but steadily balanced and realistic. He was absolutely free from neophobia as well as neophilia. As an ideal formator he maintained exceptionally cordial relationship with all the students and staff-members. For him there was no Malayalee, no Tamilian, no Mangalorian, no Tribal and no Dalit, but only humans and children of the divine 'Famother'. He would boost the gifts of the gifted students without looking down upon or showing discrimination towards the non-gifted and non-talented. In the six years I was his colleague at Ashta Seminaray I never heard any student accusing him of bias, prejudice, partisanship or parochialism. Fr. Louis was one with the students always and everywhere, whether it was garden work, wheat harvest, soybean harvest, inter-religious activities or anything like that. One would never find him in a commanding mood.

His patience and generosity to the staff members is worth recalling. There is one instance I can never forget: Fr. Paul Savio Puthussery and myself were always afraid of heat. In order to escape the scorching heat in Andhra Pradesh during the train journey to Kerala for summer vacation we booked our tickets for the middle of March immediately after the final exams, and traveled accordingly. We had thought only of the heat and forgotten the *Samavarthan*, the concluding ceremony at the end of the academic year in which the staff members also were expected to participate. Only several months after we returned from Kerala did Fr. Louis reminded us of our default. I felt ashamed of my forgetfulness but could not but admire the large-heartedness of the rector.

Fr. Louis was very keen to maintain cordial relationship to the neighbouring parish priests and the religious communities. The hospitality he showed to the visiting priests and religious from all over India was remarkable. His relationship with the Non-Christian leaders in Ashta was not only friendly but also highly effective and emulative. Through his friendship with them he could bring about a positively revolutionary change in that small town where Hindus and Muslims were equal in number and making their presence felt by feuds and frequent riots. A few murders every year was the meticulously kept divine law of this small town!! With the definite goal of making peace between the two communities he made friendship with the leaders of both the communities. He invited them as guests and chief guests to the important functions in the seminary. The fruits of his influence were visible within a few years. The tense, dangerous and volatile situation in Ashta changed so dramatically that murders and riots became quite uncommon, and peace became the law of the day. It is to be mentioned that there were a few dynamic and charismatic students like Bro. Basil from the diocese of Udaipur to strengthen the hands of Fr. Louis, the peace-maker.

As a lover of Indian culture Fr. Louis would miss no opportunity to familiarize the seminarians with Indian Philosophy and Hindu rituals and customs. Though deeply interested and involved in the Vedic heritage, he never lost sight of the tribal values and their identity, and the Dalits and their problems.

Village orientation and identification with the poor were his proclaimed ideals. Those ideals made him insist on constructing the seminary buildings always as single-storied structures. Since the lose black soil in the seminary compound was not at all suitable for such policy I used to object to it and hold my own different opinion, arguing that buildings are to remain for a long time and that multistoried buildings will be quite common in Ashta in a few years, so that our two-storied or three-storied buildings will not be scandalous to them in the future. But he would not budge a little, and remained steadily stubborn and self-willed. I would like to make it clear that this is the only point where we differed from each other and had even a bit collision. Acknowledging his sincerity and good intention with all love and respect I stick to my view that such addiction to single-storied building is sheer expensive practice of poverty. Time proved my stand to be the valid one: those who took over the seminary from the CMI Congregation demolished most of the single storied buildings and constructed a beautiful three storied one.

I think, it will be a serious omission if I do not mention the prophetic courage of Fr. Louis who was normally meek and mild to students, staff members, workers and all others he had contact with. He would show his protest in an indirect way to Joseph Pastor Neelankail the infamous bishop of Sagar by not speaking with him when he was at dining table in the seminary when he visited a couple of his theology students. Without any remorse I confess that I joined Fr. Louis. Anybody who has some knowledge of the disastrous events that took place in the diocese of Sagar at that time will understand without any difficulty the rightfulness and necessity of our uncommon and apparently impolite behaviour. It still pains me to remember how a new, vibrant diocese with more than sixty zealous and energetic priests, some of whom were exceptionally talented, was ruined to the root because of the foolish and power-crazy bishop. How horrible and terrible that all the CMI priests, who were the vast majority, left the diocese to escape from that power-inebriated jealous dictator who was also a simpleton, and the CMI Congregation renamed Sagar province as Bhopal province and shifted the provincial house from Sagar to Bhopal. The sole purpose of mentioning this historical fact here is to highlight the mental stamina of Fr. Louis who was a genuine disciple of Jesus the Prophet, and not of Jesus the Poojari.

Fr. Louis was truly wise, and consequently could change himself in accordance with the vision and instructions of the II Vatican Council. Only stones, the dead and the fools cannot change; no change means no growth; no growth means stagnation; and naturally stagnation is the beginning of death and decay.

2. Fr. Louis a Prophet of Inculturation

Anybody who knows Fr. Louis cannot but agree that his characteristic note was his passion for and self-dedication to the cause of inculturation of liturgy, to be precise Indianizaion of Mass. The Indian Mass he has prepared, and which was celebrated as group liturgy at Dharmaram College Bangalore is an eternal monument for his thirst for Indianization.

2.1. What is Inculturation?

Inculturation is the same as contextualization. The Catholic Church, the World Council of Churches and the majority of the Protestant Denominations use the word inculturation while other Protestant groups prefer the term contextualization.

To inculturate means to enter into a culture. In order to be able to enter a different place or situation one must adjust oneself. In that sense inculturation means adjusting Christian kerygma and liturgy to the culture it engages in. Adaptation is impossible without changing yourself to make yourself suitable to a new time, place and circumstances for the purpose you have envisaged. By cultural adaptation you modify Christian teaching, rituals and practices according to the locality, thought patters and mind-set of each people. The message of Jesus and the teachings of the Church should be reformulated and re-presented so that they may become appealing, attractive and acceptable to all the people she addresses.

2.2. Inculturation, Enculturation and Acculturation

Inculturation is not the same as enculturation. While the former means adaptation the latter means adoption, whereby an individual assimilates, makes his/her own, the thought-and behavior patterns of a new culture. Here one loses one's own cultural identity to a great extent, if one has own culture at all. Usually one enculturates when one has no own glorious, distinct or well-defined culture. By enculturation one does not lose much; on the contrary one gains enormously because the culture one meets is really not the second important but the first important for him/her.

For the majority of writers enculturation is the same as acculturation. However, some make a slight distinction between them. Accordingly, acculturation is more intense and comprehensive than enculturation. Those who acculturate, do not lose own culture totally, but succumb to the prevailing powerful culture; they make themselves part of the culture they have accepted voluntarily or under pressure. They may abandon even their own language besides food and clothing habits. Even their vision, values and customs undergo tremendous change. The guest culture is almost devoured by the host culture. Very often this happens through social pressure resulting from constant contact with the mighty and dominant culture. What happens in the case of migrants is acculturation.

I think, in a discussion on the inculturation attempts of Fr. Louis, the concepts of enculturation and acculturation do not deserve more than this short explanation.

2.3. *Inculturation and Catholicity*

The main characteristics of the Jesuan Community, the Church, according to the Catechism of the Catholic Church are oneness, holiness, apostolicity and catholicity. The adjective catholic is the English equivalent of the Greek word *katholos* which means universal, ecumenical, boundless, limitless, all-inclusive, all-embracing, all-comprising etc. If the Church excludes from its heart any person or any culture on the basis of race, language, country, customs or any such criteria, it ceases to be catholic, universal. Therefore, inculturation is essential for the Church to be catholic. A Church that does not enter into all cultures does not share the mind of Jesus who was literally catholic in all respects. His fundamental teaching is that each and every human is a child of God. However defective a culture is, the humans belonging to that culture are God's own children. On account of those humans each culture has to be accepted and respected. May be there are corrections to be made; for example if a culture considers human sacrifice, clitoridectomy or any such evil customs as holy and lawful, the Church has to raise its voice against it.

The importance of cultural adaptation was highly emphasized by Henri de Lubac in 1939 under the influence of John Henry Newman. De Lubac was convinced that salvation is not something abstract, hanging in the air without touching concrete human society. In his view each human is somehow part and parcel of a culture and without taking that culture into account you cannot bring him salvation. Also the Protestant thinkers like Richard Niebur and Paul Tillich have pleaded for sensitivity towards the temper and texture of each culture.

For the birth and growth of the Church in all nations, self-adaptation is absolutely necessary in all the fields like preaching, catechetics, liturgical celebration, daily practices, marriage and family life, ecclesiastical structure, administration etc.

Glorification of Western culture and its imposition on other cultures has done irreparable

Damage to Christianity and its evil effects remain as indelible stain on the glorious gown of its history. The cultural atrocities committed by the Spaniards to the South American People and by the Portuguese to the Indians, especially to the Goans, will be considered abominable by civilized and cultured humans of all time.

2 4. Inculturation in the History of Christianity

Inculturation as adaptation of gospel preaching, liturgy, catechetics etc to each culture concerned, has not yet been fully carried out in Christian Churches, especially in the Catholic Church. But, there have been several sincere attempts which are to be appreciated.

2.4.1. Paul's Attempt at Inculturation at Areopagus

Paul the apostle, the greatest of all missionaries in Christianity gives us a luminous example of relating Christian preaching to the context of the listeners Acts 14: 22-33): Standing in the middle of the Areopagus stone hill at Athens he begins his preaching by congratulating the Athenians for their deep religiosity evidenced by the altar 'dedicated to the unknown god'. He also quotes the words of the Greek poet Aratus "we are indeed his offspring". He then relates this unknown god to the self-existent, self-sufficient, omnipresent God, who is the creator of the cosmos and the provider of everything to every humans and every creature. Then he relates this God of Natural Theology to Jesus of Nazareth who is risen from the dead and the definitive judgment of mankind he will be making at the eschatological time. His preaching was not appealing to all the listeners because they were already deeply influenced by the Greek Philosophy. Only a few accepted his faith in the resurrection of Jesus and the final judgment of the world to be pronounced by him. But, Paul's kerygmatic policy has abiding significance: The preacher should begin his words by highlighting, appreciating accepting and respecting the values of the people he addresses and connect with them the message to be communicated. For, one's own culture is the medium of each human's grasping and memorizing. "Whatever is received, is received according to the mode of the receiver" (Quid quid recipitur ad modum recipientis recipitur) is an irrefutable epistemological axiom valid for all humans of all times and circumstances. Paul's stand was recognized by the Jerusalem Council held in 49/50. It declared officially that the Gentiles could be accepted to the Church without their undergoing circumcision prescribed by the Mosaic Law. Evidently the Church was acknowledging the value of the Non-Jewish cultures.

2.4.2. Early Apologists' Philosophical Approach to Inculturation

Incorporation of Greco-Roman culture into the life of the Church was an important phase of inculturation. Early Apologetic Fathers like Justin the Martyr and Clement of Alexandria implemented inculturation by connecting the Christian message to the Greco-Roman world with the Greek philosophical concept of 'logos' which was already introduced in the first chapter of the Johannine Gospel. They argued that the Logos, the eternal Word of God and the creative divine reason is present in the whole creation, albeit in a disseminated form, as '*logos spermaticos*'. Humans of all cultures perceive it in a vague manner. It becomes perfectly clear to them with the incarnation of the Logos in and through Jesus Christ.

2.4.3. Inculturation by the Missionaries

There are several important missionaries who had clear insight into the need of cultural adaptation in the process of spreading the Gospel message and establishing Christian communities. Those to be remembered in a special way with reverence and admiration are St. Patric in Ireland, Sts. Cyril and Methodius in the Slavic regions of Eastern Europe, Jose de Anchieta and Paulo Paez in Brazil, the Jesuits Matteo Ricci and Adam Schall von Bell in China, Thomas Stephens in Goa, Roberto de Nobili in South India and Alexander de Rhodes in Vietnam.

2.4.4. Promotion of Inculturation by Popes

Papal support for contextualization of the Church started with Leo XIII. He upheld the value of the Eastern Church Rites and resisted the Latinization policy of the Roman Curia. His Encyclical *Praeclara gratulationis* extolled the cultural diversity of the Catholic Church visible in the liturgical celebrations

Pope Benedict the XV concentrated his attention on the development of local clergy. In his Apostolic Exhortation on Nov. 20, 1919 he called on the Catholics of the whole world to cast aside the Eropeanization tendency in the missions and to develop the local clergy.

Pope Pius XI continued this prudent policy whole-heartedly. The Mission Congress in Rome in 1922 gave extraordinary boosting to the cause of local clergy. Each year he consecrated bishops from developing countries in Asia, Africa and Latin America. At the end of his reign 240 dioceses were administered by local bishops.

Pope Pius XII continued the inculturation policy of Pius XI still more vigorously and enthusiastically. He revoked the 250 year old prohibition of ancestor-worship in the Chinese Catholic Church, declaring openly that such Chinese customs are not superstitions but respectable manner of showing honour to own relatives. Naturally this reversal of ecclesiastical policy reinvigorated the Chinese Church.

In his Encyclical '*Summi Pontificatus*' he laid stress on the need for appreciation of the values in civilizations. The happy result of this positive attitude was twenty new arch-dioceses, seventy nine dioceses and thirty eight apostolic prefectures in the developing countries. The following words from his speech to the directors of the Pontifical Society in 1944 show his firm and unyielding conviction about the importance of inculturation and contextualization:

"The herald of the Gospel and messenger of Christ is an apostle. His office does not demand that he transplant European civilization and culture, and no other, to foreign soil, there to take root and propagate itself. His task in dealing with these peoples, who sometimes boast of a very old and highly developed culture of their own, is to teach and form them so that they are ready to accept willingly and in a practical manner the principles of Christian life and morality, principles, I might add, that fit into any culture, provided it be good and sound, and which give that culture greater force in safeguarding human dignity and in gaining human happiness."

Also his Encyclicals *Evangelii Praecones* and *Fidei donum* are clear evidence of his deep interest in inculturation. In order to foster local administration in the particular Churches he granted self-governing to the hierarchies of Western Africa, Southern Africa and British Eastern Africa. Finland, Burma and French Africa were made independent dioceses.

Ad gentes divinitus, II Vataican Council degree on the missionary activity of the Church, promulgated by Pope Paul VI validates inculturation by the Theology of Incarnation.

Several Encyclicals and speeches, especially the Encyclicals *Ecclesia in Asia* and *Redemptoris Missio* of Pope John Paul II underlines the need of integrating authentic values of all cultures into Christianity. For him dialogue between faith and culture is an indispensable ideal of the Catholic Church.

Pope Benedict XVI at the beginning of his papacy was not very much enthusiastic about the term inculturation; he was for inter-culturality. However, later he acknowledged the need of inculturation though cautioning that the integrity of faith may be compromised.

The magnificent attitude of the present Pope Francis towards inter-religious dialogue and inculturation is already world famous through his speeches and sermons. His heart is large enough to embrace all races, all nations and all cultures in the world.

2.4.5. Relevance and Significance of Inculturation from Historical Perspective

The history of Christianity in China demonstrates to what extent the rise and fall of the Church and evangelization depends on cultural contextualization.

Enlightened and prudent missionaries like Matteo Ricci and Adam Schall von Bell had deep insight into the worth of ancestor worship in Chinese culture. Therefore they joyfully allowed the new converts to continue this practice. The Chinese Emperor was so happy that he appointed them as court mathematicians, court astronomers and officials in the Chinese imperial service; these officials were known as mandarins at that time. Unfortunately the Roman Curia dissented, called ancestor worship idolatry, and prohibited it categorically. The consequence was disastrous: The Chinese Emperor felt fooled, deceived and insulted and prohibited any change in the ongoing practices. The antagonism of the Chinese rulers continued and at its climax the emperor declared Christian missions in China illegal.

2.4.6. Fr. Louis' Contribution to Inculturation

It will be an overstatement and exaggeration if somebody makes a statement that Fr. Louis Malieckal's contribution to inculturation in India is enormous, historic, stupendous, colossal, monumental etc. But, it is undeniable that he followed the footsteps of inculturation-theologians like S. Amalorbhavadas, Mathias Mundadan, John Chethimattam, Francis Vineeth, Thomas Manickom, Paul Puthenangady etc.

The most important contribution of Fr. Louis in the field of inculturation and contextualization in the Indian Church, in fact something unique to his credit, is the shaping of an Indian Mass which was celebrated at the historic All India Seminar held in 1969. I still cherish the sweet memory of celebrating it as main celebrant for a group of Philosophy students at Dharmaram College Bangalore in the year 1971-72. The lyrics and music of all the bhajans were composed by Fr. Louis. The songs were so meaningful and melodious that the listeners would feel they were written by a highly qualified and devout Hindu Sanskrit scholar. Fr. Louis celebrated this Indian Mass with such decorum and devotion as if he were a pious Hindu poojaari. His melodious singing and chanting still cling clearly and cooling in my ears. Since he was a good singer he could lead the other participants into an ecstatic mood. His elegant liturgical gestures enhanced the loveliness and attractiveness of the celebration. His incensing, flower offering and holy water springing were charming and graceful.

Fr. Louis was vehemently attracted to Indian culture; still he remained a faithful son of the Syro-Malabar Church. He was neither an antagonist nor a protagonist of Syrianization or Latinizataion. His dear dream was Indianization of liturgy. Unfortunately his expectations were disappointed and ambitions were thwarted by the octopus-grip of the conservative Oriental Congregation. Under the pressure of Vatican the Syro-Malabar Hierarchy prohibited the Indian Mass at Dharmaram College. However Fr. Louis celebrated it a few times at Kristupremalaya Seminary Ashta, while he was its rector.

3. Conclusion

When I reflect on Fr. Louis Malieckal who was my colleague in Ashta Seminary, there occur to me instantly the famous words of Henry W. Longfellow, which have eternal validity: "Lives of great men all remind us: we can make our life sublime, and departing leave behind us footprints on the sands of time". Longfellow's words, undoubtedly, express the validity of great lives but, I think, they cannot express the stability of glorious lives. For that reason I would formulate my view of Fr. Louis in the following way: Fr. Louis made his life sublime, and departing left behind him his footprints engraved on the marble of time. God empowered him to do something valuable for de-hellenization, de-romanization, de-latinization, de-westernization re-judaization and de-syrianization, and for Indianization of Christian kerygma and liturgy. He did what he could. No human can do more than that. Notable about him is that he did not identify Indianization with Hinduization, though he always acknowledged the priority of the latter. He was steadily of the firm conviction that the evangelizing culture should honour and esteem the evangelized or evangelizable culture. This conviction motivated him to dedicate his life for inculturation of Indian Church without enslaving himself to enculturarion of Indian culture.

When I think of the wisdom and broad-mindedness of Fr. Louis, I think also of the ignorance, narrow-mindedness and forgetfulness of many of the Indian clergy, especially of the Syro-Malabar bishops and priests. Ask the Syro-Malabar clergy if they can address God 'Allah' in their prayers, which is the Arabic word for God used by the Muslims. They will shrug their shoulders and say categorically 'No'. How pitiful that they forget the historical fact that till 1962 all the Syro-Malabar clergy, including some laymen, addressed God with the East Syriac word 'Alaha'. Mass, Sacraments, funeral rites, house-blessing and all other blessings, canonical payers of the clergy and everything except rosary was in Syriac language. Every priest pronounced this word 'Alaha' dozens of times every day without any constraint or inhibition. The slight difference between 'Allah' and 'Alaha' is merely phonetic. I would like to give an example from Malayalam Language to elucidate it: The word for 'he' is 'avan', and is pronounced as 'avan'(exactly as it written) by the South Keralites, but as 'oan' by the North Keralites. Not even many of the so-called highly educated Catholic clergy are aware that Syriac and Arabic are Semitic languages like Hebrew and Aramaic. It is disgusting for the Indian Christians to call God 'Vishnu'. How sad! This Sanskrit word means the same all-pervading and omnipresent God of the Christians, the same God whom Jesus called 'Abba' and the same God whom the Jews called 'Yahveh'. Vishnu means the all-pervasive one. The Christians call Jesus 'Lord' (*karthavu* in Malalyalam). They feel that the word *guru* is not sufficient to express the eminence of Jesus. But, let them remember the following facts: The New Testament is written in Greek Language and the word for lord used in it is *kurios.* It is only the Greek modification of the Sanskrit word *guru.* In Greek most of the important masculine words end in 'os'. To make the Greek equivalent for the Sanskrit word *guru* 'os' was added and thus *guruos* was formed' which in the course of time underwent a minor change and became *kurios.* If the Christian leaders had at least the basic knowledge of Sanskrit, they would feel motivated to do something for the adaptation of Christianity to Indian culture.

I hope, and am sure, that the light of Fr. Louis Malieckal's life will continue to shine, leading the Indian Church to the goal of his life, namely inculturation and Indianization of Christianity, even though more time and effort is needed to achieve this goal.

May I conclude this article with the following words of fraternal admonition to my fellow-Christians, especially to the leaders of the Christian Churches in India: Ignorance is not shameful, but arrogance is certainly shameful. Don't be so arrogant to absolutize your own religion. Uniqueness of Christ is not absolute, but relative; consequently, uniqueness of Christianity is not absolute but relative. Let Jesus be absolute **TO YOU, AND ONLY TO YOU**. Let everyone and everything else be relative. Jesus should be absolute to you, but not the way Jesus should be presented to the humankind. Jesus is unique to you objectively and subjectively, exactly as your mother is objectively and subjectively unique to you: objectively, because you were born from your own mother, and from no other mother; subjectively, because no other mother loves you so intimately as your mother and you don't love any other mother so intimately as your own mother. Your whole talk about your mother is conditioned by your birth from your mother; likewise your whole talk about Christianity is conditioned by your birth from Christianity. Your preaching about Jesus is motivated and shaped by a *theological apriori*, namely your discipleship to him. Please don't forget that there are other gurus in the world, with their own disciples. Look at Fr. Louis and try to learn from him.

PART III

CONTEXTUAL THEOLOGICAL FORMATION AND EVANGELIZATION

9

Champion of CMI Contextual Theological Formation

Sebastian Elavathingal CMI

1. Introduction

Fr. Louis Malieckal started his academic career as a theologian in Dharmaram College, Bengaluru. It was a period of intense theological reflection in the light of the Vatican II movement of updating the Church.[36] The staff and students of Dharmaram College were in the forefront of the movement called Indianization. Indian spiritual wisdom and philosophy were introduced in the teaching and learning programmes of Dharmaram. As a liturgist, Fr. Louis actively participated in the inculturation and Indianization of liturgical prayer and music. However, the real venue of Fr. Louis' teaching ministry was not Dharmaram.

36 The Second Vatican Council was convened by Saint John XXIII and lasted for four sessions from 1962 through 1965. Saint John XXIII stated that the purpose of the Council was the "modernization of the Church after 20 centuries of life." This refreshening of the Church's traditions is commonly referred to as aggiornamento ("bringing up to date" in Italian). In his opening speech to the Council the Pope emphaiszed the theme of aggiornamento by stating that "it is absolutely vital that the Church shall never for an instant lose sight of that sacred patrimony of truth inherited from the Fathers. But it is equally necessary for her to keep up to date with the changing conditions of this modern world."

2. The Ashta Years

As a young academic, endowed with a vibrant creative mind, he was sent to the newly formed M.P. Regional Theologate in Ashta, Madhya Pradesh. It was a quite unexpected appointment for him who was immersed in the life and activities of Dharmaram, backed by his European academic training. Remembering "his shock and surprise" at this unexpected appointment, Fr. Louis writes, "For me, it was a kind of 'cultural shock', because I had landed there straight from Europe after my doctoral studies, obeying the order of my religious superior, without any preparations fitting to the context. When I joined the initial team of the seminary in Ashta in 1983, a few months after its formal launching in Bhopal, I found myself in a totally disappointing and hopeless situation for the following reasons: Lack of necessary infra-structure facilities; lack of sufficient number of members on the staff and lack of a sizable number of students on the rolls".

Consequently, it took several months for him to come to terms with the 'reality of this village seminary' in Ashta. He had no preparation to live in North India and to teach a group of theology students, preparing them for their missionary and pastoral life. Besides, the task given to him was to break a new path for theological formation beginning from scratch. It was at the same time a challenge and a chance in front of him.

His efforts to reconcile himself to the new and unexpected situation began when he slowly realized the relevance of the Word of God in his life. "The Lord is my shepherd, therefore I have everything I need". In the light of this Word, he did not think of the lacking facilities and provisions of life. Rather he concentrated on the available resources which the Lord placed in front of him. It was for him a moment of deeper trust in God and in the divine plans. All the doubts about his life's future mission gradually vanished. He took up the challenge with an open mind and a generous heart.

From that time on, he started to work on the new seminary project with determination. He read thoroughly the vision proposed by the M.P. Bishops' Conference for a seminary of "contextual theological formation" in a country side, away from Bhopal. The idea was quite new in the history of seminary formation in India. It was, however, inspired by the teachings of the Vatican II and the papal teachings preceding the Council on missionary and priestly formation. The first papal document of the 20th century Maximum Illud (1919) of Pope Benedict XV onwards all the major missionary encyclicals[37]

37 1. *Maximum Illud* — On the Propagation of the Faith Throughout the World, Apostolic Letter of Benedict XV, November 30, 1919; http://www.svdcuria.org/public/mission/docs/encycl/mi-en.htm 2. *Rerum Ecclesiae* — On Promoting the Sacred Missions, Encyclical Letter of Pius XI, February 28, 1926; http://w2.vatican.va/content/pius-xi/en/encyclicals/documents/hf_p-xi_enc_28021926_rerum-ecclesiae.html 3. *Evangelii Praecones* — On Promoting Catholic Missions a. Encyclical Letter of Pius XII, June 2, 1951; http://

had insisted on indigenous hierarchy with local clergy trained according to the culture and languages of the mission areas. Again the Conference of the Metropolitans of India 1945[38] which took place just before the impending Indian independence from the colonial rule had given a blue print of formation for the indigenous clergy according the cultural and philosophical genius of India. But it was the Vatican II, which opened the windows of the Church to make its presence relevant and effective in the modern world.

In view of imparting an appropriate formation to the missionaries and priests who are sensitive to the social, cultural and religious conditions of India, a programme had to be chalked out. The plan for the new Theologate was to construct a cluster of simple buildings in the midst of a number of small villages close to the township of Ashta. Fr. Louis made the vision of the Bishop's Conference his own dream and started to realize it by adopting new methods of seminary formation, which would respond to the diversity of the social, cultural and religious contexts of India.

After giving a definite form to the formation programme in the M. P. Regional Theologate in Ashta, during his years as the Rector of the seminary, Fr. Louis handed it over to the Pallotine Fathers who continued his legacy of contextual theological formation in the Ashta seminary. The young missionaries trained under Fr. Louis even today continue to cherish their Ashta years of formation with love and gratitude to him. During his tenure as Rector and Professor in the Ashta Regional Theologate, Fr. Louis guided many candidates to priesthood. All his students have a niche in their hearts reserved for their mentor. What endeared him to the students was his ability to understand them from their viewpoints, without being judgmental. As a formator, he tried to develop a student-friendly attitude. He writes, "I have always tried to take the perspective of the other, of the students". Having held the post of a Rector for a long period, he could come down to the level of a student, a seminarian and a postulant and step into his shoes. He could mingle with all and be happy in all situations.

3. The "Samanvaya" Legacy of Fr. Louis

The Ashta experience of contextual formation of priests and missionaries was the foundation of Fr. Louis' future project of formation for the CMI missionary

---

w2.vatican.va/content/pius-xii/en/encyclicals/documents/hf_p-xii_enc_02061951_evangeliipraecones.html 4. *Fidei Donum* — On the Present State of the Catholic Missions Especially in Africa; Encyclical Letter of Pius XII, April 21, 1957 b. http://w2.vatican.va/content/pius-xii/en/encyclicals/documents/hf_p-xii_enc_21041957_fideidonum.html. 5. *Princeps Pastorum* (Prince of the Shepherds) – On the Missions, Native Clergy, and Lay Participation; Encyclical of Pope John XXIII, November 28, 1959 b. http://w2.vatican.va/content/john-xxiii/en/encyclicals/documents/hf_j-xxiii_enc_28111959_princeps.html.

38 *Conference of the Metropolitans of India*, (Madras, 1945).

priests. The great legacy bequeathed by Fr. Louis to the CMI Congregation is the concept of "Samanvaya" contextual theological formation, which envisages a programme of formation for missionary priests. It is intended to make future missionaries capable of proclaiming the Good News, responding to the actual contexts of life through action and reflection.

Fr. Louis with his collaborators launched the programme 25 years ago. In visualizing Samanvaya the whole Congregation participated. It was the fruit of several discussions, live-togethers and seminars conducted in preparation for this new venture.[39] Hence, it was in continuation with the CMI tradition of seminary formation which was already begun in the early years of the Congregation in Mannanam.

The first batch of Samanvaya students started their course in Jagdalpur. They were accommodated in the small Provincial House at Jagdalpur, which was generously made available specifically for this purpose. The students had voluntarily opted for the programme which had an entirely new theological formation concept, developed after many discussions and deliberations by the CMI scholars and missionaries involved in formation.

The Samanvaya method of teaching and learning is contextual and participatory, that is, eliciting questions from the context and finding answers in the light of the Word of God. Its concept is different from that of the traditional method of theological formation based on fixed texts and predetermined questions and answers. It is a challenging method which demands a critical and creative involvement of the students in learning the theological subjects. They cannot remain passive listeners as in the traditional system of learning theology. It is challenging also to the teachers who are supposed to accompany the students helping them to interpret the experiences of the contexts. The Word of God is the backbone of contextual theological learning.

In the early years of Samanvaya, there were some uncertainties regarding the movement of the students from place to place. The original idea was not to have any established seminary for the students. Instead, they would be hosted by the mission provinces according to the availability of the space for accommodation. It was felt to be impractical and finally it was decided to build a Centre for Samanvaya. The Poornodaya campus provided space to construct a modest structure as the Coordinating Centre. Now there are Samanvaya centres in Bhopal, Jagdalpur, Rishikesh and Bengaluru. Fr. Louis worked in association with the Jesuit scholars to give the Samanvaya programme a good academic standard. More than two hundred and fifty CMI priest missionaries belonging to different CMI Provinces have come out of Samanvaya in the past 25 years.

---

39 See Cyril Kuttiyanickal CMI, Ed. *Theological Formation in Context: A CMI Initiative,* (Bhopal: Samanvaya), 2009.

4. "Samanvaya" Vision of Theological Formation

Samanvaya envisages small communities of more or less 15-20 students each. The purpose is, on the one hand, to avoid the anonymity and depersonalization of big communities and, on the other, to foster genuine community spirit through common undertakings and shared responsibilities. Each student is personally attended to through appreciation, correction and assignment of tasks. There is necessary and sufficient space for interaction and involvement. Small communities enable mobility and adaptability to different conditions. They are ideal for fostering creativity among the members. Each batch of students is guided by a Master who is directly responsible for the formation in the given context.

During the three and a half years of priestly formation the students involve themselves in four contexts moving from one to another. They begin with the rural and tribal life situations of Jagdalpur, confronting the questions of subaltern cultures. In the second year they are to rediscover their faith in the light of the inter-religious context of Rishikesh, where they have a number of opportunities to confront Indian religiosity and spirituality in the practices of different religions. During the third year of theology the students are transferred to Bangalore Dharmaram College, where they have opportunities for various pastoral experiences. They live one semsester in the Dharmaram community. The second semester of the third year and the first semester of the fourth year the students live in Bhopal studying topics of pastoral importance and involving themselves in various social and pastoral sensitization activities.

Each of the contexts has a specific academic thrust spelled out by a theme.

- The subaltern context in Jagdalpur has the theme of **God and the World** with a focus on Scriptural subjects
- The Inter-religious context in Rishikesh has the theme of **Christ and the Human** with a focus on systematic theology
- The socio-pastoral context in Bangalore and Bhopal has the theme of **Spirit and the Church** with a focus on pastoral theology

Contextual Theology method considers culture and social change as resources of theology. It is faith-reflection on reality – the world and the conditions of human life, seen from the "God-perspective". It is not a purely rational, intellectual exercise, but an activity involving human experience in its totality. The students begin their theological reflection responding to the questions raised from their experiences of the context. Following are the exposures given to the students in the three and a half years of their formation:

THEOLOGY YEAR I: <u>Formation in the Rural/Tribal Context</u>

1: Participation in Rural Life through Daily Life Activities

2: Learning about the Art and Culture of the Area
3: Living Experience with the Rural/Tribal Families – Three Weeks
4: Participation in the Life of the Local Church

THEOLOGY YEAR II: Formation in Indian Religiosity and Inter-religious Dialogue

1: Efforts to Explore the Religious Context of Rishikesh
2: Dialogue on Religious Experience in a Hindu Ashram
3: Two Weeks of Christian Ashram Experience at Jaiharikal
4: Pilgrimages to the Dhams (Shrines) of Himalaya
5: A Closer Look at Islamic Religiosity

THEOLOGY YEARS III & IV: Formation in Social/Pastoral Context

1: Pastoral Service Among Migrant Christians
2: Pastoral and Social Sensitization Activities – Ministries Among the Marginalized

5. Samanvaya Spirituality of Integration

Samanvaya spirituality is a spirituality of integration, as expressed in the logo: "*samanvayena sakshatkarah*". Integration has to take place at different levels and in different spheres of life. In the area of academic formation, integration has to take place between life and learning. Theological education should not be limited to an intellectual exercise aimed at academic perfection. It has to be a means of spiritual awakening. It has to answer questions arising from day to day realities of life and authentic human experiences. This experiential content of theology demands involvement, participation and commitment. Thus, theology evokes emotional responses which are expressed in prayer, praise and thanksgiving, besides many other creative forms of expression. Samanvaya is integration of *karma-jnana-bhakti.*

Another sphere of integration is the sphere of individual-community relationship. Such integration is at the root of the participatory life style envisaged by Samanvaya. Individual's identity and inalienable qualities are to be discovered, recognized and fostered. There should not be any undue emphasis on uniformity. Individual initiatives should be encouraged. At the same time, the achievements of the individual must contribute to the realization of the ideals and goals of the community.

The habit of prayer life is inculcated in the students in view of the missionary and apostolic life they will have to live at the completion of seminary formation. The Samanvayic spirit of prayer life demands a basic attitude of communion with the Church, entire humanity and Nature, for which Jesus Christ is the inspiration, motivation and finality. This spiritual outlook centred on Christ and nourished by the Word of God has to be manifested in all forms of prayers and spiritual exercises practiced in the seminary. It is essentially praying with Jesus - "Abba" and singing with Mother Mary the "Magnificat".

In tune with the cultural and inter-religious thrusts emphasized in Samanvaya formation, students are encouraged to squat on the floor during prayers. Besides the traditional Christian prayers, *yoga*, meditation, *namajapa, bhajan, arti, tilak* and other typical Indian forms of devotion and spiritual *sadhana* are accepted and practiced with proper understanding of their significance.

6. Goal of Samanvaya Formation

The final goal of formation in Samanvaya is to help each student **to become a man of God with pastoral compassion, missionary spirit, capable of living in solidarity with common people, especially the poor and the less privileged ones, adopting a simple life-style, grown up in mature freedom and able to work as a team-member for building up the Kingdom of God.**

The conditions of life in different Samanvaya Centres and the opportunities given there are deemed to develop in each student a fine sensitivity to the world, nature and human conditions. The blending of theoretical learning with practical field experiences is the way to activate personal reflection on theological questions. It is also possible to rediscover one's faith with greater fervour, when confronted by the challenges from outside, as it happens in the context of interreligious relations in the second year. Different social and pastoral sensitization programmes make the students attentive to the problems of the poor and the socially marginalized people. The students in the third and fourth year, besides doing pastoral assistance in different communities, are regularly visiting prisons, hospitals, old age homes, shelters for street children etc. in view of sharing the lot of the poor and the needy.

The success of Samanvaya programmes depend almost totally on the motivation of the students to make use of the opportunities given to them. It is something that has to grow from within rather than imposed from outside. Our efforts in this regard are limited to giving opportunities which are conducive to develop in the students many qualities such as:

- Integration of spiritual life with active life
- Christ-centred and Word-nourished life
- Ability to dialogue with people of other faiths
- Sensitivity to social issues
- Readiness to side with the poor and the marginalized
- Total dedication to the given mission without reservation
- Developing a broader world-view
- Having a sense of belongingness to the community

- Hard work with commitment
- Accountability and transparency
- Courage to take risks and challenges to fulfil one's mission
- Ability to organize and manage activities
- Preparedness to do any task given in the mission
- Ability to communicate with ease and confidence

Tools of self-evaluation are given to the students periodically which would make them aware of the opportunities in front of them. We find considerable progress in the students year after year as they move from one stage to the other.

7. Conclusion

Fr. Louis' long years of missionary life in North India, experimenting with the action-reflection method of theologizing has much to contribute to the efforts of making the Church truly Indian and truly Christian. The overpowering of a monolithic Church which suffocated the creativity of its members had been done away with by the Second Vatican Council by introducing the notion of a pilgrim Church, giving greater space to the people of God, their cultural diversity and creativity. The concept of pilot seminaries in priestly formation was also a daring experiment which was gaining support as a means to understand social realities and adapt priestly formation to down to earth values with the "odour of the sheep". Dharmaram College was at that time the breeding ground of many revolutionary ideas, especially under the influence of the All India Seminar of 1969, which unleashed many soul-stirring thoughts on an Indian Church by the great theologians of the time, assembled in Dharmaram. Some of the values, which Fr. Louis held as dear to his life were the ideals of an ashram life, its simplicity and hospitality, a deeper understanding and appreciation of the Indian cultural, philosophical and artistic values, the *yogic* spirituality of integration and universal communion and the *gurukula* ideals of spiritual and intellectual formation. In revamping the "classical" method of theological learning and teaching for envisaging the tenets of a *samanvayic* formation, Fr. Louis drew inspiration from the values he had imbibed from the Dharmaram of the post-Vatican II times. Samanvaya theological formation programme incarnates these values as the spiritual legacy of Fr. Louis to the CMI Congregation. He stood by Samanvaya and upheld its method and values of priestly formation from its inception till the day he breathed his last.

10

Growing Up Young

Dr. Anto Amarnad CMI

Introduction

Growing is an amazing process we begin right at the moment we are being conceived at the wombs of our mothers. As a result of our growth we become fully developed human beings and then we are born to our creaturely existence in the world. Growing gets new dimensions after our birth. The infant must grow physically, socially and psychologically and should attain a stature of maturity as a grown up and matured person. Thus, human development can be explained in terms of several processes of biological, psychological, social and spiritual maturation over the human life span. It is an incessant process of alteration and modification. We can better explain it as a series of distinct transformations determined by the genetic programme fixed at the time of conception which we call inheritance or hereditary, and added by the external environmental state of an individual.[40] Maturation indicates a development of our inner structuring capacity for life oriented activities. Erik Erikson, the eminent figure in the field of psychoanalysis and human development, defines human development as a synthesis of developmental and social tasks.[41] Erikson explained his fundamental premise that "a human being's existence depends at every moment on three processes of organization which must virtually

40 Cf. J. N. Hall, Human Development, in Atkinson D. J., Field D. F. Holmes A. O'Donovan O. (eds.) *New Christian Ethics and Pastoral Theology*, Intervarsity Press, London, 1995, 461.

41 Cf. E. H. Erikson, *Childhood and Society*, Harper & Row, New York, 1950.

complement each other. There is, in whatever order, the biological process of hierarchic organization of organ systems constituting a body (*soma*); there is the psychic process organizing individual experience by ego synthesis (*psyche*); and there is the communal process of the cultural organization of the interdependence of persons (*ethos*)."[42] Integrating all these three components one should resolve to grow as a matured human being. The developmental block defeats the functional harmony and crops a defective person. Hence, we must insist on the biological, psychological and social proportions for a true mature growth in every human person.

1. What is 'Growing Up Young'?

After conception and development into a mature human being, the process of 'growing up young' is a third dignified evolution in human person. Here, a man/woman grows old but with a set of abilities that makes him/her to acquire the most beautiful aptitudes of the young and satisfy the ever green aspects in life. It is natural to a human being to grow old. And every living organism is destined to grow old. As the old age takes its own traits and unique physiognomies in human beings, it is not easy to keep psychological and spiritual magnanimity and social altruism unless one cultivates the values of 'growing up young.' Growing up young is a challenge to possess the noble and open character. A society based on fair and just laws, providing the best possible psychological, cultural and economic conditions, makes its members more creative and benevolent individuals. So too, the individual who grows up young must have a beautiful community life, a support and mingling of matured human persons, knowledge of positive values of one's own culture and above all an openness to be creative and benevolent.

2. Steps to Mature in 'Growing up Young'

One thing is certain-as the years pass by, our lives will be filled with multiple transitions and modifications. Some we can plan, others just happen to us; some alterations are positive and others negative. Transitions are inevitable events. We might carry the accumulation of years in our body and on our face, but we can stay young at heart and not let the years weigh on our spirit. That's one of the most beautiful things we can imagine to do. So many things are more important than our age. For instance, more wisdom, more learning, sights seen, friendships made, the love of a community one serves, to be at help to so many people in numerous ways. As Frank Lloyd Wright opined: "The longer I live the more beautiful life becomes." But then how to stay young? Let us here ponder on few pertinent aspects which will help us stay young.

42 E. H. Erikson, *The Life Cycle Completed: A Review*, W. W. Norton, New York, 1982, 25-26.

2.1. Conducive Resources and Circumstances

As Franklin D. Roosevelt advocated, human beings will strive toward nobility and creativity in a society which possesses four freedoms-freedom from fear and want, freedom of speech and worship. He says that it is difficult to believe that if people are in dire danger, or hungry, or sick, or in a state of slavery that they can write symphonies or poems.[43] Growing up young also necessitates freedom *ad extra* and *ad intra*. Freedom in land and community is also important as a freedom within from the fear, childhood regressions, inner mental wounds and other psycho-spiritual entanglements. Only a truly free person can imagine of 'growing up young' in a society with complex activities and interactions. 'Growing up young' is also the result of the milieus and circumstances. According to Arieti[44] it is easy to understand why no musician like Beethoven could flourish in a place such as Africa in the eighteenth century, where there was no possibility of studying music effectively. There is no likelihood also even in England for a Beethoven to grow and to be a great composer, although England was so great in literature, philosophy, and science. England did not have enough cultural patrimony to have a Beethoven be emerged.[45] The availability of resources also extends to physical means to achieve greatness and quality in behaviour.

2.2. Openness to the Fresh Trends

Another important feature for 'growing up young' is to have an openness to the fresh and newly emerging trends and thought patterns. Every generation holds on their own few sets of interpretations of meaning and standards about the life lived. The generation gap usually shuts its iron doors against understanding of new generation's fresh way of approaching the values and attitudes. 'Growing up young' invites to have a sincere love to welcome the new generation's way of thinking, rationalizing and dreaming. The outgoing generation should not focus exclusively on one way of knowing and interpreting the human life and its truths. For example the Europe in Middle Ages was called the 'Dark Ages' because there was no openness to the cultural changes and nuances but much of the creativity was focussed on the aspects like that of faith, theological philosophy, clergy, religious life and salvation of the soul.[46] There was a great

---

43 Franklin D. Roosevelt, quoted in Silvano Arieti, *Creativity: The Magic Synthesis*, Basic Books, Inc., Publishers, New York, 1976, 313.

44 Silvano Arieti is a world renowned psychiatrist and psychotherapist who made intensive study and research on the concept of creativity and intrapsychic self.

45 Cf. Silvano Arieti, *Creativity: The Magic Synthesis*, Basic Books, Inc., Publishers, New York, 1976, 313.

46 Cf. Silvano Arieti, *Creativity: The Magic Synthesis*, Basic Books, Inc., Publishers, New York, 1976, 314.

clash between the secular and sacred aspects and a ferocious fight against all that is not coming under the purview of religion. The new generation could not find support from the powerful lobbies of authorities and governance. In each generation we can detect a free and creative growth which brings forward the humanity towards the new horizons of maturity and growth. The clash begins when the declining generation vehemently hold on to their old visions and values. Both the old and new generations will not be able to compromise each other's position and thus they would strongly attack each other to maintaining their own visions and practices. The same story would repeat when the new generation becomes the old generation in the course of time.

2.3. Not Just on Being but on Becoming

A culture that puts emphasis only on immediate gratification of sensualism, cosiness, and peripheral cosmetic dimensions does not promote the hard toiled outcome of 'growing up young' in attitudes and life style. The contrast between *being* and *becoming* invites variety of challenges. *Being* is one way an easy posture but *becoming* is, very often, filled with uneasiness and complexity in picking up a dependable posture. *Being* will keep tomorrow changeless but there is an inherent urge in *becoming*, to look for an existence appropriate for tomorrow. There is lot of trust and confidence with *being* aspect but *becoming* aspect is filled with innumerable angsts. Further, 'growing up young' will bid for the dimension of *becoming*. Arieti says that a "mature man is always *becoming* because he is constantly affected by a universe of changing symbols. Today he is somewhat different from the way he was yesterday, and tomorrow he will be different from the way he is today. He listens, reads, learns, feels; he observes daily events that are personal or collective, private or public, scientific or experiential, practical or theological, rational or irrational, moral or immoral."[47] He must be always open to the ever changing context of his surroundings in order to have a right *becoming* aptitude and attitude. He has to combine his present and future in the process of *becoming*. *Becoming* is not a losing and failing to acquire a self-identity but synchronizing one's *being* and *becoming* experienced together for greater achievements and coordination in life.

2.4. Openness to Learn from the Cultural Realities

Culture is the medium we make use to become what we are in our own context and express ourselves within the society as an extension of a united group of people with same identity, tradition and style of life. A nation has a culture and a community has a culture and as a reality, each family has its own peculiar

47 Silvano Arieti, *Creativity: The Magic Synthesis*, Basic Books, Inc., Publishers, New York, 1976, 314.

culture and rituals. It is difficult to define culture with all its complexities. Culture provides us tools to deal with different avenues of life and stylize our life in relationships with the groups of people with a given circumstances. Our true and full identity comes out from our own unique culture and beliefs. According to Christopher Dawson culture is "an organized way of life which is based on common traditions and conditioned by a common environment. It is the sum-total of nation's thinking and living, transmitted for a long period of time so as to form a tradition capable of influencing society."[48] Here we see that the styles of behaviour which the culture creates are built up by the acquired and transmitted symbols and signs. The physical aspects of culture could be seen in the habits of clothing, eating, customs, use of peculiar technology and tools. The non-material aspects of culture are values, world-vision, language, symbols, role systems, art forms etc. K. M. Panikkar defined culture as "the complex of ideas, conceptions, developed qualities and organized relationships and courtesies that exists generally in a society."[49] 'Growing up young' will happen only in the background of culture. Hence, a true knowledge of one's own culture is essential to make it creatively young and novel by adapting many things with the young generation who shapes the numerous elements of culture through their innovative and original ideas. Very often, there is a normal tendency in the elderly people to perpetuate the old culture, symbols, rituals, language and tradition. But, new generation innovatively and innately work on the culture and shape for themselves every aspect of it with novel transformations. The elder generation's ability to comprehend and accommodate to the nuances of young generation will make them to come forward with more easiness in the interpersonal relationships and in becoming acceptable to the young generation. The arrival of a new generation in the society necessitates hoisting of a green flag of change in the attitudes and outlooks of elderly generation. In one sense, the 'growing up young' is an ability to appropriate the cultural changes that the young generations bring in forefront.

2.5. *Awareness of Repression on Young*

The young people are, very often, discriminated and they sometimes undergo severe oppression or outright exclusion in an insensitive society or a tradition-ruled community. Even because of moderate disparity shown to the young, it may seriously damage their human spirit. A matured person who wishes to grow in the process of 'growing up young' must desire to challenge the existing degradation towards the youth and must struggle to give what the

48 Christopher Dawson, *Religion and Culture,* Catholic University of America Press, Washington D. C., 1948, 47.

49 D. S. Amalorpavadass, *Indian Culture*, in NBCLC: 'Inculturation' Pamphlet Series No. 16, p. 2.

young was previously denied in dignity and self-worth. The ability to be with the young is a marvellous talent. Of course, the young lack life-experience of an adult world and their concentration fluctuates frequently and perhaps they are drawn up by their dreams or imaginations rather than by a matured and seasoned outlook in life. All these drawbacks should not condemn them and reduce their goodness in prospering to a promising future with magnanimous commitment and charisma. 'Growing up young' means to be in the shoes of the young! It is difficult for a matured old person to come to the style of youth and dance, sing, clap the hands, make merry and letting oneself in the free spirit of expressions and adjustability. The fixed nature of the adult world would frighten the young people who would dynamically imagine of their future with lots of colour, amusement and laughter. The youth spontaneously inherit the quality of flocking together with the people who have the same viewpoint in the life. A person who is willing to 'growing up young' must merge into the young people's world and into their positive qualities.

2.6. Acquaintance with Contrasting Cultural Stimuli

According to Arieti in most cultures, both the valuable and the not-so-valuable features tend to remain steady.[50] When they are well-imbedded, these features usually tend to be static. Since they have won the tests of time, they earn esteem and prompt people to preserve them in their life. But, when new inducements are acquired and added from diverse cultures, the growing-up-young-person will flourish in all his/her abilities to be creative and efficient with traits of the young. It is said about ancient Greece that they acquired a cultural prominence due to their openness to different cultures and receptivity to some of their elements. Arieti is of opinion that some historians trace back the commencement of Greek's decline to a decree made by the great Pericles which prohibited foreigners to live in Athens.[51] It is said that Hellenism was not only artistically but also politically reborn in Italy and Hellenism and Christianity had fought each other for a millennium but they could finally meet and merge. Thus, Christianity gave up its fear of pagan world and because of that it could accept and assimilate the greatness of the ancients.[52] Whenever there are contrasting elements meet together a new synthesis would emerge as a sign of greater growth and development. A 'growing up young' person will have a privileged position by virtue of his/her integration of various generations, their aspirations, traits, thought patterns, principles and standards to shape a

---

50 Cf. Silvano Arieti, *Creativity: The Magic Synthesis*, Basic Books, Inc., Publishers, New York, 1976, 320.

51 Cf. Silvano Arieti, *Creativity: The Magic Synthesis*, Basic Books, Inc., Publishers, New York, 1976, 320.

52 Cf. Silvano Arieti, *Creativity: The Magic Synthesis*, Basic Books, Inc., Publishers, New York, 1976, 321.

better and qualitatively rich personality. The consolidation of divergent and complimentary features will give shape to a more integrated and inclusive nature for the transmission and exchange of higher growth and civilization.

2.7. Gift of Tolerance for Diverging Views

'Growing up young' speaks about the capacity and giftedness in the virtue of tolerance. The word "tolerance" originated from Latin word "*tolerantia,*" which means "to bear," "to endure," "to overcome." It is an ability or willingness to tolerate the existence of opinions or behaviours that one dislikes or disagrees with, and is estimated to be a top virtue of a matured person. Tolerance is also an attitude of a wise-man. Toleration is the allowing, permitting, or acceptance of an action, idea, object, or person which one dislikes or disagrees with. Thus, being tolerant is a sign of a mature and reflective personality. Usually, most of the humans undergo a threat when a divergent thought emerges in the conversation. People think that deviating and differing attitudes jeopardise unity and cooperation. But, for a broadminded and forward-thinking person, the value of tolerance is a pertinent trait. In other words, it is a moral obligation or duty which involves respect for the individual as well as mutual esteem and consideration between the people. Tolerance between the people makes it possible for conflicting claims of beliefs, values and ideas to coexist as long as they fit within the acceptable moral values. For example: to have respect and love towards people belonging to different religions and even to make friends those who are atheists, is a beautiful sign of living the tolerance. Tolerance is our aptitude to show a fair and objective attitude towards those whose lifestyles differs from that of ours. As researchers tell us the tolerant people are happier than intolerant ones.[53]

People are not at ease with all kinds of divergences. Every particular personality often disturbs others because of the question of unfamiliarity of that typical person with others. Persons are more comfortable with whom they already knew or are in a known category. Nobody welcomes an unpleasant surprise from any one whom one meets. To 'grow up young' one needs tolerance and attitudes of accepting the otherness with a benevolent approach. Arieti says that "If sufficient Christians of the thirteenth century had not developed a tolerance for the Hellenic age, no Renaissance would have emerged. If a French elite had not acquired a tolerance for unrealistic representation, modern art would not have developed."[54] In the world of Technology and Science, Philosophy and Theology and Anthropology and Communication Media,

53 https://study.com/academy/lesson/what-is-tolerance-definition-types-examples.html retrieved on 21/11/2019.

54 Silvano Arieti, *Creativity: The Magic Synthesis*, Basic Books, Inc., Publishers, New York, 1976, 322.

the divergent thoughts paved new paths of discovery and resulted with great enhancement of humanity. Tolerance must be encouraged in all the communities and societies for welcoming new developments. A 'growing up young' person must have the tolerance to invite different ideas, beliefs, customs, practices and styles of life to make societies and communities grow and be appreciated.

2.8. Communication with Remarkable Persons

We might have seen in our human history that the highly talented people would very easily influence the community and individuals. Socrates, Pythagoras, Homer, Virgil, Dante, Gandhi, Mother Theresa, A. P. J. Abdul Kalam etc., have influenced thousands of people in the world. Their encounters have crucial importance and will bring about numerous changes in the attitudes of human beings. These prominent people carry in them a great lot of 'growing up young' qualities in their thinking and activities. They adopt a universal and inclusive approach in their outlook which goes along with 'growing up young' persons. Thus they are able to welcome any situation, people, and programme for the unity and harmony of humanity. A place which provides amble occasions for the highly talented people to assemble and interact each other would afford more refined growth of personality and talents. 'Growing up young' persons grow in the frequent communication of significant people renowned for their special giftedness. The importance of the contrasting socio-cultural and psychological elements in the highly remarkable persons would enhance best exchange and building up of creative human spirit. Thus the encounters with significant people would prepare a best arena for personality development and maturity and the qualities of 'growing up young.'

2.9. Recognitions and Incentives

In every community we see that a great recognition and appreciation is given to those who have a creative blend of mind to live 'growing up young.' This 'growing up young' people have positive attitudes towards people and to their own lives. Having a life style with this quality is not so common but rare and is appreciated by most of the people at least in their conscience. The so-called external incentives and respect given by the community would become an added charm in the personality which would cause in many, to follow the lovely model of 'growing up young.' The external recognitions and incentives strengthen the motivation of the 'growing up young' people and that would work with a reinforcing effect in them. "In the ancient Greece, the prizes given to athletes and playwrights served to promote athletics and the theatre."[55] Plato's famous statement that "What is honoured in a country will

55 Cf. Silvano Arieti, Creativity: The Magic Synthesis, Basic Books, Inc., Publishers, New York, 1976, 324.

be cultivated there."[56] When we honour and encourage 'growing up young' attitudes in human beings, it is most probable that many may try to imbibe the attitudes and grow higher and higher in human conscious development.

2.10. Chronological Age and Subjective Age

In the postmodern times we read that 'feeling young' could mean that our brain is aging more slowly. While some people are young at heart, others feel older than their age-and a recent study finds that this 'subjective age' may reflect brain-aging. The elderly people who feel younger have less signs of brain-aging.[57] While everyone gets older, not everyone feels their age. The study results suggest that elderly people who feel older than their age should consider caring for their brain health. We tend to think of aging as a fixed process, where our bodies and minds change steadily. Nevertheless, the passing years affect everyone differently. How old we feel, which is called our subjective age, also varies between people – with many feeling older or younger than their actual age.[58] People often go through some cognitive impairment as they age. In fact, the brain shows a variety of age-related changes that are reflective of declining neural health, including reductions in gray matter[59] volumes. The researchers hypothesize that those who feel older may be able to sense the aging process in their brain, as their loss of gray matter may make cognitive tasks more challenging. MRI brain scans in 68 healthy people whose ages ranged from 59-84 years and looked at gray matter volumes in various brain regions. Critically, those who felt younger than their age showed increased gray matter volume in key brain regions. One fascinating possibility is that those who feel younger are more likely to lead a more physically and mentally active life, which could cause improvements in brain health.[60] After analysing the mental and physical health of test, subjects who feel younger than their chronological age, scientists are in agreement that our chronological age is irrelevant and our subjective age is what matters. Our subjective age is not how old we wish to be, but how old we feel. It is a multidimensional construct marked by one or more of the following indicators: felt age; biological age (looks and physical health); societal age (how we act and what we do); and intellectual age (interests and pursuits). Consider oneself lucky, if one feels young, looks young, participates in youthful activities and have the curiosity

56 https://www.pressreader.com/canada/toronto-star/20170107/282827895827107 retrieved on 22/11/2019.

57 https://www.sciencedaily.com/releases/2018/07/180703110014.htm retrieved on 20/11/2019.

58 https://www.sciencedaily.com/releases/2018/07/180703110014.htm retrieved on 20/11/2019.

59 Gray matter is a major component of the central nervous system, consisting of neuronal cell bodies, neuropil (dendrites and myelinated as well as unmyelinated axons), glial cells (astrocytes and oligodendrocytes), synapses, and capillaries.

60 https://www.sciencedaily.com/releases/2018/07/180703110014.htm retrieved on 20/11/2019.

of a child-because those are the indicators for how old you really are.[61] Feeling younger has many benefits. According to an article in the Journal of Personality by researchers from Florida State University and Montpelier University, it makes us into better people because it fosters "openness, conscientiousness and agreeableness."[62]

3. Young in the World

According to a United Nations' report published in 2014 revealed the countries with largest youth population in the world. According to the reports, there are 1.8 billion young people in the world between the ages of 10 and 24. Interestingly, 9 in 10 of the world's young population live in less developed countries. With 356 million 10-24 year-olds, India has the world's largest youth population despite having a smaller population than China, a latest UN report stated.[63] It said that developing countries with large youth populations could see their economies soar, provided they invest heavily in young people's education and health and protect their rights. In the same report we read that "Young people are the innovators, creators, builders and leaders of the future. But, they can transform the future only if they have skills, health, decision-making, and real choices in life." UNFPA Executive Director Babatunde Osotimehim said "Today's record 1.8 billion young people present an enormous opportunity to transform the future. Never before have there been so many young people. Never again is there likely to be such potential for economic and social progress. How we meet the needs and aspirations of young people will define our common future."[64] There is more migration of young people happening and the biggest motivations for them are the search for jobs, decent livelihood and the search for security and freedom from violence and discrimination. Critical youth investments needed to reap a demographic dividend and they are those that protect rights, and provide skills and knowledge to build young people's capabilities.

---

61 https://www.thedailybeast.com/the-cliche-is-true-you-really-are-as-young-as-you-feel retrieved on 21/11/19.

62 https://www.thedailybeast.com/the-cliche-is-true-you-really-are-as-young-as-you-feel retrieved on 21/11/19.

63 https://economictimes.indiatimes.com/news/politics-and-nation/india-has-worlds-largest-youth-population-un-report/articleshow/45190294.cms?from=mdr retrieved on 23/11/2019.

64 https://economictimes.indiatimes.com/news/politics-and-nation/india-has-worlds-largest-youth-population-un-report/articleshow/45190294.cms?from=mdr retrieved on 23/11/2019.

3.1. Young and Their Worlds

We live in the middle of worlds! Although the young live in 'one world' they have to respond to many other "worlds!" Young need to find unity in diversity like in one universe containing billions of stars linked together mysteriously! Everything is connected to each other and make a beautiful cosmos in spite of the individual differences. Young people enter into a complex reality of various dimensions of human life. Here, they need an assistance of matured leaders and animators to frame a successful concept of life and grow splendidly. Below we make an analysis of different types of world within the world of a young person so that there would be an awareness of the complexity and the need for competence in serving the youth.

3.1.1. Intellectual World

For every youth there is a world of intellect which demands engagements in critical thinking and reading, research, and human self-reflection about one's life and society. Through this intellectual world they may propose solutions for their problems and gain authority as a public figure. An intellectual person is someone with a reasonable extent of intelligence, capable of thinking and resolving matters rationally, as well as solving difficulties. Usually, intellectual people are highly adaptable, they understand how much they don't know, they have insatiable curiosity, they are open-minded, they like their own company, they have high self-control, and they are sensitive to other people's experiences.[65] A young person has to develop his intellectual ability to enhance his potentials in a creative way. Like climbing of the mountain top, the individuals create new knowledge basing on their elders' experiences and expertise together with the reservoir of traditional know-hows and towards a greater acquisition of new intellectual prospects.

3.1.2. World of Culture

Culture is the womb where an individual is shaped and maintained. A young person enters into a world of culture by being part of a society. According to Tylor "Culture is an umbrella term which encompasses the social behaviour and norms found in human societies, as well as the knowledge, beliefs, arts, laws, customs, capabilities and habits of the individuals in these groups."[66] Culture is considered a central concept in Anthropology, encompassing the range of phenomena that are transmitted through social learning in human societies. Cultural universals are found in all human societies; these include expressive forms like art, music, dance, ritual, religion, and technologies like tool usage, cooking, shelter, and clothing. The concept of material culture

65 Cf. https://en.wikipedia.org/wiki/Intellectual retrieved on 23/11/2019.

66 Tylor, Edward. *Primitive Culture.* Vol. 1. New York: J. P. Putnam's Son, 1871.

covers the physical expressions of culture, such as technology, architecture and art, whereas the immaterial aspects of culture such as principles of social organization, including practices of political organization and social institutions, mythology, philosophy, literature-both written and oral, and science comprise the intangible cultural heritage of a society.[67] A young person will have to acquire culture through the learning processes of enculturation and socialization, which is shown by the diversity of cultures across societies. A cultural norm codifies acceptable conduct in society; it serves as guideline for behaviour, dress, language, and demeanour in a situation, which serves as a template for expectations in a social group.[68] For every young person culture is a complex field for interiorization and growth.

3.1.3. Moral World

For a young person, moral world is a complex appropriation of values and virtues by which one is asked to develop one's conscience and discern one's course of actions in life. Morality speaks what is right and wrong. The moral learning prepares an individual to choose what is good and avoid what is bad. Morality speaks of a system of behaviour with regards to standards of right or wrong behaviour. The word carries the concepts of: (1) moral standards, with regard to behaviour; (2) moral responsibility, referring to our conscience; and (3) a moral identity, or one who is capable of right or wrong action. Common synonyms of morality include ethics, principles, virtue, and goodness. Morality has become a complicated issue in the multi-cultural world we live in today. It describes the principles that govern our behaviour. Without these principles in place, societies cannot survive for long. In today's world, morality is frequently thought of as belonging to a particular religious point of view, but by definition, we see that this is not the case. Everyone adheres to a moral doctrine of some kind.[69] The moral world introduces a comprehensive and diverse perspectives of major ethical codes and theories nurtured by one's own clan or community. The Moral World enables a young person to understand the place of ethics, religion, and helps recognize the value of integrity in the material world. As part of good moral contact, the young man is asked to possess personal beliefs and values, such as: Always tell the truth, do not destroy other's property, have courage, keep one's promises, not to cheat anyone, treat others as one wants to be treated, do not judge, be dependable etc.[70] This is a highly complex area of formation that is necessary for every young person to undergo. Our world

67 https://en.wikipedia.org/wiki/Culture retrieved on 23/11/2019.

68 https://en.wikipedia.org/wiki/Culture retrieved on 23/11/2019.

69 https://www.allaboutphilosophy.org/morality.htm retrieved on 23/11/19.

70 https://www.google.com/search?q=What+are+some+good+morals%3F&sa=X&ved=2ahUKEwiLuL367 Retrieved on 23/11/19.

will become less happy as we neglect the aspects inherent in the sound moral vision.

3.1.4. World of Fears

Stepping into an unfamiliar place is always threatening to a young person. Fear comes automatically into human mind especially when it is dark and lonely space. Fear is usually a feeling induced by perceived danger or threat that occurs in certain types of organisms, which causes a change in metabolic and organ functions and ultimately a change in behaviour, such as fleeing, hiding, or freezing from perceived traumatic events.[71] Fear of the unknown or irrational fear is caused by negative thinking or worry which arises from anxiety accompanied with a subjective sense of apprehension or dread. Irrational fear shares a common neural pathway with other fears, a pathway that engages the nervous system to mobilize bodily resources in the face of danger or threat. Many people are scared of the "unknown."[72] Especially the young people are victims of: 1. The fear of inadequacy; 2. The fear of uncertainty; 3. The fear of failure; 4. The fear of rejection; 5. The fear of missing out; 6. The fear of change; The fear of losing control; 8. The fear of being judged; 9. The fear of something bad happening; 10. The fear of getting hurt.[73] But, the positive aspect of human nature is that all the fears can be solved with correct leaning about them and by gaining courage of one's self. We see thus the young people are vulnerable with their world of fears.

3.1.5. World of Dreams

Every young person is filled with a lot of dreams and imagining a wonderful future. Dreams give an impetus to walk through newer and tougher paths. Dreams also shape individuals to grow great and contribute abundant potentialities. One widely held theory about the purpose of dreams is that they help someone store important memories and things one learned, get rid of unimportant memories, and sort through complicated thoughts and feelings. Dreams are hallucinations that occur during certain stages of sleep. They are strongest during REM stage of sleep, or the rapid eye movement stage, when one may be less likely to recall one's dream. Much is known about the role of sleep in regulating our metabolism, blood pressure, brain function, and other aspects of health. But, it's been harder for researchers to explain the role of dreams.[74] "In fact some of the biggest inventions of our time came

---

71 https://en.wikipedia.org/wiki/Fear Retrieved on 23/11/19.

72 https://en.wikipedia.org/wiki/Fear Retrieved on 23/11/19.

73 https://www.cnbc.com/2017/05/18/the-10-biggest-fears-holding-you-back-from-success.html retrieved on 23/11/19.

74 https://www.healthline.com/health/why-do-we-dream Retrieved on 23/11/19.

about through daydreams – the Internet, robots, rocketry, test tube babies, the list goes on. All these things were dreamed up by imaginative people; people who went beyond facts and thought globally and synthetically, made serendipitous associations and came up with surprising and novel solutions."[75] Dreaming about the future is connected to our own subconscious mind. If one thinks of dreaming as associated with a higher sense of awareness it is not uncommon that dreams actually can predict the future. Such dreams are known as precognitive dreaming.[76] Dreams are essential. It is only when we dream big with all our heart, we will be able to achieve bigger things in life. Young persons through their dreams try to achieve good marks, have good friends, get support from the family and make it big in life. Dreams also can nurture a beautiful career from an early age. Dreams can inspire us, but goals can change our lives. Goals are all about action. Goals turn dreams into reality. Goals change a young person in his/her life. The world of dreams are complex because of its mystery and non-availability of correct or true interpretations. But, dreaming is not bad because it has the potential to heal and encourage.

3.1.6. World of Emotions

Every human person is blessed with the gift of many emotions. They sometimes control humans but a true maturity is an ability to control one's own emotions in an appropriate way. Emotions penetrate every aspect of our lives. Interwoven with memory, attention, cognition, and decision making, they determine our interpersonal relations, our private life, the public sphere, and religious worship. According to Nicole Gravagna "An emotion is our human way of putting a meaningful label on experiences. We do it unconsciously. Emotions are experienced as a sense of urgency directly tied to a physical sensation in the body."[77] When we enter the world of emotions we find plentiful of them: Acceptance, affection, amusement, anger, angst, anguish, annoyance, anticipation, anxiety, apathy, arousal, awe, boredom, confidence, contempt, contentment, courage, cruelty, curiosity, depression, desire, despair, disappointment, disgust, distrust, ecstasy, embarrassment, empathy, enthusiasm, envy, euphoria, fear, frustration, gratification, gratitude, greed, grief, guilt, happiness, hatred hope, horror, hostility, humiliation, interest, jealousy, joy, kindness, loneliness, love, lust, outrage, panic, passion, pity, pleasure, pride, rage, regret, rejection, remorse, resentment, sadness, self-confidence, shame, shock, shyness, social connection, sorrow, suffering,

75 https://dowhatyouloveforlife.com/your-dream-your-future/ Retrieved on 23/11/19.

76 https://www.auntyflo.com/dream-dictionary/dreaming-about-future-and-it-comes-true Retrieved on 23/11/19.

77 https://www.forbes.com/sites/quora/2018/01/04/how-emotions-shape-the-way-retrieved on 23/11/19.

surprise, trust, wonder and worry. This enquiry into the world of emotions tell us how brilliant is every human being with his/her variety of emotions. In a right proportion and in a right place when the emotions are being used then there is best scope for a lively human existence. Young people are afraid of their emotions because very often they are being controlled by their own emotions. It is a complex capacity to become a matured person in controlling one's own emotions. Emotions make us true human beings and we become sensitive to the events that happen in the relationships every now and then.

3.1.7. *World of Needs*

Usually, the young people are being controlled very much by different types of needs in their personal life. Needs are again like a world! The time one gets up in the morning from sleep and until one goes for sleep at night, hundreds of needs are being satisfied to make one's life realized. From physiological needs to the transcendental needs every person search for fulfilment. According to Sperling A "drive is a persistent stimulus, usually of physiological origin, which demands an adjustive response."[78] Abraham H. Maslow believed that "Human beings have an innate tendency to move towards higher levels of health, creativity, and self-fulfilment."[79] In his basic need hierarchy, Maslow proposed an ascending order of need satisfaction. Here the gratification becomes as important a concept as deprivation in his theory.[80] Maslow believes that every human being goes through a ladder of needs starting from the physiological Needs. Then the next set of needs he calls the safety needs and further the belongingness and love needs reaching the next step as the esteem needs and then finally the self-actualization need.[81] Every young person has needs, interests, desires, values, strengths and weaknesses, which are going to affect his/her behaviour. While all youth have different personalities, they are alike in many ways. All young people have five basic needs: The desire to belong, Becoming independent, Achievements in life, Need for New experiences, and Need for affection or love.[82] Our discussion on needs unfolds before us a big world of different varieties of needs which every young person will encounter in the process of his/her growth in human maturity.

---

78 A. P. Sperling. *Psychology*, Butter Worth-Heinemann Ltd., Oxford, 1982, 187.

79 R. Frager, *Foreword*, A. H. Maslow, *Motivation and Personality*, Harper & Row Publishers Inc., New York, 1970, xxxv.

80 Cf. A. H. Maslow, *Motivation and Personality*, Harper & Row Publishers Inc., New York, 1970, 17.

81 Cf. A. H. Maslow, *Motivation and Personality*, Harper & Row Publishers Inc., New York, 1970, 16-22.

82 Cf. http://4h.okstate.edu/literature-links/lit-online/others/volunteer/ 4H.VOL.102 Retrieved on 23/11/19.

As we perceive the worlds of the young there are still further many items appear important like: A World of Sickness, A World of Fun and Pleasures, A World of Fashion and Dressing, A World of Sickness and Ill-health, A World of Achievements and Failures, A World of Prayer and Spirituality, A World of Sacrifices, A World of Friendships, A World of weakness and Deviations, A World of Compassion and Charity, A World of Competitions and A World of relationships and groups. These details of variety of features paint an integrated and holistic picture of the worlds within the world of young people. A mentor of young people should get the knowledge and tools to deal with these issues, if at all he/she needs to help them grow positively.

4. Fr. Louis an Excellent Mentor of Youth

Aforesaid details on the youth were well taken care by the great personality of Fr. Louis Malieckal CMI in his life-style and attitudes. He was a mentor par excellence. He was a veteran Indian theologian, who loved the challenges and opportunities given by the Second Vatican Council in the areas of inculturation of Liturgy and contextualized priestly formation. Much of his life he spent as an accompanying mentor of priestly students and he genuinely possessed a young heart to deal with the young. Even in his matured age he had the quality of 'growing up young' for the mission entrusted with him by the Church and his Superiors. He is well-known as one of the architects of contextualized theological formation in North India. His refined and dignified vision has made an enormous and enduring impression on the minds of young generation in the ecclesial and religious circle.

Soon after the II Vatican Council, the Church in India organized the well-known "All India Seminar on Church in India Today" in the year 1969 in Bangalore in which about 600 people participated, representing all sections of the people of God–lay people, sisters, priests, and bishops. During the seminar many issues pertaining to the life and mission of the three Churches in India were discussed. High on the agenda was the issue concerning the transformation of a post-colonial Church into an Indian Church. It laid stress on spirituality, dialogue with other religions, evangelization and Indian culture, education, socio-cultural activities, communication media etc. However, at the seminar itself not much was said about priestly formation and theological education.[83] This famous 'All India Seminar' of Catholic Church which was held at Dharmaram College, Bangalore, from 15 to 25 May, 1969, in fact gave a great impetus to the Indianization process of faith expressions, theology, sacraments and sacramentals and particularly the Eucharistic Liturgy. Mario I. Aguilar wrote in his famous book-*Christian Ashrams, Hindu Caves and Sacred*

83 Errol D'Lima, "Priestly Formation for Service to the World," in Jacob Kavungal et al. Eds. Vatican II: *A Gift and a Task*, St. Pauls Bandra, 2006, pp. 226-245.

Rivers: "Late venerable Abhishiktananda worked particularly with a group of priests of the Carmelites of Mary Immaculate from Kerala who had been encouraged by their bishop, Joseph Cardinal Parecattil, on the development of an Indian Liturgy for the Syro-Malabar Rite" (page 74). Here we find the wholehearted involvement of Deacon Louis Malieckal who appropriated the great clarion call of Vatican II to update Church's worship and later to become a great catalyst for shaping of a contextualized priestly training.

The young Louis joined in the creative group of Dharmaram to give shape to an 'unknown' rite of Indian Mass. The history tells us that at the request of Joseph Cardinal Parecattil, the Rector of Dharmaram College organized a group of staff and students to take up the task of preparing a complete order of the Eucharist in the Indian style in view of the forth coming All-India National Seminar. Accordingly, a group was set to work for studying Eastern/Indian Character of Holy Eucharist, Hindu ritual worship, *bhajan* singing and Vedic prayer recitation. As a deacon, Louis joined with Fr. Vineeth and visited the Ashram of Vinoba Bhave which was called *Brahmavidya Mandir* in Maharastra. The team's stay in that Ashram, sharing meals with the Ashramites, doing Ashram-seva, praying with the inmates, listening to the way they were reciting the prayers and chanting *bhajans*, and above all trying to understand the Hindu world-vision through reading and discussing with the members of Ashram, the group got confidence to venture upon shaping an Order of the Eucharist in the Indian style.[84] In 1983 when Fr. Louis completed his higher studies and returned from Belgium, he was appointed at Ashta Regional Seminary. He asked himself: What is the task assigned to me by God's providence in this particular context? He then developed a new methodology for Seminary training which he called Action-Reflection-Action and Village living. Being the Rector he served Khrist Premalaya two terms. During his time, he also begun the *Sarvadharma Samiti*-Interreligious Association in 1988 which played a very vital role to bring peace between communities of diverse religions.

These historical milestones speak volumes on the personality of Fr. Louis. He became an inspiring figure amidst the youngsters and could achieve a lot of transformation both in the worship pattern of Catholic Church as well as in the formation of a mission oriented theological priestly training. All his students have a loved and admired space in their hearts reserved for their mentor. What endeared him to the students was his ability to understand them from their viewpoints, without being judgmental. As a formator, he tried to develop a student-friendly attitude. He writes, "I have always tried to take the perspective of the other, of the students." As we have noted at the first part

84 Cf. Fr. Louis Malieckal CMI, (Editor: Cyril Kuttiyanikkal CMI), *Interface of Cult and Culture: Essays on Inculturation, Liberation and Mission*, ISPCK, Delhi, 2019, p. 142.

of this article, the important traits of a 'growing up young' were significantly present in the person of Fr. Louis Malieckal.

Conclusion

I hope, this remarkable book would be the best way we can celebrate the life of Dr. Louis Malieckal who was the source of inspiration for thousands of priests, religious and lay people. I read in a Newspaper advertisement which I would like to rephrase for Fr. Louis: A cloud can turn out to be a nurturing rain; a simple humming could turn out to be a most beautiful melody; a simple whisper can turn out to be a sweetest memory in the mind and a simple person can turn out to be a great history of a community. This is true in Fr. Louis. Looking at his personal history, one can admire profoundly Fr. Louis. He was a great history of a true Indian theologian who worked indefatigably for the emergence of a new Indian Church with her own unique treasures of theology, liturgy, music, and formation of priests. He was a visionary and reconciler for unity and harmony within the Church and Society. Fr. Louis was a noble soul who served as a bridge between God and humanity; between literate and illiterate people; between privileged and underprivileged ones; and between the culture and Christian faith.

Through his unique personality, talents, wisdom, knowledge, creativity and by his selfless and genuine commitments he made our world a better dwelling place and thus realized the dream of God through his educative, formative, and theological pursuits. With Fr. Louis our world was more dignified, reconciled, more creative and enchanting. Now in his absence, it is our duty to continue and foster his values, attitudes and legacy. We need to dispense the fragrance of his visions and merits in Indian Church by having more and more will for studying the Indian ethos, philosophy, spirituality and making our Christian faith more indigenized. He loved the land and people locally as well as globally; he learned Sanskrit, read Indian Sacred Scriptures and tried to bring out the most profound aspects of 'soul of India.' He had his unique views and perspectives in life but he was very simple in his life-style and open to understand others with gentleness and respect. His cordiality, care, and happy nature will be remembered always not only by the young generations but also the elderly. My salutations to him who tried to write new scripts in inculturation and theological formation of priests and religious.

We need more people like Fr. Louis who have an intimate love with Jesus and an ardent love towards the Church and People of God. The culture is the best medium and language through which a Christian can translate and transmit the Good News and bring the effectiveness of the Gospel of Jesus of Nazareth in the society. Inculturation is not a luxury to the theologians and Christian believers but an obligation by which Christ will be more heard, loved and known in our world. The Indian Church needs a greater conversion to make herself authentic in her own soil. More and more dedication, study, and contemplation are desired to make our people to grow into the consciousness and stature of a true Indian follower of the Gospel. Let us pray to Fr. Louis for his powerful intercession to have more theologians and leaders with his mind and vision.

11

Dismantling Class Room Theology for Mission

Dr. Davis Varayilan CMI

The Church is missionary in spirit and nature. She needs committed and risk-taking missionaries to continue the mission of the Lord in today's challenging context. It requires a theological formation that ignites fire to inflame the hearts and sentiments of the students. If theological seminaries have lost fire to inflame the hearts of the students to take risk in life, it is an indication that theology has become too static; it has lost touch with the contextual realities; it has stopped reading and responding to the signs of the times. Theology must interact, challenge and integrate faith with life, text with context, and classroom with the field. Fr. Louis Malieckal, the former rector of two theological seminaries in North India, was very much concerned with the method of theological education and formation. He gave the highest value to the work of priestly formation because it is linked to the very mission of the Church, especially the evangelization of humanity (PDV 2). According to him, the formation of a priest is not just an academic programme to be taught in the class rooms but to ignite fire in the students for mission of the Lord by exposing them to the contextual realities.

Fr. Louis was convinced that the need of the time was not a repetition of traditional method of theological formation, nor a rejection of the past but a re-formulation of the content and the method to attain the goal of formation. His effort was to go beyond the class room academic theology to contextual theology. The importance of context is highlighted in *Pastores Dabo Vobis:* "God always calls his priests from specific human and ecclesial contexts, which inevitably influence them; and to these same contexts the priest is sent for the service of Christ's Gospel" (PDV 5). He experimented and proved the relevance of contextualized theological formation in two seminaries: Khrist Premalaya Regional Theologate (KPRT), Ashta and Samanvaya Theology College, Bhopal. In this article, we shall deal with his method to contextualize theological formation in KPRT, Ashta where the author was a student for his theology. It is brought out in four points: towards dismantling class room theology, contextual method of theological education, factors that contributed to contextualize theology in Ashta and the impact of contextual theology.

1. Towards Dismantling Class Room Theology

Until Vatican II, the theological formation given in the seminaries was based on the canon 18 of Reformatory Decrees passed on the 23rd session of the Council of Trent held on 15 July 1563.[85] The focus of theological formation during the Tridentine period was to make sure the availability of a law-abiding and obedient group of clerics. According to Isaac Padinjarekuttu, "The strictly orthodox, celibate priests trained in the newly established seminaries became the bulwarks of Roman Catholicism and its centralized system in the following centuries."[86] In this style of formation, there was a complete isolation of the candidates from their environment for the entire training period so that they did not succumb to the world's pleasures.[87] They were segregated with a special dress and tonsure. The theological presuppositions were very narrow.

The Tridentine method of theological formation was influenced by the classical theology. The subject matter of classical theology was revealed truths contained in the Scripture and Tradition because revelation was understood as God communicating a set of basic truths about Himself to a privileged people. These truths were written down in a human language and passed on in Scripture and Tradition of the Church to succeeding generation. This supernatural revelation is necessary for salvation. And so the task of theology was to define, explain and teach the revealed truths authoritatively for our better understanding. The faith was understood as an intellectual assent to those revealed truths. Consequently, theological education in the seminaries was in tune with the classical theology and the teaching was confined to class room in an atmosphere insulated from the social and cultural realities of the world. Theology was primarily concerned with eternal truths valid for all places and times, and life beyond death. The context, space and time where one theologized did not affect the truth that the doctrines presented.

---

85 Isaac Padinjarekuttu, "Priestly Formation: Historical perspectives," in *Shaping Tomorrow's Church: Formation of Priests and Religious for India,* ed. Kurien Kunnumpuram (Bombay: St. Pauls, 2006), 147.

86 Isaac, "Priestly Formation", 148.

87 Ibid.

In the Indian context, the St. Thomas Christians had a unique system of seminary formation called Malpanates where the disciples lived with the Malpan and studied under his care. The priests were part of the life of the people and were held in high esteem and enjoyed a prominent position in society. After the arrival of Portuguese, during the period of Vicar Apostolic, Bernardine Baccinelli, the ancient system of Malpanate was legally abolished and made seminary education compulsory.[88] The seminaries introduced a systematic training of the priests according to Tridentine reforms but in a secluded atmosphere without much connection with the context and the people.

The **Post-Conciliar period** was an attempt to move away from the heavily centralized system of formation to a decentralized system of formation by recognizing the variety of peoples and places. The Second Vatican Council came as a game changer in the understanding of priesthood, priestly ministry and priestly formation and paved the way for theological education and formation in context. It was influenced by the new understanding of revelation and faith in *Dei Verbum*. The revelation is explained in *Dei Verbum* as personal self-communication of God to human beings in the history of salvation, which reaches its fullness in the person of Jesus Christ (DV 2). When we understand revelation in interpersonal terms or a personal self-offer of God's very self to men and women, the context becomes important because this offer becomes meaningful only in terms that men and women could understand. God's revelation to the men and women of India has to be in terms of categories, language and forms that really speak to the Indians.

The faith is a total and personal response to God's Word, the Word incarnate (DV 5). Pope Benedict XVI says that the Word that we follow is Jesus Christ and we are drawn to him by both Tradition and Scripture. In his Apostolic Exhortation *Verbum Domini,* Pope writes that Christianity is not a "religion of the book" but of the Word of God, "not of a written and mute word, but of the incarnate and living Word" (VD 7). In his encyclical *Deus Caritas Est*, Pope Benedict XVI writes: "Being Christian is not the result of an ethical choice or a lofty idea, *but the encounter with an event, a person,* which gives life a new horizon and a decisive direction" (DCE, No. 1). In other words, the focus of theology has to be shifted from the revealed truths to God the Revealer and from the focus on Scripture and Tradition to encounter with the person of Jesus through them. The document *Presbyterorum Ordinis* speaks about priests as instruments of Christ (PO 12), ministers of Jesus Christ (PO 2), and representatives of Christ (AG 39). Priests are not ministers of the Church but ministers of Christ who act in the name of the Church. Therefore, the primary objective of theological education is not just faith in Christ but configuration to Christ. This new, interpersonal notion of revelation and faith

88 Ibid., 152.

points to the necessity of a theology that takes seriously the actual context in which men and women can experience the person of Jesus.

The changing cultural, social and religious scenario of contemporary India, marked by acute awareness of the multi-religious experiences, awakening of the subaltern groups and the increasing influence of globalized world and media thrust upon seminaries to respond to them creatively by contextualizing the theological formation and revamping the existing paradigms of theological education. Considering the pluralistic contexts of the world the Council document *Optatam Totius* stated: "In such a great variety of peoples and regions only general laws can be laid down; so in each nation and rite a special 'programme of priestly formation' is to be initiated and determined by the Episcopal Conferences.... so priestly formation may always match the pastoral needs of those regions in which their ministry is to be exercised" (OT 1).

Following the instructions from the documents, the CBCI produced a provisional draft in 1971with the title "Programme of Priestly Formation in India." In this document the CBCI stated: "Concretely and in particular, our seminary studies must prove themselves relevant and meaningful in the actual Indian context."[89] This has been reaffirmed in the Charter of Priestly Formation for India approved by the CBCI in 1988.[90] This document highlights three important contexts of India: the socio-economic, the religio-cultural and the scientifico-technological which are "constitutive factors in the theological process."[91]

The rectors of North Indian Region met at Allahabad seminary in 1980 and decided to undertake a serious study on 'missionary formation' in seminaries and a memorandum of recommendations was submitted to the bishops of the region. Once the bishops endorsed the memorandum, the rectors met again in March 1981 and prepared the guidelines for wider consultation. After collating all the views they organised systematically and sent to the Regional Consultation held at Navsadhana, Varanasi in 1982. The fruit of the consultation came out as a series of recommendations on seminary training related the content and methodology. The Consultation recommended the 'action-reflection-action programme for theological formation at least for one month each year as part of the curriculum. "We recommend the starting of a new formation set up with a small number of suitable students and competent

89 *Programme of Priestly Formation for India* (Madras: Commissio Technicia for Seminaries, 1970), 31.

90 *Charter of Priestly Formation for India* (Madras: CBO Commission for Clergy and Religious, 1988), 18-19.

91 Samuel Rayan, "Theological Education in the Social Context of India Today," in *Theological Education in India Today,* ed. Felix Wilfred (Bangalore: ATC, 1985), 28.

formators with the mandate of working out new and integrated courses by test-teaching. A feasibility study of this project is to be initiated."[92]

Fr. Louis Malieckal states that "It is largely in the light of these recommendations that Khrist Premalaya Regional Theologate (KPRT), Ashta, started in 1982-83 with just six seminarians and four staff-members including this writer."[93] KPRT began functioning in July 1982 in Bhopal with Fr. Eustace Thottan CMI as the first Rector. In July 1983, the Theologate was shifted to Ashta. Then Fr. Louis Malieckal who returned after his studies in Louvain joined the staff and became the Rector from 1986 to 1994. He studied the recommendations of the bishops thoroughly and put them into practice in the seminary at Ashta. Under his leadership the KPRT took a definite shape in contextualised theological formation.

2. Contexutal Method of Theological Education

Fr. Louis was convinced that the class room theology taught by armchair theologians is not the need of the time for the mission in North India. The theology taught in the seminaries has to be related to the context where the priests would do the ministry. Asian bishops clearly affirmed that "Seminarians and religious in formation should not be taken out of their cultural environment, but be in continual contact with their living traditions. Formation is not so much information about the past but an introduction into new possibilities for the future."[94] But, what we see today in seminary formation is as Sebastian Kappen puts it succinctly: "The first part of the formation is creating a gulf between seminarians and the world, and the second part, in fact the rest of life, is an attempt to bridge the gulf."[95] There had been numerous pronouncements and initiatives by the Indian hierarchy regarding priestly formation in India like seminarians "should not be isolated from the mainstream of life,"[96] "at every stage of their formation, the seminarians should be in touch with the societal, cultural, and religious realities in which they are…"[97] but the tendency

92 *Priestly Formation in North India: Problems, Challenges Hopes* (Varanasi: Navsadhana, 1982), 3.

93 Louis Malieckal, "Theological Education in India since Vatican II," in *Theology of Wheels: A Movement for Contextualized Theological Education*, ed. Davis Varayilan (Delhi: ISPCK, 2011), 43.

94 FABC Office of Evangelization, "Conclusions of the Theological Consultation," 1991, in *For All the Peoples of Asia: Federation of Asian Bishops' Conferences Documents from 1970 to 1991,* Vol.1, eds. Gaudencio B. Rosales and C. G. Arévalo (Quezon City: Claretian Publications, 1992), 20. (Henceforth cited as *FAPA,*1).

95 Kuncheria Pathil, "Rethinking Theological Education in India: New Models and Alternatives: A Discussion with Sebastian Kappen," *Jeevadhara*, 14 (July 1984), 285.

96 *All India Seminar: Church in India Today*, (New Delhi: CBCI Centre, 1969), 316.

97 Charter of Priestly Formation for India, 1988, 21.

in the seminaries is to go back to the Tridentine model of formation based on classical theology. Fr. Louis took initiatives to change this trend by focusing on contextual method in theological education.

2.1. Theology is Contextual

The theologies that were developed in the West have been wrongly regarded as universal and standard to judge the theologies developed in other parts of the world. The theologies emerged in the developing world have been regarded as contextual and considered as optional extra or secondary in the western academic circles but there is no universal theology. There is no such thing as 'theology' for theology happens only from a particular perspective which is influenced by theologian's biological and cultural heritage and conditioned by the time and place which are his *Sitz in Leben*. To be relevant, a theology must be particular and specific, seeking to answer the questions of the context. Every theology is elaborated within the context of a specific situation.

The New Testament portrays diverse images of Jesus which is an indication of the possibility and necessity of articulating the Christic experience from different worldviews and communicating them in a language meaningful to those to whom it is addressed. Both Paul and John show us how the mystery of Jesus Christ can be experienced, articulated and proclaimed using both Hebrew and Hellenistic world-views.[98] Paul addressed his Jewish listeners quoting Scripture but when he addressed Gentiles, he began with general revelation. The focus of Paul's preaching remained the same, the Gospel. However, Paul shifted his presentation of the Gospel to fit the worldviews of his listeners. Augustine theologized in the context of controversies regarding the validity of Baptism, the necessity of grace, etc. Aquinas's context was the new culture of thirteenth century Europe, Luther's context was widespread corruption in the church and Karl Rahner's context was a world torn apart by war. Theology is and has always been contextual. According to Bp Desmond Tutu "Theology seeks to make sense of the experience of a particular Christian community in relation to what God has done, what he is doing in the present, and what we believe He has promised to do in the future and the ultimate reference point is the man Jesus Christ."[99]

98 Jacob Prappally, "The Contribution of Indian Theology to the Universal Church," in *Doing Theology in India: 40 Years of ITA Milestones and Signposts,* ed. Jacob Parappally & Vincent Kundukulam (Bangalore: ATC. 2018), 76.

99 Desmond Tutu, "Towards a Relevant Theology," in *Confronting Life: Theology out of the Context,* ed. M.P. Joseph (Delhi: ISPCK, 1995), 155.

2.2. Contextual Realities as Resources of Theology

The Church affirms God's presence and activity in the world through the Spirit. Therefore, the contextual theology follows the inductive method where the contextual realities are taken not as *background* for developing theology and evangelization but as *resources* of theology together with Christian sources of Scripture and Tradition.[100] They become resources of theology in so far as they embody and manifest the presence and action of the Spirit.[101] The resources of Indian contextual realities for doing theology are culture with its manifold expressions; religions with their scriptures, oral traditions, rituals, and popular religiosity; economic and political realities and world events; social movements, in particular women's, tribal, ecological, and popular movements.[102] The Office of Theological Concerns of the FABC acknowledges that this method has been accepted in Asia and is bearing fruit in the life of the Church.[103]

2.3. Theological Method to Interpret the Signs of the Times

Contextual theology has to dialogue with two realities: the experience of the past recorded in Scripture and the Church's Traditions and the experience of the present or the context in which theologians live. The 'signs of the times' is the key to dialogue with these two realities. Pope Paul VI provides clear guidelines for the proper use of the signs of the times as a theological methodology. In his address at the general audience on 16 April 1969, the Pope notes that from the time of Vatican II, this phrase has "taken on a current use and a deep, very wide and very interesting meaning, that is, that of the theological interpretation of contemporary history."[104] This phrase "refers to those events in history characteristic of an epoch, which, if properly read, can reveal the presence or the absence of God."[105] Pope Paul VI suggests that scrutinizing the signs of the times "is a question of detecting 'in the times,' that is in the course of events, in history, those aspects, those 'signs' . . . that can be indications to us . . . of some connection with the 'kingdom of God,' with its secret action, or . . . with

100 Ibid.; see also *FABC* V, 9.4, *FAPA,* 1:288.

101 Office of Theological Concerns (OTC), "Methodology: Asian Christian Theology," 3.1 in Franz-Josef Eliers, ed. *For All the Peoples of Asia: Federation of Asian Bishops' Conferences Documents from 1997 to 2001* (Quezon City: Claretian Publications, 2002), 3:356 (henceforth cited as *FAPA,* 3).

102 Ibid., 3.2, *FAPA,* 3:356-62.

103 Ibid., 3.1, *FAPA,* 3:356

104 Pope Paul VI, "Signs of the Times," *L'Osservatore Romano*, English edition (24 April 1969), 1.

105 M. Heath, "Signs of the Times," in *New Catholic Encyclopedia,* ed. Thomas Carson and Joann Cerrito (Farmington Hills: Catholic University of America, 2003), 117.

the possibility, the availability, the exigency of an apostolic action."[106] From these guidelines, one can identify three stages: (1) detecting or scrutinizing the signs of the times; (2) theological interpretation of these signs by seeing their connection with the kingdom of God; and (3) appropriate apostolic action. In the Conciliar documents, *Gaudium et Spes* clearly follows the theological methodology of the signs of the times and emphasizes that "the Church has always had the duty of scrutinizing the signs of the times and interpreting them in the light of the Gospel" (GS 4).

Scrutinizing the signs of the times can be neither an academic exercise nor merely by an exposure to the field; it requires knowing the times.[107] It means that one should know the great changes that are taking place in the modern world. In the words of Paul VI, "the world becomes a book for us."[108] The Christian mystic Meister Eckhart says, "Apprehend God in all things, for God is in all things. Every single creature is full of God and is a book about God. Every creature is a word of God." A close reading of this book demands, first of all, an *immersion* in the realities of the context or first-hand experience of the realities of the times accompanied by an attitude of reflective knowledge. The purpose is to provide us with an experiential knowledge of the people from their perspective. It helps us to feel the pulse of 'what is going on' in the world in order to discern 'what is pushing forward God's plan for the world and what God is telling the Church today. This can be identified only by means of the aspirations and dreams, "joys and hopes, griefs and anxieties" (GS 1) of human persons in society.

Secondly, discovering the signs of the times requires a *sociological analysis* of facts from the field which includes social, economic, political, cultural and religious systems in society as well as the needs and aspirations of the people. This analysis examines what effect these facts have on human consciousness and on social life and what arises from there is, properly speaking, the locus of the signs of the times.[109] Paul VI cautions about the danger of identifying the signs of the times on the basis of a purely phenomenal observation or purely technical and sociological schemata of facts surveyed and classified. Thus he points out the need for a theological interpretation of the signs of the times with the guidance of the Spirit in the light of the Gospel.

For a theological interpretation of the signs of the times, Paul VI suggests that the Church must compare "faith with life" or discern their connection with the Kingdom of God. In a comparison of faith with life, the Church is

106 Paul VI, "Signs of the Times," 12.

107 Gerald O'Collins, *Fundamental Theology* (New York: Paulist Press, 1981), 106.

108 Pope Paul VI, "Signs of the Times," 12.

109 C. G. Arévalo, "On the Theology of the Signs of the Times," *Philippine Priests Forum* 4 (1972), 18.

called to avoid pious interpretations to the cases of its experience and see the direction to which these signs point. Do these signs "spontaneously meet higher plans, which we know to be Christian and divine (such as the pursuit of unity, of peace, of justice)"? Do they suggest "that the time has come for a simultaneous step forward of the kingdom of God in the human kingdom"?[110] Do they further God's plan for human history? This is the theological level of discernment indicating how these signs become carriers of divine intentions.

To interpret the signs of the times we need to listen to what the Spirit speaks to the Church through the people, especially the poor, other religions, the secular movements and the events of history and discern them in the light of the Scripture, the Tradition and the magisterial teachings. Paul VI calls attention to the ambiguity of interpretation of signs. He acknowledges the reality of the *sensus fidei* which may confer the gift of wise insight for the interpretation. However, he affirms that "the assistance of the magisterium will always be provident and decisive when the ambiguity of the interpretation deserves to be solved either in the certainty of truth or the benefit of the common good."[111] Reading the signs of the times is precisely to discover what God is communicating to us through the events and experiences of today. "We must, therefore, recognize and understand the world in which we live, its expectations, its longings, and its often dramatic characteristics" (GS 4). According to Samuel Rayan, "Theology is done by bringing faith-experience with its interpretations and symbols face to face with real life with its problems and sufferings; by letting them meet, clash, question and challenge each other, illumine and interpret each other, and encounter God as judgement or as grace in each other's depths. The sparks born of the contact and the flame leaping from it will be the seeds and the buds of a theology making for social transformation."[112]

3. Factors that Contributed to Dismantle Class Room Theology in KPRT, Ashta

I was a student of theology in Khrist Premalaya Regional Theologate, Ashta from 1989-1992 when Fr. Louis Malieckal was the Rector. In KPRT, the theological education and priestly formation was integrated, the text was a response to the contextual realities, the class room was extended to the villages and parishes, and the community was inclusive of the people around. The factors that contributed in dismantling class room theology at Ashta seminary were the rural setting of the seminary, non-Christian surroundings, weekly

110 Ibid.

111 Paul VI, "Signs of the Times," 12.

112 Samuel Rayan, "Decolonization of Theology," *Jnanadeepa* 1, 2, (1998), 149.

visit to the villages, action-reflection-action programme, day scholars in the seminary and simple structure and life-style with focus on vernacular language.

3.1. Rural Setting of the Seminary

The Khrist Premalaya Regional Theologate began in Bhopal, the capital of Madhya Pradesh in 1982 but a year later it was shifted to a village two kilometres away from Ashta town. There was no good tarred road in our times to travel from Ashta to the seminary. Travelling to the villages as well as to the seminary became all the more difficult during the rainy season. The entire buildings of the seminary were single floored. There were no single rooms for the brothers until we became deacons. We were staying in the dormitories partitioned with curtains. There was no boundary wall for the seminary. Fr. Louis always insisted to have single floor for the buildings to identify with the poor people in the villages. This kind of simple structure of the seminary and the frequent contact of the brothers and the staff with the people in the villages made them feel at home with the seminary campus. In his Apostolic Exhortation *Evangelium Gaudium*, Pope Francis says, "I want a church which is poor and for the poor" (EG 198) The Church should be a place where "the poor feel at home" (EG 199).

3.2. Non-Christian Surroundings

There were no Christian families in the villages around or in the Ashta town except a few families who settled for the work. We were living in the midst of the followers of other religions mainly Hindus, Muslims and Jains. Our relation with them was not based on class room theology but by the concerns and needs of the context. We looked at the context not as religious diversity but as religious pluralism. The religious diversity means different religious traditions exist side by side without knowing or engaging with one another or even detached from and indifferent to each other. In Ashta we were practising religious pluralism, which means we were trying to know, engage and build relationships with the neighbours of another faith. This engagement with the followers of other religions motivated us to take initiative to organize *Sarva Dharama Sammelan* involving the members of all religions of Ashta. Communal riots between Hindus and Muslims were common in Ashta town. Gradually, a *Sarva Dharma Samithi* was formed involving members from different religions and it continues even today. Fr. Louis played a key role in constituting this *Sarva Dharma Samithi*. He always encouraged the brothers to take such initiatives.

3.3. Weekly Village Visits

There was weekly exposure to the villages on every Friday afternoon after the class. This weekly exposure was meant to keep in touch with the realities of the context while pursuing academic studies. The weekly exposure to the villages and constant interaction with the people destroyed our deep-rooted prejudices and overthrew certain narrow outlooks and helped us enter into the inner world of the "other" and appreciate and appropriate the richness of the other religions and cultures into our own spirituality. These village visits helped us to familiarize ourselves with the social life and customs and religious practices and traditions of the people in the villages. It also brought us closer to the stark realities of their life. These weekly village exposures enriched our academic studies in the class rooms by raising new questions from the field.

3.4. Action-Reflection-Action Programme

Action-Reflection-Action is the method employed in the seminary formation in Ashta. To apply this method concretely three weeks live-in experience is provided to the students as part of the academic programme. The students were free to choose any diocese of Madhya Pradesh or even outside for particular experience like Hindu ashram in Rishikesh. Fr. Louis gave freedom to the students to choose the places and areas of involvement according to each one's interest in the field of mission. The students used to spend about three weeks in the field collecting data and gaining first-hand experience of the situation of the people. These experiences and facts were further analyzed by using the tools of social analysis to find out what effect they have on human consciousness, on family, spiritual and social life. Then by the guidance of the Spirit these effects were interpreted in the light of the Scripture and Tradition (GS 44) to discern where the Spirit is leading them and what actions are called for. The findings of study and experiences in the field were presented in a written report. The sharing of the variety of experiences by different groups enriched one another. This method provided the students with an experiential knowledge of the people from their perspective. The findings of the ARA raise questions for theology. It is in responding to these questions a living theology is born. It is an attempt to interpret the Christian faith in the light of today's experience and to understand the events and experiences of today in the light of faith.

3.5. Day Scholars in the Seminary

Fr. Louis was always open to the initiatives of the students. He encouraged the students to live in groups in the villages for a month and attend the daily classes in the seminary. Together with Fr. Joseph P. P. and Fr. Simon, I stayed in a village called Kilcrama, four kilometres away from the seminary, for a month. We stayed in a rented house with single room and kitchen in the village. There was no toilet in the house so we had to go to the open field. We went to the seminary everyday in the morning by bicycle and returned in the evening to the village. We spent time with the villagers in the evenings by taking tuition for the children, conducting awareness programmes and visiting the houses. Initially they looked at us as strangers but gradually they welcomed us and made us to feel as one of them. Immersing ourselves in the context challenged us to get out of our comfort zones and made theological classes more interactive by bringing questions from the context. Challenges from the context make students creative, innovative and dynamic. Bp Gratian Mundadan says, "Class room lectures on propositions, formulations and defense of doctrines might reduce theological education just to an intellectual exercise. Theological education should enable the students to discuss courageously the problems of the Church, of the context and to intervene in that context. This would offer them the confidence and the strength to confront the challenges in the future ministry."[113]

3.6. *Lifestyle in the Seminary*

Fr. Louis created a positive, open, understanding and encouraging atmosphere in the seminary for practising contextual theological method. He respected the conscience of the individual, giving them freedom to take individual and group initiatives. There was an atmosphere of freedom and mutual trust between the staff and the students. In the past, the style of formation was more of a uniform pattern. It was seen in terms of big structures, of rules and routine exercises. The lifestyle in the seminary was attuned to the context. During the harvesting season of wheat and soyabean, the routine exercises of prayer and classes were postponed and all of us went to the field in the morning at 06.00 am to harvest. Fr. Louis encouraged us to have freedom with responsibility which helped us to grow in maturity and discernment. Where there is freedom for initiative and creativity, there is also risk and uncertainty. He was ready to take the risk for the sake of students' growth. The mature growth takes place only when there is enough freedom to discern the actions.

4. The Impact of Contextual Theological Education

It is not easy to assess the impact of contextual theological education since theologizing contextually is itself an ongoing process and the context keeps changing. By and large contextual theological education still remains a class room exercise. To a great extend, the success depends on the students' openness to the context and willingness to take up the challenges and constant accompaniment of the staff. I have not done any survey to evaluate the outcome of such theological education but from my experience as a student in Ashta and as a member of the staff in Samanvaya Theology College, Bhopal, I can point out some of the possible outcomes in contextual theological education.

---

113 Bp Gratian Mundadan, "Theological Education for Mission in Context," in *Theology of Wheels: A Movement for Contextualized Theological Education*, ed. Davis Varayilan (Delhi: ISPCK, 2011).

The first outcome is growing in wisdom by merging class room and the field. Jesus said, "I came to the world to "throw fire" and how I see it burning." To have fire in theology and to keep that fire burning throughout the life and ministry of the students or to create passion for Jesus and compassion for people, the academy and the field, text and context should merge. The students explore their capacity, capability, passion, energy and the real purpose of their lives by implementing the knowledge they gain from the class, experimenting with it in the context, innovating, renovating and continuously repeating it during their theological formation, they grow in wisdom rather than merely in intelligence. Intelligence is when we have an understanding of Jesus from the studies, whereas wisdom is when we have implemented that knowledge in our life and for the good of others. In other words, the contextual theology helps the students to convert the data they acquire from the class, books, etc., into information and by practising it in the context they gain knowledge. In spite of the inner struggle, outer challenges, and failures, those who increase their efforts to implement it repeatedly, the size of the success become larger and knowledge turns into wisdom where they know what exactly need to be done, how to convert failures and challenging situations into opportunities, how to be sensitive to the context and do the mission.

The second impact is growing in creativity by raising questions through exposure and immersion in the context. Questions make us different and creative. Questions provide the key to unlock our unlimited potential and maximize our life. A well-asked question is already half the answer. Raising new questions in the class makes the class more interactive and participatory. It also helps the students to develop the skill to ask the right questions. Being a student in Ashta and a member of the staff in Samanvaya Theology College for 11 years, I can say that contextual theological method helps to bring out new questions to the class. The classical theology strips the students of their freedom to think differently because it gives answers and answers make everyone the same. That is why the candidates who enter in the seminary with lot of initiatives and creativity come out after 14 years of formation thinking the same and doing the ministry the same way bereft of all creativity and the capacity to think differently. It is not an abundance of answers that makes us creative, but the quality of our questions.

The third strength is the attitudinal changes in the students towards the contextual realities. The prolonged exposure and constant interaction with the context destroys deep-rooted prejudices about the culture and people and helps them enter into the inner world of the "other" and appreciate and appropriate the richness of Indian cultures and religions into one's life, spirituality and ministry. They develop the ability to dialogue with the people of other faiths and sensitivity to social issues. The students move from rigidity to flexibility. They show interest and openness to unlearn and relearn according to the signs of the times. It enables them to be critical, creative, open, flexible and daring to take risk. It enriches, deepens and purifies their own faith and enables them to maximize the divine within them.

The fourth outcome in Regional Theologates is integration of theological education and theological formation. There is no separation between academic and personal formation like specialists impart theological knowledge on a variety of subjects and some others give guidance towards personal formation. All are educators and formators. Formation is a matter of being caught rather than taught. Priesthood is not a matter of getting a degree or diploma but having passion for Jesus and compassion for people.

Conclusion

Theology is not meant to be purely academic discipline. Theory and praxis must go hand in hand. Every theory must be tested in action and every action must be reflected upon and integrated into theory. "It is only by being with the people, by sharing their joys and hopes, their tears and struggles, their failures and frustrations that one can begin to theologize meaningfully."[114] Therefore, contextual theology is the right response to the changing context of the present world. Context redeems theology from being an ideology, from monolithic absolutism and staling stagnation. Relating theology inextricably to the context means to let theology become a dynamic force. Such dynamic theology will have fire to inflame the hearts and sensibilities of the students. Static theology is not only dangerous to the growth of religion, but also breeds fundamentalists, whereas contextual theology keeps growing according to the signs of the times and creates prophets who keep religion relevant to the times.

Fr. Louis Malieckal is one of the pioneers in the field of contextualized theological education in North India. It is right and fitting to bring out a book to commemorate his first death anniversary. He should be remembered for his contribution to the priestly formation which was very dear to him. He was a risk-taker in the field of theological formation because he was landed in an unexpected place after his doctoral studies in Louvain. But he tried to bloom where he was planted by the Lord.

114 Kurien Kunnumpuram, "Theology in India at the Crossroads," in *Theologizing in India*, ed. M. Amaladoss, T. K. John and Gisper-Sauch (Bangalore: TPI, 1981), 214.

12

An Ode to Louis Malieckal His Contextual Academic Contributions

Benny Thettayil

1. Introduction

It has been almost fifty years since theologians first began talking about contextual theology. Theoretically, at least in the developing countries today, the Church requires of the centres of theological education to contextualize it and construct contextual theologies that are helpful in the local churches. However, there are only a few helps available. The expectation is clear, but an understanding of the process by which this may occur is lacking. Practically, some of the teachers and most of the students of theology, often complain that they are led to adapt Western theology to their context rather than developing theology for their churches. Demands for contextual theology are made and arguments in favour are proposed often, but there has been little debate explaining and defending the methods involved and a very few attempts to meet the demand. Louis Malieckal, like several before him, entered the debate and invited his students and colleagues alike to appreciate the gravity of the ecclesial situation and join the conversation because he knew that only a healthy contextual theology can shape the future of theology by reviving biblical images and perspectives found in world Christianity.

Theology has always been contextual. There is a wrong but general assumption among the Asian students of theology that all of Christian orthodoxy has been developed and articulated by the privileged, powerful, "Western" people out of speculation. Many of the early influential theologians were non-European. For example, Arius, a Libyan ascetic was an Egyptian. His teachings about God the Father's uniqueness and Christ's subordination to the Father, and his opposition to what would become the dominant Homoousian Christology, made him a primary topic of the First Council of Nicaea, in 325. Similarly, Athanasius of Alexandria was a Christian theologian, a Church Father, the chief defender of Trinitarianism against Arianism, and a noted Egyptian leader of the fourth century. He was called by his enemies "the black dwarf", which indicates a non-European ethnic heritage and he was anything but part of the "ruling elite" of the Constantinian and post-Constantinian Roman Empire. He was exiled by Roman emperors five times including one exile among the "desert fathers." And yet he was crucial in the development and preservation of Nicene orthodoxy. In the following century, there was Augustine, a Roman African, the bishop of Hippo in North Africa, an early Christian theologian whose writings influenced the development of the Western Church and all of Western Christianity. We could come up with numerous examples of great defenders of Christian orthodoxy who do not fit the profile of the privileged, European, white people who most people think are the progenitors of theology.

The earliest theological works in Christianity were written by these Church Fathers who attempted to construct coherent frameworks through which people could better understand the nature of God's revelation to humanity in Jesus. However, admittedly, there was a time when for centuries, the doing of theology had been shaped by Western theological imperatives. Today the decline of the institutional religion in the West, and the extraordinary growth of the church of the East call for a recapture of theology that is contextual. A rereading of the gospel through specific cultural contexts can advance a critical and contextual theological development.

2. The Indian Theological Scenario and Louis

The last few decades of the twentieth century and the first decade of the twenty-first century have witnessed a great shift in Christian theology in India. This is a shift from the singular Indian Christian Theology to the plural Indian Christian Theologies. It was only natural for an Indian Christian Theology that came of age. It was also necessitated by the multiplicity of the experiences of the religious communities and the recognition of this multiplicity by those thinkers in the area. The acknowledgement of the multiplicity of religious experiences and their influence on theology are further enhanced by the voices of those who are at the margins. They bring their own perspectives to theological thinking. This paper is an attempt to highlight the theological contributions and engagements of Louis Malieckal, an Indian Christian theologian, poet and thinker who left an indelible mark on the Indian Theological horizon, especially through his attempts to bend the trajectory of Indian liturgical thinking and action.

In his articulations, Louis expressed his views with a vision, and in this way, and through his academic pursuits he transformed the world around him. There is hardly any branch of theology that he did not touch. He made significant contributions on Cultural Studies, Dalit Studies, Tribal Studies, Christian Social Ethics, Mission and Ecumenism and Practical Theology. In all these diverse disciplines, he offered methodological insights especially from the awareness of the methodological shifts in these disciplines.

3. Louis the Theologian

Louis is one of the Indian theologians who struggles with the provisions of the Vatican II in the second half of the twentieth century and the first quarter of the twenty first. He became a teacher of Systematic Theology. However, he maintained the mathematical expertise, which was his first love. A mathematician turned theologian, he sustained a mathematical precision in all his theological writings and talks.

Since his first major work on Eucharist in which he viewed sacrifice in the light of the Indian concept of *yajna*,[115] which was ground breaking in its time and was instantly recognized as such, his contributions have continued to be profoundly original and constantly creative, while also continually resourced from the theological tradition.[116] The creative features of this work have been so influential that they have become common, even taken-for-granted features of much subsequent Indian theological discussions. Some key themes, such as sacrificial dimension of the Eucharist, give a characteristic shape to his whole theological development. However, his work has continually moved on, and at every stage of his teaching career, he has not only rethought major Christian doctrines, but also related them to one after another key contextual issue that has arisen in the contemporary world like politics, legislation, ecological issues, inter-faith dialogue and so on. The originality of Louis becomes evident when he brought together the Christian theological tradition, and the confronting culture and the demands and insights of the contemporary world presented by the context.

His contextual theological contributions have been important not only for fellow theologians and students of theology, but also for very many leaders of the various Indian churches, clergy and interested lay people. This is not only because his work relates the central theological themes of Christian faith to the contemporary world and its concerns, but also because, alongside his

115 Louis Malieckal, *Yajna and Eucharist: An Inter-Religious Approach to the Theology of Sacrifice*, Bangalore: Dharmaram Publications, 1989.

116 Louis Malieckal, *Interface of Cult and Culture: Essays on Inculturation, Liberation and Mission*, Cyril Kuttiyanikkal (ed.), Delhi: ISPCK, 2019, pp. 34-37.

major works, he has written many shorter and more accessible articles that communicate his best thinking in a readable style without much technicalities.

Often in these shorter works in journals, meant for a wider readership, he expands on the practical implications of his main thought. The spiritual and socio-political implications of his ideas are expressed in these short works more than he does it in the major works. As a review editor of a few journals, he kept himself abreast with various important thoughts and thinkers in the field and this made his own contributions really substantial.

4. Contextual Theologizing

Theology is a response to God's revelation to his people in the concrete contexts of life. Stephen Bevans argues that there is no such thing as one normative theology, and that "doing theology contextually is not an option"[117] since it is a human enterprise which is created within a particular human context. Contextual theology refers to the manner in which the Church in every age, in the light of the gospel message, has adapted its teachings to the culture in which it found itself. Bevans defines contextual theology "as a way of doing theology in which one takes into account the spirit and message of the gospel; the tradition of the church; the culture in which one is theologizing; and social change within that culture, whether brought about by western technological process or the grass-roots struggle for equality, justice and liberation."[118]

Contextual theology is an umbrella term and as it arises from the confrontation of the gospel and context, there are many, not one, contextual theologies. For instance, Black theology (Africa and US), Minjung theology (Korea), Dalit theology (India), theology of struggle (Philippines), liberation theology (Latin American) and feminist theology are contextual theologies that have emerged out of concrete historical realities that were touched by the liberative aspects of the Christian message of the gospels.

5. The Contextually Shaped Theologian

Louis woke up to the call of the Vatican II for renewal in the Church and was fascinated by the euphoria created by the open approach of the Council. The buzz of renewal was everywhere. This was specially seen in the liberal approach of the theologians and historians who were at the helm of affairs in the institution where he had just begun his theological studies as a young man. Fascinated by the contextual approach that they were spearheading, he joined

117 *Stephen B. Bevans, Models of Contextual Theology, Maryknoll, NY:* Orbis Books, 2002, p. 3.

118 Stephen B. Bevans, *Models of Contextual Theology, Maryknoll, NY:* Orbis Books, 1992, p. 1.

the band wagon.[119] Once he was part of the group, he got himself fully involved in the process and the whole project bore fruits that made others envious.[120]

Although he started out his ministerial career as a mathematician, and he had a secure career going, the community would give him another mandate. His early contributions and interest in the area of liturgy, especially the "Indian Liturgy", and the need of the community for a committed liturgist, set him on another course of academic involvement – Theology. For this reason, he was sent for higher studies in Liturgy, which he completed commendably. His choice of specialization in theology would again be dictated by the context that he was part of - *Indian*. In all these ways, the theologian in him was being shaped by the context that he found himself in.

This is also the case with the field of formation in which he would test and perfect his theological views. Although, he did not have a clue regarding the arena of his academic ministry until the end of his higher studies, towards the end of his studies, he was informed that he was to go to Khrist Premalaya, the M. P. Regional Theologate at Ashta, entrusted to his community, the Carmelites of Mary Immaculate a few years earlier. Providentially, this was an institution that was far more rural than what he had bargained for. Characteristically, after his appointment, Louis went around learning the methodology from the Jesuits who had already established a few contextual theology centres in several parts of India. Backed by sufficient theoretical know-how, he plunged into the context, dived deep and brought out precious pearls of contextual theology. With the students and the colleagues, Louis developed a theological engagement cum study programme in which the students and teachers were placed directly in the context in which they were to do theology confronted by the hard social, cultural, religious, economic and political realities of life.[121]

Later, the methodology for contextual theological engagement that was developed there would be cloned in Samanvaya Theologate[122] where he was appointed the first Rector. In Samanvaya, he furthered the concept of contextual theological formation of the priestly students. In the altered scenario, the students are doing theology in four specific contexts with adequate theoretical and conceptual backing. Once again, the North Indian Context that Louis found himself in, shaped his theological mind and the theologian in him responded to the context positively. However, of late, like the liturgical renewal that he was part of, this venture also came under the scrutinizing radar of the Congregation for Catholic Education, Rome and objections were raised regarding the mode

119 Louis Malieckal, *Interface of Cult and Culture*, p. 147 No. 10.

120 Louis Malieckal, *Interface of Cult and Culture*, p. 224 No. 23.

121 Louis Malieckal, *Interface of Cult and Culture*, p. 165.

122 *Samanvaya Theologate* was Rechristened *Samanvaya Theological College* and Further Rechristened *Samanvaya Theology College* Later.

in which education in the first cycle of theology in Samanvaya is carried out. This hitch notwithstanding, the legacy that Louis left in the area of Contextual Theology is of immense value.

6. Danger of Half-baked Contextual Theology

Context refers to the circumstances that form the setting for an event, statement, or idea, and in terms of which it can be fully understood and assessed. Contextual theology, therefore, is theology that asserts the necessity of social, cultural, political, economic and religious context to fully understand any text that is produced on God in a given space, which then is taken to another space. Hence, contextual theology is born when these two historical horizons meet. When these poles of interpretation are kept apart either on account of ignorance or convenience, the exegete tends to distort the message for the interpreting community.

Contextual theology in the modern times, seeks to include the realities of contemporary secularity, technology and the struggle for human justice in its range of theological investigation and the subsequent articulation in the light of the gospel message.[123] However, in general, the principle of contextual theology has to be applied carefully if the teachings of Christ are to be accepted by any culture. There is a danger that the truth can be accommodated to the culture to the extent that it becomes compromised instead. For example, the cultures which are predisposed to the plurality of gods can accept Christian teachings and even faith to the extent that it becomes acculturated and never truly effectual in turning people to the God the gospels. When theologians are vague on this, or when they are compromising in their views and teachings, the effect is that the God of the gospels becomes just another addition to the plethora of deities that are worshipped. Plurality is so ingrained in the psyche of people who belong to some cultures that when relating to them it is all too easy to cross the line and fall into syncretistic[124] positions, especially on the plurality of saviours. This is sadly wrong.

Another beautiful biblical example of contextualization is found in Paul's sermon at Areopagus found in Acts 17:22-31. Speaking in Athens, Paul quoted Greek philosophers and poets to prove that Jesus Christ rose from the dead. By using familiar poets, Paul made it easier for the Athenians to become open to his message, albeit without any immediate positive effect. Whether it be in a religious or secular milieu it is a similar type of

123 *Charles E. Van Engen, "Toward a Contextually Appropriate Methodology in Mission Theology", in Charles H. Kraft (ed.), Appropriate Christianity, Pasadena: William Carey Library,* 2005, p. 194.

124 I am aware of the fact that the term *syncretism* is almost completely dropped from contemporary liberal theology; only the ultra-conservatives use it occasionally.

contextualization that is employed when somebody quotes a current movie or a bestseller to illustrate a point that he wants to drive home.

Louis was convinced of the need of contextual studies that are necessary in order to make sense of the text and then make a practical application of the text to the context taking into account the present context. In this application, neither the *core* of the message of the text is adversely affected nor the *garb* of the applied context is harmed. It is in order to avoid this pitfall, that Louis would take recourse to his predecessors in the field of both Contextual Theology and liturgy. One of them is John Britto Chethimattam for whom he had great admiration.[125] In this way, with the help of several mentors in the field, Louis made his own mark.

The development of Contextual Theology has occurred as a result of a shift in the understanding of revelation. In the classical theology, revelation is understood in the form of "eternal truths handed down to us from Christ and the Apostles. Faith is understood to be the intellectual assent to those truths. All these are systematically arranged and presented as the... Faith."[126] The understanding that has undergone a shift speaks of revelation as God's ongoing act of self-disclosure in inter-personal terms. According to this view, revelation means God offering himself to us "by means of concrete actions and symbols in history as God's self-communication to men and women."[127] This calls for faith as a response from the people as a gift to the revealing personal God. Contextual theology looks for ways and means to articulate the message of this self-revelation of God in *local idioms* that they can understand within their cultural contexts. Theology takes seriously the contexts in which women and men encounter God.

7. Louis and his Subaltern Bend of Mind

Originally, subaltern is a term that refers to a person of inferior rank in the military circles. It was Antonio Gramsci, an Italian Marxist who used this term for the first time to designate the subordinated social groups and oppressed classes. The awakening of the suppressed masses and the philosophical articulation of their feelings that transpired in the underdeveloped world in the 90's, used this category to refer to the general attribute of subordination. This subordination is expressed in terms of class, caste, age, gender and office or in any other way.[128] Ever since, Indian social analysts and thinkers

125 Louis Malieckal, *Interface of Cult and Culture*, p. 155.

126 Jose de Mesa and L. Wostyn, *Doing Theology; Basic Realities and Process*, Manila: Maryhill School of Theology, 1982, p. 80.

127 Bevans, *Models of Contextual Theology*, p. 9.

128 Ranjith Guha, "Preface," *Selected Subaltern Studies*, (eds.), Delhi: Oxford University, 1999.

have been using this category in their discussions to delineate the political, aesthetical, epistemological and theological engagements of the marginalized human minority segments such as Dalits, Tribals, Adivasis, women and other overlooked people of Indian social history.

When he was sent to the M. P. Regional Seminary in a very rural area, Louis promptly entered this subaltern politics in order to interrogate the knowledge and institutional practices of any kinds of domination and hegemony. The time-line of Louis and his subaltern discourses given to his students reflect the history of the struggles of the subjugated rural people. In these discourses and the subsequent actions, his students created constructive encounters with the power structures of domination that was apparent everywhere. All dominations are power structures where some kind of knowledge systems is embodied and they are manifested through certain kind of social practices of marginalization and subjugation. Some of those structures that Louis, his colleagues and his students encountered were caste, patriarchy and hierarchy. In the light of the engagement of Jesus of the gospel with these sections of the society in his time, they told the rural people that life could be different and better in many ways.

Louis drew knowledge and insights from other disciplines such as sociology, anthropology, psychology, political science and economics that describe, analyze and interpret the experience of the villagers. *Theology* done in *context* offered his students a clear survey of the field of contemporary Liberation Theology and provided them with a sound understanding of how Contextual Theology worked in practice. Another recognizable fact is that grass-roots people in the village have been enabled to articulate their world views through their stories, myths and symbols, which according to him the "reality itself,"[129] even though these have remained in the form of oral tradition, which in turn is taken as a basic source of theological construction.

8. Methodological Challenges to Christian Theology

The subaltern cannot speak because in his subaltern consciousness he bears the imprints of several thousand years of servile psychological sediments and somebody else must wake him up from the slumber and speak for him and further enable him to speak for himself. Beginning with his students, Louis deconstructed the psychological edifice of the subaltern state of the villagers where his institution was situated. In this process, the subaltern people were enabled to re-image their subjectivity and speak of it. In this renewed and altered subjectivity, their social engagement would be on an egalitarian basis rather than on the basis of a victimised status that they had entertained so far.

129 Louis Malieckal, "Symbolism in Hindu Worship," in *Journal of Dharma* 9 (1984) 261-273, p. 266.

This led the entire group to envisage new ways of being an altered people and to resist the oppressive dominant powers in the contemporary context of plurality.

In the missions Louis encountered suffering among the rural people, which, he considered, had to be part of his theological thinking. This suffering was unique; was different from the suffering found in the rest of the world. The reality of suffering in this part of the world is described by Julio Labayen, which is more relevant today than in 1977 when he wrote it:

> Most obviously it is the extent, the sheer magnitude of the suffering. More Asians are hungry, homeless, unemployed and illiterate than all the rest of the world put together. More men and women are despised, humiliated, cheated; more suffer the tyranny of governments and oppressive elites, and the fear and shame that tyranny brings than in all the rest of the world combined... There may be areas of poverty around the world as bad as Asia... but there is nothing anywhere to match the sweep and unrelieved misery of Asia's suffering.[130]

Louis rejected the universal, monolithic and homogenizing methodology of a theology that did not have any touch with the suffering masses of India. It is this kind of shift in understanding that had, even before his arrival on the scene, provided the space for the emergence of various Contextual Theologies. The subaltern aspirations for a pluralistic, just, democratic and dialogic civil society led him to join hands with people of various walks of life and faith backgrounds. Theology as he visualized and understood it, attended to a passion for justice and transformation and thus opened a new face in the religious history in that part of India.

9. Context and Liturgical Overtones

Louis was a theologian who was always led by the contextual awareness that enabled to transcend the narrow confines of the classical definition of life and the various modes of its relationship both with the divine and the human beings. Liturgy was his forte. Traditionally, liturgy is the customary public worship performed by any religious group. As a religious phenomenon, *it* represents a communal response to and participation in the divine through activities reflecting praise, thanksgiving, supplication or repentance. However, he gave a whole new meaning to certain aspects of liturgy as he reflected on *sandhya* and the liturgy that is performed at various twilights. Transcending the monastic understanding of the schedule for prayer, he would consider these *sandhyas* not only as a time of prayer, but also as a prayer of time.[131]

---

130 Julio Labayen, "Asian Suffering and the Christian Hope", in T. K. Thomas (ed.), *Testimony Amid Suffering*, Singapore: CCA, 1977, p. 9.

131 Louis Malieckal, *Interface of Cult and Culture*, pp. 1-11.

9.1. The Liberative Liturgies

Louis would further explore the liberative overtones of the Eucharist. The Bible has a collection of contextual readings and liberative texts that have encapsulated the memories of subaltern people encountering the dominating elites. There is a great parallel between the biblical liberation and the liberation that people are in need of today. These stories and the liturgies connected to them provide immense inspirations for social engagement and possibilities for liberative applications. The Biblical hermeneutics that Louis followed for a subaltern theology for a broken people looked at the Church as a Eucharistic space for the celebration of *the broken body*, which has immense possibilities.

Furthermore, with his background research on the Eucharist, Louis was able to tap the abovementioned possibilities when he explored the potential of the sacrament of reconciliation. In the breaking of the bread, done with the grace of the sacrament of reconciliation, both the subaltern and the elite find a theological space for a dialogical community experience. It was in this kind of dialogical experience that alternative liturgies and ecclesiologies that were part of the subaltern theology were born.

9.2. Contextual Experiments in Liturgy

Louis lent a helping hand to the liturgical renewal efforts of his teachers in the light of the provisions of Vatican II. He narrates the details of the works they did in his article on the experiment.[132] *Swami Abhishiktananda had an appreciation for it. James Stuart notes that at the All India Seminar, held at Dharmaram College, Bangalore on 6-9 May, 1969, on 'The Church in India Today' Abhishiktananda "encouraged the efforts of a group of priests from Kerala (Carmelites of Mary Immaculate), who at the request of their bishop (the late Joseph Cardinal Parecattil) had been working on the development of an Indian liturgy, inspired by the Syro Malabar rite."*[133] In spite of all his efforts and studies in liturgy, his dream project of an Indian Liturgy, which had redirected the trajectory of his scholarly destiny, would not be fully accomplished. The conservative forces in the Church would neither understand nor endorse the Indian liturgical initiative that he was part of.[134]

---

132 Louis Malieckal, *Interface of Cult and Culture*, pp. 138-148.

133 James Stuart, *Swami Abhishiktananda: His Life Told through his Letters*, Delhi: ISPCK, 1989, p. 213; *Report, All-India Seminar, Church in India Today, Delhi: CBCI Centre, 1969;* Mario I. Aguilar, *Christian Ashrams, Hindu Caves and Sacred Rivers: Christian-Hindu Monastic Dialogue in India 1950-1093*, London and Philadelphia: Jessica Kingsley Publishers, 2016, p. 74.

134 Louis Malieckal, *Interface of Cult and Culture*, p. 144, 147 n. 16, 148 n. 19. He would discuss the liturgical experimentation in a detailed manner in Louis Malieckal, "Liturgical Inculturation in India: Problems and Prospects of Experimentation", in *Jeevadhara*, July 1988, 279-292.

9.3. Louis and his Liturgical Convictions

In spite of the setback that the liturgical initiative suffered, Louis, a practical theologian, kept the fire burning. Louis and his companions wanted to bring in more expressions in the liturgy, adapted from the context of the various cultures. Speaking of various models of contextual theology, Bevans notes:

> The praxis model gives ample room for cultural expressions of faith, while providing exciting new understandings of the scriptural and older theological witness. In some ways this model takes the concrete situations more seriously than any other model, since it regards theology not as a generally applicable, finished product that is valid at all times and in all places, but as an understanding of God's presence in very particular situations.[135]

Despite its limitations as pointed out by its critics, the liturgical initiative commended itself in a compelling manner to those, like Abhishiktananda, who were serious about their task of doing theology by means of liturgy in the Indian context. As a missionary theologian, Louis continued his liturgical efforts for the mission until his last breath,[136] because he believed that the *restored liturgy* was more suitable for a stagnant Church and offered no challenge to a pilgrim and missionary people; it does not inspire especially the young.[137] He longed for a *renewed liturgy* rather than a restored liturgy.

9.4. Louis the Praxis Theologian

A praxis theologian as he was, Louis learned to be humble in the face of the surprising ways by which God's will and ways are disclosed in the world and, through the world, to the Church. Through the various experiences, he learned to accept the contextual missiological fact that not only does the church have a mission to the world, the world, which is the context too, has a mission to the Church. Hence, until his passing, he continued to celebrate the Ashram Liturgy, which was an adapted version of the *Bharatiya Puja* (Indian Liturgy), at the same time, faithful to the Syro-Malabar liturgy.[138] His theological acumen in this field is evident in the fact that like several theologians with imagination in

135 Bevans, *Models of Contextual Theology*, p. 71.

136 See Louis Malieckal, "A Liturgy for Mission that Proclaims Jesus Christ to all Peoples and Cultures", in *Third Millennium II* (1998) 2, 8-24, where he is exploring the mission to look at the liturgical implications for the mission and vice versa. See also Louis Malieckal, *Interface of Cult and Culture*, pp. 85-90.

137 See Louis Malieckal, "Liturgical Inculturation and the Mission", in Bosco Puthur (ed.), *Inculturation and the Syro Malabar Church*, Kochi: LRC Publications, 2005, 183-205, pp. 203-204.

138 See Louis Malieckal, *Interface of Cult and Culture*, pp. 107-111, where Louis engages in a detailed discussion on the manner in which the liturgy of the Eucharist is to be celebrated in the church *sui iuris* of which he was a member.

the past, he was able to translate his thoughts into poems that were introduced into liturgy.[139]

Reflecting on the notions of pilgrimage and rituals, and delineating the various aspects of the religious ritual Louis notes that some of the rituals lead to fellowship and dialogue bringing down the "caste barriers, which are often visible in the everyday life"[140] resulting in a change of heart,[141] which is much longed for.

10. In Dialogue with the Context

When doing theology in a milieu of religious pluralism, the pluralistic perceptions of people regarding the Reality that we call God, need to be taken into consideration. Theologizing in a context of plurality demands engagement with others and finding connections between the differences. Christian theology in India finds itself in the midst of spirited and influential non-Christian religious systems, especially Hinduism, which claims the allegiance of 84% of Indians. Hindu religio-cultural factors have, therefore, played a decisive role in the emergence of several significant issues of Indian theology. According to ITA statements 2003,

> Indian theology seeks to interpret the Christ-event in dialogue with the religions of humanity. The Logos that is immanent in this universe as Life and in human history as Light has become flesh; this is the foundational experience of the Christian community. This kenosis of the Divine in Jesus Christ invites us to see the mystery of the divine turned towards humanity and reflected in the person of Jesus, crucified and raised from the dead. It ill-accords with claims that are triumphal, exclusivist or suggestive of 'fulfillment'. We realize that we now experience the mystery of the Divine in signs and symbols. It is in the Eschaton that we see God face to face. Until then all our perceptions continue to have a fragmentary character.

---

139 He "adapted and Christianized" Hindu bhajans "for our purpose" of Christian liturgical music. See Louis Malieckal, *Interface of Cult and Culture*, pp. 142, 147 n. 12, 225 n. 26. However, here Louis makes a factual error stating that the bhajan he adapted was "one of the oldest Christian bhajans". However, at least a century prior to his efforts, Brahmabandhab Upadhyay, an Indian Christian theologian, journalist, Indian freedom fighter and a "Hindu Catholic", composed among others, a bhajan in Sanskrit in praise of the Holy Trinity. See Julius J. Lipner, *Brahmabandhab Upadhyay*, New Delhi: Oxford University Press, 1999, p. 201. Further back, three centuries prior to Upadhyay, there was Thomas Stephens SJ, an English missionary, who was engaged in great Indian Christian literary activities. Among his works, the ground breaking *Kristupurana*, an epic poem both in Marathi and Konkani, which also needs to be taken in to consideration. See Francis Correa, "The Shakespeare of the Konkan Coast: Fr. Thomas Stephens SJ (1549-1619)", in *Vidya Jyoti* 83 (2019), 461-471.

140 Louis Malieckal, *Interface of Cult and Culture*, p. 21.

141 Louis Malieckal, *Interface of Cult and Culture*, p. 20.

Consequently, Indian theology considers persons of other religions as co-pilgrims and respects their religious faith.[142]

A viable base for dialogue exists in the NT synthesis of Hebrew and Greek culture for synthesizing Christian and Hindu culture in India. Hinduism and its scriptures are treated as counterparts to Judaism and the Hebrew Bible in relation to the gospel. Louis has always tried to listen to God who speaks through other religions also. Raymond Panikkar's theologies emerge in this context of religio-cultural pluralism. They advocate letting Christ reform Hinduism from within and so unveil the Christ who is already present there, though hidden and unacknowledged.[143]

Louis, in his theological sojourn, especially in the inter-religious contexts like Rishikesh, gave expression to the dialogical potential that the gospel carries. In his engagements with the various gurus of Rishikesh, it is not the *alterity* that he sought, but the mutuality, relationality and fraternity that are so explicated in the *Trinity*. This is also how he looks at the pilgrimage of John Paul II to India and his meeting with 200 religious leaders at an inter-religious meet in Chennai. Louis calls this a unique event in the history of inter-religious pilgrimage of dialogue.[144] Moreover, listening to the stories of the struggles of the several inter-religious seekers for transfiguration and resurrection, he celebrated a new kind of relationship where the 'Other' is re-visited and the ways of talking about him (theology) is re-invented. The differences of life in various worlds including inter-ecclesial world and intra-ecclesial world are to be acknowledged. Along with the assessment of the world outside, we need to attend to the 'politics of difference' within the church and the politics of indifference in the society. The hermeneutics of mutuality provided Louis with new possibility of multiple ways of being.

11. Bending the Text to Meet the Context

Contextual Theology attempts to view the Bible within its cultural context. Some of the aspects of Contextual Theology include adapting non-Christian and even secular practices for Christian purposes, testing them with help of the general message of the Bible, especially in the light of those biblical statements that are apparently applied only to the original culture, and determine how the biblical principles that are derived from these statements apply to new a

142 ITA statements 2003, "Society and Church: Challenges to Theologizing in India Today."

143 Raimundo Panikkar, *The Unknown Christ of Hinduism: Towards an Ecumenical Christophany*, London: Darton, Longman & Todd, Limited, 1981.

144 See Louis Malieckal, "Syro Malabar Mission: New Challenges in Perspective", in G. H. Ambooken (ed.), *Mission and Community Building*, Kochi: CMI-CMC General Department of Publication, 1990, p. 172.

new context. As a matter of fact, this is the process that we see in most of the sermons and in almost all the letters of the New Testament.

In theologizing, one needs to be ultra-vigilant not to bend the Scripture to fit a current cultural context. There is great danger in biblical truths being watered down in order to accommodate cultures. It has been observed that in our pluralistic culture where people engage in polytheistic worship, perhaps for lack of solid biblical teaching, Christians end up adding Mary to the pantheon of gods, which is a deceptive mistake. In the prayers that we make and in the prayers that we let the faithful make, in many cases, these unwarranted initiatives go unnoticed. Christianity's encounter with cultures and religions that believe in a plurality of saviours, tends to make Jesus one of them, which at least in some unseasoned theological mind, would seem better than nothing at all or at least a stepping stone to a better understanding later. Jesus is "the way, and the truth, and the life" and no person comes to the Father except through Jesus (Jn 14:6) who is the unique incarnation of God. The quest for relevance in theology, whether classical or contextual, should not be at the expense of commitment to the finality of the written and living Word of God.

Christian theologians also must encourage great caution when engaging in contextual theology. First of all, while reading the Bible today, the differences between the first century and modern culture must be taken into consideration. Secondly, any theological statement that is made as a result to a biblical interpretation, must be considered universally relevant and contextually applicable unless there is very strong evidence to the contrary. When we bend the text and make it speak what it does not, the text gradually becomes irrelevant. When this happens, the faithful might ignore those commands that they find most difficult to follow, making Christian life banal.

12. Louis on Contextual Biblical Understanding

Any contextual theology that legitimately claims to be *Christian* must be based on the Scripture. The distinctive experiences of a subaltern people can and should point everyone toward the experience of the lost, forgotten or neglected people who are found in the Scripture. Christian theology, like all forms of knowledge, thinking and practice, arises from and is influenced by the context in which it is done. Louis, in his varied theological contributions, analyses how various theological expressions assert a clear and persistent link to the Scripture and how should these expressions should be contextualised. Unlike many other traditionalist thinkers, he does not fear that a radically contextual reading of Christian Scripture will lead to a relativist understanding of Christianity. Since theology is born when the Bible is read and understood in the light of the present reality in context, various branches of theologies can share some form of common identity both despite their remoteness of origin and because of their present understanding which is contextual in nature.

Under the general umbrella of contextual theological discussion, can be gathered anything that the Bible does not directly and specifically address. Today, Contextual Theology seeks to find the underlying principles of Biblical commands and apply them to the postmodern culture. However, in theologizing, care should be taken not to add to or override the Scripture and the basic orthodoxy derived from the Scripture in the first formative centuries of Christianity.

13. Louis and his Cautious Theological Approach

The role of a theologian is to point out whether the articulation is keeping with the gospel and the basic Christian orthodoxy and needing correction. In his enthusiasm for contextual inculturation and adaptation, especially in liturgical matters, Louis does not become blind. Like any conscientious theologian who is aware of the implications of the result of his thoughts and his writings, he would scrutinize and analyse the context and shape a view that is conforming to the orthodoxy of faith and practice in the Church. He was not naïve in his adaptations. It is with this caution that he approaches the rituals practised by the followers of other religions. In his analytical considerations of Hindu pilgrimage, he notes some extreme penitential rites and questionable expressions of devotion in some of the pilgrim centres.[145]

Similarly, Louis approaches a theological issue from various angles. When he reflects on religious rituals, he would do it from as many perspectives as possible in order to keep himself away from falling into false theological assumptions. Taking a cue from the historical experience of the followers of the mystery cult in the Greco-Roman world whose rituals degenerated into many abuses, he delineates both the enslaving and liberating characteristics of the rituals and cautions his readers of the jeopardy.[146] Any theology that does not stand the test of orthodoxy is risky. Hence, Louis would make a journey through the extant cultures and cults in order to assess his theological positions in the light of the aberrations that have occurred in the history of theology.[147]

14. De-contextualization of Contextual Theology

In Louis' postmodern subaltern contextual theological discourses, he assumed that theology was a response to God's revelation in the concrete contexts of life and neglected the micro power relations inherent in them. This is usually a by-product of the concentrated stand that one takes on any issue. While the

145 Louis Malieckal, *Interface of Cult and Culture*, p. 25.

146 Louis Malieckal, *Interface of Cult and Culture*, pp. 52-53.

147 Hence, Louis would explore the various cultural currents and the emergence of sects and their distinctive cults in various religions and cultures. His approach here would both be inter-religious and intra-religious. See Louis Malieckal, *Interface of Cult and Culture*, pp. 55-76

subaltern is empowered, the subtle power politics exerted by them silences another group and the whole dialectical process is set in motion. In this seesaw game of the oscillating power, the theologian can, for his predilection for the oppressed or the perceived oppressed, place self at the centre, and define the perceived groups as binary opposite. The question that always loomed in Louis' social theology is of the empowerment of the powerless (and he was, to a great extent, successful in bringing that about). In the process, he overlooked the possibility of the overturned power equations making the now-empowered subalterns bring about a scenario in which they make their erstwhile elites subaltern. This vicious circle is usually inescapable as long as the controlling factor in the society is power. The empowering articulation for the subalterns should always have a third position where both the factions are empowered in such a way that they could live amicably and leave no room for *subalternity*.

The above-said polarity was the major methodological challenge that Louis faced as he lived his contextual subaltern theology. Contextual Theology, with all its contributions so far, has yet to make an attempt to define the fulcrum of social engagement and to have a dialogue between the subaltern and elitist discourses in order to suggest alternatives to the practices of domination in the familial, social, ecclesial, religious and political systems.

15. Conclusion

Any meaningful theological engagement with the experience of the real people today, poses new methodological challenges to Christian theology. Postmodern epistemological shift in understanding the socio-religious interplay provides theoretical possibilities for subaltern discourses to come forth. It calls for new theological engagements that transform the *contexts* and bring forth *texts* that are appropriate for the present and the future. As postmodernism defines itself, in the light of the Spirit who is free moving, the subaltern discourses, contextual affirmation and liturgical activities are open ended. They are ever open for interrogation, dialogue and change.

Louis was essentially a religious priest from whose prayer and meditations emerged his theology. He mined the resources of scripture and tradition for a fuller understanding of the God of the Hebrew prophets and of Jesus Christ, a God who, rather than being remote, uninvolved and transcendental is found "in the midst" of the world and in the suffering of God's people. The fullness of the faith that he thus communicated was evident in all his works. Contextual Theology for him was through and through congruent with the themes of the Christian Scripture and tradition.

As a missionary, he was led to confront the receptive hearts ready for the Kingdom of God, but often he found that the "non-believers" were already in the Kingdom of God in their own way. For him, the Kingdom of God is ultimately God's gift rather than a human achievement. This idea constituted his theological framework for doing the work of evangelization. While most theologians found it challenging to transpose this framework into a context, it was easier for Louis to relate to any people of any religion in any context, for they were perceived to be either co-citizens of or co-pilgrims to the Kingdom of God.

Louis is a modern prophetic voice that is crying to the church to become more contextualized and less Western or Eastern. However, there are not many, books that demonstrate how to use contextual methods to accomplish that task, to think theologically and act missiologically in different cultural contexts filling gap, in the articulations. He does not advocate catchy slogans and trendy techniques to create contextualized expressions of Christianity, but he underscores the importance of relying on Scripture and engaging ecumenically and inter-religiously in demonstrating the universal nature of Christianity that finds many expressions in numerous local communities all over the world, across space and time while living out their faith in particular local settings.

Although, the epicentre of Christianity has shifted to the East, yet, contextual theology, which, in its own way, seeks to preserve the integrity of the faith, has not been met with generosity among the Western scholars in general. The humble attempts of people like Louis were to burst the bubble of the overrated Western academy. He shows that to take context seriously in conversation with the Christian 'text' is a mark of all authentic theologizing, whether in a seminary or in a slum.

13

Tender Hands
Forming with Gentleness
Towards a Loui-Way in Formation

Joshy George Pazhukkathara CMI

A few leave their presence powerful in their absence. Such people are remembered due to the impact or the impression they create in the hearts of others during their life time. Some create impression through their extraordinary behaviour, some through their provoking thoughts, and some through their consoling and loving words. In Jesus' story, people were impressed, because of the authenticity and authority of his words (Lk 4:32). The impression that Fr. Louis Maliekal left in the hearts of many stems from his amazing personality, loving nature, and accompanying leadership. Louis was an able leader, who never walked before, nor followed behind, but who walked side by side, holding the hands of the sojourners. Louis was a true pastor, who cared for the needs of the people than the regularity of such an office. He was a formator, who owned the heart of Jesus, a loving and accompanying Shepherd. The qualities of tenderness and gentleness are those factors that proffered an enduring mark in the hearts of many. Indeed, the words, actions and approach of Louis have created an impression that keeps his memory alive in hearts of many, particularly his students. It is because Louis handled formation as a "delicate mission."[148] In this paper I would like to describe my memories with

148 Congregation for the Clergy, *The Gift of the Priestly Vocation: Ratio Fundamentalis Institutionis Sacerdotalis*, *L'Osservatore Romano* (8 December 2018), 132.

Louis, as a person with a loving heart. All of his students admire this quality of Louis, an ever smiling formator.

I have undertaken this task under six headings. In the first part, an attempt is made to narrate how Louis was able to append a colourful face for the seminary, which carved a lasting memory in his students. Secondly, I try to draw the way Louis envisaged an ideal seminary and how he accomplished it. Third part is an attempt to narrate those qualities of Louis which made him a formator par excellence. Fourth part explains what I term as *Loui-Way* in formation. In the fifth part, a description is given on how *Loui-Way* becomes effective through its future proof trajectory. And lastly, reflecting on the *Loui-Way*, I propose certain tactics for the present and future formators.

1. Charting a Colourful Face for the Seminary

I have heard people saying highly positive about their seminary formation; not just from those insiders, but even by those who chose not to be in priestly life. At the same time, I also have heard people speaking so negatively about their seminary life. I remember to have heard one speaking so negatively about his seminary life; he is full of anger and frustration. As he described, the formators wasted their colourful youth in the seminary. As I evaluated these two differing views on formation, one about the positive side and the other about the negative side, I found, for some it is a place where they grow more mature, more loving, happier and more God-centered persons; and for a few, it becomes a place where they turn to be more aggressive and segregated with one's own unhealthy tendencies. The latter category often comments that they were better at home, seminary made them worse. There could be many reasons for such differing views about the seminary. Most of these, in the latter category, point their finger towards the formator, who in their view, turned seminary a dark place. Indeed, more than anyone else the Rector and the staff members play a major role in making seminary a place of love and joy. My warranty for this observation is none other than Louis who turned seminary a 'love home.'

The students of Louis belong to the first category that still holds a reminiscence of a loving *papa* in the person of Louis. Definitely, because of the behavior of Louis he could chart a Good Face for the seminary wherever he was. Writing on the essential of formation, Joe Mannath observed that "the formator's main responsibility is to create a good atmosphere,"[149] a feature that made Louis a successful formator. His care and concern for the students, his ability to understand individuals, made the seminary a place of joy and happiness for all his students. Wherever he was, whether in Ashta or in

149 Joe Mannath, "Formation: The Essentials in a Nutshell," *Sedos Bulletin*, Vol. 50, No. 3/4 (2018), 37-43, 41.

Samanvaya, through his impressive approach, he could create a bright face for the seminary. As Pope Francis admonished, Louis was successful in becoming a merciful face all through his life. Students approached him without any hesitation because of this extraordinary feature of compassion and mercy. All of them were "edified and encouraged"[150] by the life of Louis.

Louis was convinced that "the priest of tomorrow, no less than the priest of today, must resemble Christ."[151] Hence, he always took pain to be empathetic towards his students and colleagues. Louis, as *Pastores Dabo Vobis* instructs, was particular to stress that "priests are called to prolong the presence of Christ, the one high priest, embodying his way of life and making him visible in the midst of the flock entrusted to their care."[152] It is this conviction that enabled Louis to be an icon of harmony and peace, becoming a Christ for others.

Louis always believed that Holy Spirit is the one who transforms believers into the image of Christ (2 Cor 3:17-18).[153] His conviction that the Divine Trinity and particularly the Holy Spirit is the ultimate formator, made him a compassionate formator. Louis had the broadness of heart to leave the task of formation to the Real Formator. Hence, he always respected the freedom of the students, with an assurance that this freedom is exercised with responsibility. Louis realized that "all formation, priestly formation included, is ultimately a self formation. No one can replace us in the responsible freedom that we have as individual persons."[154] This is seen repeated in the new *Ratio Fundamentalis* where we read, "each seminarian is the protagonist of his own formation."[155] Therefore, Louis took ultimate care to form pastors with responsibility, because he knew, as Pope Francis said, if not we "form their hearts … we are creating little monsters."[156] Subsequently, we do see that Louis gave more prominence to creating in the formees the ability to discern. It is these paternal features of Louis' person that help in charting a colorful face for the seminary. Definitely, all students of Louis cherish their seminary life as a time of sweet memories.

150 *Ratio Fundamentalis*, 132.

151 Pope John Paul II, Post Synodal Apostolic Exhortation, *Pastores Dabo Vobis, AAS* 84 (1992), 729-778, 5.

152 *Pastores Dabo Vobis*, 15.

153 See, *Ratio Fundamentalis*, 125.

154 *Pastores Dabo Vobis*, 69.

155 *Ratio Fundamentalis*, 130.

156 Jeffrey A Kramers, *Lead with Humility: 12 Leadership Lessons from Pope Francis* (New York: Amacom, 2015), 76.

2. Louis' Vision on Ideal Seminary

Louis' vision of the seminary can be summarized along the lines of *Ratio Fundamentalis*. Accordingly, "the Seminary community is indeed a family, marked by an atmosphere that favors friendship and fraternity."[157] Because of this vision, Louis always wanted to be an agent of peace, harmony, and joy. He seemed to be an icon of peace incarnated. To me, Louis was an ambassador of peace in the seminary, in the parish, and in all other offices he held. Through peace, he believed, we could create healthy pastors for the future. Hence, he took initiative to make the seminary an abode of peace. In fact, Louis wanted to make seminary a replica of life to come. I am sure, it is with this idea in mind Louis tried to convert the seminary to home of love and peace. Indeed, the presence of Louis made Samanvaya, a place of love and peace.

I assume that Louis had clear idea about what an ideal seminary is. He did his level best to make seminaries abodes of human and Christian values. He was careful not to make seminaries rehabilitation centers, where people are trained to reform themselves according to the changed situations. For Louis, instead of making seminaries remedy centers, they should be places where students discern and decide for oneself, what, why, and how. It is not a place, where one is kept in some predesigned tracks, and all those who tread out of the track are punished or dismissed. Louis knew this is possible only if each individual discern for oneself. Hence, instead being a course corrector, Louis showed how he forms himself.

An ideal seminary for Louis is a place of collaborative work; the work undertaken in the name, and for the sake of Christ. Therefore, as he regarded, formation is not a unilateral act, that is undertaken from the part of the formators alone. Rather, for him it is a mutual and collaborative project; collaboration between the staff, and among the students. Where such a collaborative work takes place, Louis deemed it to be the ideal seminary. As *Pastores Dabo Vobis* noted, "often the world of young people is a 'problem' in the Church community itself."[158] However, for Louis young people were an opportunity to instill love and care through his special approach, which I would like to call as *Lui-Way*.[159] It was through this *Loui-Way*, that he tried to make the seminary an ideal place.

3. A Formator Par Excellence

According to *Pastores Dabo Vobis*, "The Church's work of formation is a continuation in time of Christ's own work."[160] Moreover, as we have mentioned

157 *Ratio Fundamentalis*, 52.

158 *Pastores Dabo Vobis*, 8.

159 For an explanation of the *Loui-Way* refer the fourth part in this article.

160 *Pastores Dabo Vobis*, 2.

above, the Holy Spirit is the ultimate formator – a realization that helped Louis to form himself as an authentic formator. In the following we analyze a few major qualities that make Louis a formator par excellence. Mannath summarizes these qualities in three words, namely: inspire, interact, and instruct, which we would describe in detail.[161]

Louis was an undeniable source of inspiration. His life not only motivated others, but also challenged them. The joy and happiness in the life of Louis had such a deep sense of impact in all those who came in contact with him. About today's formees it is told, they do not have ears to listen to the advices, but have only eyes to see. For this reason, formation becomes a process of transformation only if it is carried out through a life of witness. Repeated advices or admonitions can generate only ill or bad feeling in the formees. Louis seems to have realized this truth because his life was an open book that could be read and imitated by the students. As Mannath says, "There are no short cuts. We learn the best lessons of life by experience and example, not through exhortations. A formation house must be a setting where younger people live with persons they can look up to and learn from."[162] Mannath continues, "Inspiring members are the best advertisement for a religious order or diocese."[163] The life of Louis was a source of inspiration for all of his students. He realized that what is required in formation today is not 'information packages' but 'living experience.' Today's generation turns suspicious if such information packages are provided without substantiating life witness. I am sure that Louis had the conviction that "every authority is exercised in a spirit of service as 'amoris officium' and unpretentious dedication for the good of the flock."[164] The spirit of service that one notes in Louis was such that even in his grown age, he always tried to serve others than to be served. I am sure, it is this service mindedness that has inspired and influenced me personally.

The second feature of a good formator is the ability to interact with others. Mannath notes, "Formation, like parenting, is a twenty-four-hour task. You can be a part-time professor; you cannot be a part-time formator."[165] Louis was not a part timer in formation, but rather he was a full timer. This very feature enabled him to make himself available to everyone. He liked to interact with each of the student irrespective of their differences. He was with them all through, in the chapel, in the class room, in the garden, in the play

---

161 Joe Mannath, "Formation: The Essentials in a Nutshell," *Sedos Bulletin*, Vol. 50, No. 3/4, (2018), 37-43, 38.

162 Mannath, "Formation: The Essentials in a Nutshell," 39.

163 Mannath, "Formation: The Essentials in a Nutshell," 38.

164 Congregation for the Clergy, *Directory for the Ministry and Life of Priests* (11 February 2013), 25.

165 Mannath, "Formation: The Essentials in a Nutshell," 38.

ground, and even beside the bed when they fell sick. His presence was a loving presence, which the students cherished even after their time in the seminary. Thus, disproving the proverb, in Louis, familiarity never created contempt, but rather it generated a filial love as in a home.

The third feature is the role of instruction in formation. The formator has a definitive role to play through the instructions that he imparts to the students. Louis instructed his students, on various theological topics. However, his instructions had the color of loving persuasion, which left no room for the students to react or retort. His instructions were accompanied by his own living example. As *Ratio Fundamentlis* points, he was a formator "distinguished by prudence, wisdom and balance."[166]

Louis could thus, inspire, interact and instruct the young ones, because the initial fire in him was still burning with zeal. Often with many of us, the initial fire does not burn, or it is in a state of dormancy. The zeal and the fire in the life of Louis made his life meaningful, inspiring and challenging. Even at the age of 80 he was young at heart, burning with the initial and original zeal of a young religious. This is the prime reason why I have presented him as formator par excellence, because this is the quality that is required in every formator, namely, staying young in the heart, and burning with the zeal.

In his article Mannath narrates nine qualities of a good formator: Inspiring Personal Life, Team Work, Sound Judgment, Fidelity to the Church, Enthusiastic Familiarity with the Charism, Effective Communication, Intelligence and Academic Preparation, Pastoral Experience, and Some preparation for this ministry.[167] All these qualities are blended in Louis, which made him a composed formator. Moreover, Louis made sure that the new wine is preserved in the new wine skins. It is this ability of equipping himself according to the signs of the time that kept Louis a relevant formator until the last breath of his life. He had realized that "today's young people, with the vigor and vitality typical of their age, are also bearers of ideals which are coming to the fore in history: the thirst for freedom; the recognition of the inestimable value of the person; the need for authenticity and sincerity; a new conception and style of reciprocity in the rapport between men and women; a convinced and earnest seeking after a more just, sympathetic and united world; openness and dialogue with all; and the commitment to peace."[168] Louis was never an outdated formator, he always moved along the signs of the time.

---

166 *Ratio Fundamentalis*, 134.

167 Mannath, "Formation: The Essentials in a Nutshell," 40.

168 *Pastores Dabo Vobis*, 9.

4. The *Loui-Way* in Formation

In the traditional point of view formation is seen as an interruption in the unformed. However, for Louis, formation was never interruption in the individuality of the other, but rather loving perception of the other. He adopted the method of love and tenderness in forming and shaping the young minds. He never believed in compulsive rectification in formation. According to him, course correction can be made possible and effective only through love and tenderness.

As the statement of the US Bishops' Conference notes, "There is a temptation to use a basic plan to establish an ideal type of priest, an unrealistic, unattainable, and therefore unhelpful goal. A more realistic aim is to identify the true formative points of human, intellectual, spiritual, and pastoral encounter that priests must face in their ministry and lives and that are the privileged places where God's transforming grace touches them."[169] Louis from the very beginning of his career wanted to move beyond this temptation of traditionalism. Therefore, he wanted formation to be uninterruptive, but realistic and touching the core of the formee.

Moreover, Louis always warned his students not to fall into the problem of clericalism; instead he admonished them to be agents of collaborative action. He had a similar view on clericalism as Eugene Duffy described: "Clericalism obscures the reality of the ordained ministry in the Church. Clericalism is a kind of club mentality where the interests, privileges and status of the clergy are promoted and safeguarded. It exudes a hierarchical and authoritarian view of leadership and gives the impression that the clergy can monopolise and control the work of the Spirit. Clericalism tends to put grace in short supply."[170] In clericalism there is the absence of love and tenderness; and therefore, it can make one stubborn and assertive. According to the *Loui-Way*, there is no room for any monopolizing or hegemonic tendencies of clericalism in formation.

Louis always wanted that a priest must be, as *Pastores Dabo Vobis* explains, "a man of communion, in his relations with all people he must be a man of mission and dialogue. Deeply rooted in the truth and charity of Christ, and impelled by the desire and imperative to proclaim Christ's salvation to all, the priest is called to witness in all his relationships to fraternity, service and a common quest for the truth, as well as a concern for the promotion

169 *A Statement of the U.S. Catholic Bishops, issued 2001*, http://www.usccb.org/beliefs-and-teachings/vocations/priesthood/priestly-life-and-ministry/national-plan-for-the-ongoing-formation-of-priests.cfm, accessed on 11 January 2020.

170 Eugene Duffy, "I Will Give You Shepherds: The Formation of Priests" *The Furrow*: A Journal for the Contemporary Church (Maynooth: Vol 43, No.11, November 1992), 597-606, 597.

of justice and peace."[171] According to Louis, communion and fraternity are the hallmarks of a priest. He should be able to oppose all types of divisive tendencies in and outside the community. According to Louis, ability to accept and if possible incorporate the varying views and ideologies is an important characteristic feature of a priest. For him "the 'seminary' in its different forms - and analogously the 'house' of formation for religious priests - more than a place, a material space, should be a spiritual place, a way of life, an atmosphere that fosters and ensures a process of formation, so that the person who is called to the priesthood by God may become, with the sacrament of orders, a living image of Jesus Christ, head and shepherd of the Church."[172] In every sphere of his life, Louis could become a living image of Christ; and everyone could experience love and tenderness through his words and actions.

All through his life as a formator, Louis made sure that the future priests are able to respond positively to the question, 'Do you love me?' (Jn. 21:15). He taught them to love the Lord, not through instructions, but by way of his living example. He was sure of the present feature of the students, who are viewers than listeners. Louis, in this sense, was a living model of formation, an example to follow. He did not make many instructions, corrections, but he became a copy to be emulated. This is what I call the *Luoi-Way*. Accordingly, the formator needs to become the message, before imparting it to his students.

Finally, the biblical image of clay "in the hands of the potter" from the book of Jeremiah is the right image that could clearly portray the *Loui-Way* of formation (*Jer* 18:1-10). In formation, Louis allowed himself to be like the image of God as a potter, who "discovers that Israel is conserved in the loving hands of God Who, like a patient potter, takes care of His creature, places the clay on the wheel, models it, forms it and, in that way, *gives it shape*. If He realizes that the vase has not turned out well, then the God of mercy once more puts the clay into the mass and, with the tenderness of the Father, begins to mold it again."[173] Such an impeccable mercy and care is the attractive feature of *Loui-Way*.

To wrap up, the characteristics of *Loui-Way* are: love and tenderness in the approach, uninterruptedness and aloofness from the ideal type, collaborative interactions, harmonious communion with neighbours, alluring life model, and enduring patience of the potter.

---

171 *Pastores Dabo Vobis,* 18.

172 *Pastores Dabo Vobis,* 42.

173 Jim Fair, "Pope: Priestly Formation Decisive to Mission of Church," (October 7, 2017), https://zenit.org/articles/pope-priestly-formation-decisive-to-mission-of-church/, accessed on 10 January 2020.

5. Future Proof Formation

It is my feeling that the *Loui-Way* has a lasting effect, in terms of its influence and impact in the students. Hence, adapting the *Loui-Way* can create a "future proof formation,"[174] because formation as described by various people is a lifelong process. Therefore, it has to foresee the challenges of tomorrow. According to Louis, such a 'future proof formation' with lasting effect can be generated only in an atmosphere of a loving community. He always saw that no external or internal factors, whether it be financial, social, cultural or even individual factors destroy such a homely atmosphere of the seminary. Maintaining such an atmosphere of calmness and serenity in the seminary was the success of Louis.

Another element of the 'future proof formation' is his presentation of himself as continuously being formed and grown on a daily basis. According to Louis, religious and priestly life is a life long journey of discipleship. Because of this reason, the roles, the distinctions, the tasks, etc. that every person play, he thought, are with one purpose, namely in completion of the journey of discipleship. It is this awareness that enabled him to be always open and receptive even to disagreeing views. He welcomed differences and appreciated such differing views if found healthy and encouraging.

A third and the most important element of the 'future proof formation' is to train the students to be part of the community. That is, not to be "lone rangers," or simply "rugged individuals of the past."[175] Louis never entertained one-sided tracks in the community. He was always keen to inculcate the culture of the community in each of the students, because he thought only a 'we-feeling' would be successful in the future. Formation, according to him, should never be a one-act play; the community has a significant role in the formation of the individual. He was quite sure that if one is formed by and in the community, he or she learns the principle of solidarity. The 'give and take' nature of the community, he thought, can make formation a future proof one.

6. Tactics for Formators based on the *Loui-Way*

The life particularly the formative style of Louis, which I termed as the *Loui-Way*, puts forward certain tactics to be a good formator. As described above, for Louis life was a continuous learning and forming of oneself. Therefore, according to him, every formator must keep in mind that formation is forming oneself along. In the following, I try to sketch those characteristic features of the *Loui-Way*, which would fashion one a good formator.

---

174 Declan Marmion, Michael Mullaney, and Salvador Ryan, eds., *Models of Priestly Formation: Assessing the Past, Reflecting on the Present, and Imagining the Future* (Collegeville, Minnesota: Liturgical Press, 2019), xviii.

175 Marmion, *Models of Priestly Formation*, xxii.

a) Be Authentic: This is the greatest quality of a formator. He must be genuine to his own call. Formator is the open book for the formees to learn for themselves. Today's generation easily spot the humbugs; and your speeches will never be effective without accompanying life. You words should present the authenticity of life. If they feel that your words are empty, then any amount of corrective measures you apply on them will not make any difference.

b) Be Open to Criticism and Correction: I think, this is the greatest quality one might observe in Louis. He was open to criticism and was ready to accept any correction. He allowed the students to challenge him. He never felt offended even when he had to face disparagement from the students. He was always ready and available for dialogues. Formation, he believed, is a two sided movement carried out through open dialogue.

c) Trust, Entrust: As *Ratio Fundamentalis* describes, "the programme of formation should explore and outline the concrete ways in which this trust can be encouraged and safeguarded."[176] This I feel is the key of formation in the *Loui-Way*. Louis always trusted his students. This trust was clearly expressed through his magnanimity to entrust great responsibilities to them. He never entertained doubts, but rather he always placed hope in the students. According to him, the past events in the life of the students, or the previous corrections, were not the decisive factors in the process of evaluation. He always encouraged the students for a change, and the trust he placed on them really worked. Indeed, Louis valued each of his students. According to him, one is able to entrust the duties to the students only if one realizes that Jesus never followed a one-way traffic. Jesus never said, 'follow me and I will teach you,' but rather he said, "come and see" (Jn 1:39), an expression of love and trust.

d) Spirit of Appreciation: Louis never seemed parsimonious in appreciating the other. Even if, it was a matter of trivial importance the efforts of the other was appreciated by Louis. This created an ambiance of happiness in the community. He never spoke ill of the other. Faults committed by one, he considered, are steps towards maturity and change of action. He was so generous in appreciating everyone, including the domestic staff. Speaking about the seminary formation, Archbishop Eamon Martin said, "the most basic task of a Church leader is to discern the spiritual gifts of all those under his authority, and to encourage those gifts to be used to the full benefit of all. Only a person who can discern the gifts of others and can humbly rejoice at the flourishing of these gifts is fit to lead the Church."[177] In this sense, Louis was

176 *Ratio Fundamentalis*, 47.

177 As quoted in Marmion, *Models of Priestly Formation*, p. xxii. Cf. John Chrysostom, *Six Books on the Priesthood*, trans. G. W. Butterworth (Crestwood, NY: St. Vladimir's Seminary Press, 1964), 44. This is a quotation from St. John Chrysostom.

a person with right discernment, who encouraged the students to develop into their full vigor.

e) Caring Confrontation: Calm and caring confrontation seemed to be a healthy way in course correction. Louis never lost temper or felt anger; but he made sure that he confronts such situations without evading them where corrections are required. Method of 'let go' was not of Louis. He expressed his difference of opinion calmly and in a caring fashion, without offending the perpetrator. Confrontation was never done publically, but he met such persons personally and through coercing dialogue he assured a change in the pattern of the students.

f) Flexibility and Openness: Being one of the pioneers in contextual formation in the CMI Congregation, Louis favored openness to other cultures, persons, and beliefs. Flexibility in our worship pattern was a fascinating feature of Louis' person. He knew the heart of the young people, that is, sameness and stagnancy lead them to boredom. Hence, Louis opened ways to exhibit their innovativeness and creativity, in class rooms, and in other pastoral avenues. Rigidity according to him, opposes the quality of our Lord, who was open to the outcastes, oppressed and abandoned. As a matter of fact, Louis practiced openness in every realm of formation and allowed flexibility in the manner of discernment.

g) Giving Feedback Effectively: When and wherever it was required, Louis did not hesitate to give feedback, because he cared the other. Many of us do give feedback, but such feedbacks do not meet the requirements of effectiveness. He knew, feedbacks become effective only if we make them in proper way. Moreover, effective feedback depends on the context and the manner. For example, if a correction is not given at the proper time, it is correction denied. If the correction is not given privately, that do not bring expected result, but rather that might bounce back. Therefore, examining the *Loui-Way* is the easiest means to learn how to give feedback effectively.

h) Allowing Students to be Exposed: Overprotection and recessed setting do not let students grow in a mature way. Making the seminary a ghetto would not help in the formation of the students. They need to be exposed to the real life situations, knowing the struggles and problems the ordinary people face in their lives. Louis promoted occasions that would allow students to be exposed to the hard realities of life. Maturity, he thought, is not spoon fed, but dynamically generated from an open life situation, where students are provided occasions to get mingled with different kinds of people.

i) Maintaining Confidentiality: Betraying confidentiality is annihilating healthy formation. There are many religious and priests who do not trust their superiors, because of their experience of breach of confidentiality. Trust in the formator is created through the assurance of confidentiality. For all of his students, Louis was a paradigm of confidentiality. Hence, as they were with Louis the students were open, without any mask. According to Louis, pretense is something created in the formees through their experience of non-confidentiality in the superiors. Becoming a good friend and a confidant is the best way of giving formation.

j) Daily Submission in Prayer: Lastly, I feel, one of the most important factors that Louis wanted to propagate through his life example is the habit of praying for his students daily. Once he said to me that a prayer for your students can make you a good master. This, he said because he believed that Jesus is the true formator. Hence, Louis would admonish every formator to submit each candidate to the care of Jesus, and he will do his job faithfully and effectively.

Conclusion

Louis had realized that formation is to help us in becoming Christ like. As observed by Mannath, "After all, we do not join religious life to become geography teachers or nurses or school principals. For doing any of these 'jobs,' a person does not need to join an order or a seminary, and spend years in spiritual practice – daily Eucharist and other prayers, sermons, retreats, spiritual direction, times of silence. If the goal is forgotten, or is pushed to the periphery, we will end up with smart and ambitious men and women who pursue worldly goals."[178] Apparently, Louis was clear about the purpose and goal of formation. Every inch of his life was spent for this great cause. Through his committed life and example he could achieve it to the maximum possible level.

At the end, I would like to summarize the personality of Louis quoting *Pastores Dabo Vobis*. Accordingly, he was "capable of loving people with a heart which is new, generous and pure - with genuine self - detachment, with full, constant and faithful dedication and at the same time with a kind of "divine jealousy" (cf. 2 Cor 11:2) and even with a kind of maternal tenderness."[179] To conclude, tenderness was the hallmark of *Loui-Way*, the formative method he has left for the formators around the globe.

178 Mannath, "Formation: The Essentials in a Nutshell," 39.

179 *Pastores Dabo Vobis*, 22.

PART IV

ADMINISTRATION AND VISION FOR COMMUNITY LIFE

14

Celebration of Communion

Fr. Shepherd Thelappilly CMI

1. Introduction

Altruistic minds, liberated from the narrow confines of worldly attachments are truly rare. They can look beyond the world around them, being endowed with an inspiring vision of the future. Their exemplary personal profile includes uncommon mentoring skills, which demand a rare ability to channelize God's power. They are graced with winning generosity and sublime holiness. Fr. Louis Malieckal was such a great soul, a rare gem of the contemporary world.

A person's history is the evidence to show him/her as a holy person or a great soul. Posterity continually examines and discovers his/her greatness. Blessed are those souls who can render lifelong noble services to fellow beings by conquering self-centred thoughts. Their graceful presence signifies an endorsing signature of the Creator. Fr. Louis belongs to this category of noble souls.

The blessed souls who are liberated from the yoke of selfishness and lure of desires deliver succour to selfish mortals who wallow in the confines of worldly desires. A massive banyan tree offers shade and re-energizes exhausted travellers, trying to escape the scathing sun. In the process of offering shade, the tree absorbs the scorching heat of the unrelenting sun. It musters the sun's energy and transforms into harvests of bounty with delectable solace for the exhausted birds and humans, providing rest. Plants and trees collect sun's energy not to satiate their own hunger. They do not misappropriate the energy for the benefit of their own offspring.[180] Fr. Louis was such a banyan tree who offered himself in complete selflessness.

2. Fr. Louis' Love for His Dear Ones

Ms. Annie Varghese, niece of Fr. Louis who loved him dearly wrote, "It's really difficult to explain the pain that hit me as I heard that my uncle passed away to eternity. But, it was for a glorious resurrection with Jesus Christ, my Lord and Saviour. He was really a person who did not care for appreciation. But he followed the call of God, to love and serve Him, with total dedication and prayer. Wherever he put his footsteps, success followed. Every piece of his advice had great results. I really admire the simplicity and humility of my uncle. His unassuming nature is evident in all his dealings. While travelling, he used to carry some newspapers to use it as his' sleeping mattresses, if needed. If berth wasn't available during a train journey, he would unfold the newspaper; spread it like a bed sheet to sleep on it for the night's travel. He was always seen silently remaining in the midst of his family when he visited Kerala, where his near and dear ones lived. Last but not the least, I thank God for giving me a wonderful person as my maternal uncle, He was a caring and loving person like my own daddy and mommy. I know and understand; crying and weeping over the past, will not help in the present. But a fervent prayer, trying to follow his life's example and the advices given by him will help me to grow closer and closer with deep intimacy to the Holy Trinity".

3. Teacher Par Excellence

Fr. Louis had an astounding grasping power of issues. He was a man of great intelligence and immense clarity of thought. As the seminary professor, he taught Liturgy in Dharmaram College, Bangalore. During his time, in the spirit of the Vatican II, he contributed to the development of an "Indian Liturgy". It was for this liturgy that he wrote the *bhajan 'Om Jagadeswara sadapi chinmaya anavaratam vande'*. It was one of the earliest Christian bhajans which the seminarians used to chant during meditation and prayer services. His dealings were always genuine and noble, imbued with great humility. He deeply respected the freedom of others and gave them space to grow and flourish, and encouraged to maximize their talents and abilities to utilize them for the betterment of society.

One of my friends, Joy shared his experience about Fr. Louis, "He taught us and loved us very much; he won the respect of learned people as well as the affection of children. He rightly earned the approbation of honest critics; and endured the betrayal of false friends. Fr. Louis appreciated beauty; found

180 Leelavathy, M, "Immortal Thou", article in "The life and legacy of Saint Kuriakose Elias Chavara, edited by John Mannarathara, Viva Books, New Delhi, 2015, page, 145.

the best in others. He was sensitive to the social condition of the poor and the disadvantaged. He could be playfully relaxed and enthusiastically active with his students, participating in all their works. He was always aware to make the lives of all joyful".

4. Community Life: An Expression of Self-Transcendence

I remember the Renewal Retreat conducted in Poornodaya Training Centre in Bhopal in 2003. Fr. Louis was one of the resource persons and his favourite subject was communion/community Life. For him community life is an expression of self-transcendence and an experience of pro-existence. He explained community life with the help of the root meaning of community: *cum+ unitas* = togetherness; cum+munus= mission. He thus explained the two-fold fundamental characteristics of the religious community.

He went on explaining the four-fold community at different levels as: religious level, ecclesial level, human level and cosmic level. The essence of community on earth is defined as communion, which is God's vision of humanity. At all levels, community is founded on God's will. We pray for this uniting spiritual foundation in Lord's Prayer: "Your will be done on earth as it is in heaven". Fr. Louis explained that the nature of our religious community requires a process of building up by loving, caring, sharing, bearing the burdens and serving selflessly. Secondly, there are the ecclesial level communities. Ecclesia is a symbol of the Kingdom of God. Basic Christian Communities witness the Kingdom of God in their life of Gospel praxis amidst the world. They fulfil the "*Mission Ad Gentes*"- the mission entrusted to the Church by Jesus Christ.

With regard to community on human level, our community consciousness must penetrate to embrace the whole humanity, proclaiming universal brotherhood with peace and harmony. To promote communion, dialogue has to become a way of life. Mahatma Gandhi said, "I would like my house open to all sides so that winds from all directions can enter and play around; but I would be the master of my house". Fr. Louis added: "We must have roots at the centre and be open to other religious and cultural traditions to absorb what is good in them".

With regard to community at cosmic level, Fr. Louis explained that our community experience must embrace the whole cosmos/universe. The eastern mentality of looking at reality is not anthropocentric, but rather characteristically cosmo-centric and nature-bound. The nature is our cosmic body, extended self and source of vital energies. I live in the same home of the Lord, "with the birds of the air and the lilies of the field" (Cfr. Mt 6: 25-33). "*Isavasyam idam sarvam yat kim ca jagatyam jagat, tena tyaktena bahujinita, ma girdhah kasyasvid dhanam*" (Isavasya Upanishad chapter 4:1-2) "The Creator pervades the whole universe", so it is dependent upon primordial nature, which in turn is also pervaded by Him; he alone is thus independent, do not seek anyone/anything else such as wealth etc". This *upanishadic* view rhymes with the Pauline view of the fulfilled universe, in which God becomes "all in all" (1 Cor 15:24-28). We should view God and the universe as being in a state of harmony. Fr. Louis even thought of creating a "*Cosmic Liturgy*".

Fr. Louis concluded his talk quoting from Henry Nouwen's famous book, *Intimacy* where the author explains five circles: "Intimacy circle, friendship circle, acquaintance circle, associate circle and all-embracing circle"[181]

5. Kingdom Ideal vis-a-vis Community life - Scriptural Basis

Fr. Louis drew inspiration for the communion/community life from the kingdom ideal of Jesus: the fatherhood of God and brotherhood of all human beings. In the third and last temptation of Jesus (Mt 4:1-11) the devil took the Lord to a high mountain and showed him all the splendour and offered him the kingship of the world. Isn't that precisely the mission of Jesus in the world? Isn't he supposed to be the king of the universe who unifies the whole world in one great kingdom of peace and well-being?[182] Pope Benedict XVI in his famous book, *Jesus of Nazareth* narrates that the temptation to turn stones into bread has two remarkable counterparts in Jesus' story: the multiplication of bread and the Last Supper.

The same thing is true for the third temptation; the risen Lord gathers his disciples "on the mountain" (Cfr. Mt 28:16) and he said, "All the authority in heaven and earth are given to me". Two details are here new and different. The first, the Lord has power on earth, not earthly power which is fragile and ambiguous but God's power for the good of men and for the blessings He gave. Second, Jesus has this power by the virtue of his resurrection, which presupposed the Cross and his death on the other mountain – Golgotha. The kingdom of God is different from the kingdom of the earth which the Satan parades before Jesus. Jesus' kingdom grows through the humility of the proclamation in those who agree to become his disciples, who are baptized in the name of the triune God and who keeps the twin commandments (Cfr. Mt 28:18-19 f). The first one: "You shall worship the Lord your God and Him only shall you serve" (Mt 4:10; Deut 6:13); this is also the fundamental commandment of the Christians: God alone is to be worshipped. It is followed by the second, "Love your neighbour as yourselves".

Fr. Louis took the ideal of the kingdom of God as the fundamental vision of the community in religious life and worked hard in his tenure as provincial, encouraging the members to practice these two precepts: to become deeply

---

181 Nouwen, Henry, "**Intimacy**", Hawthorne Academics, New York, 1975, page, 123.

182 Ratzinger, Joseph, (Pope Benedict XVI), "**Jesus of Nazareth**", Bloomsbury, New York, 2007, pages, 38-45.

spiritual persons as men of God and to grow in fraternal love through various ministries, shedding all kinds of disunity and disharmony among them. To a great extend he succeeded in bringing all members into a single flock.

6. Fr. Louis Was a Problem Solver

Fr. Louis was acknowledged as a man of reconciliation who could deal with individuals and communities to solve disputes and dissensions among them. His clarity and conviction, his discerning mind and ability to speak clearly on the most difficult issues were inspiring. He was always ready to go where he had never been before. He was never bothered of what others thought and said about him. He refused to be discouraged when others misjudged his motives.[183] As Provincial, he treated each member of the Province warmly and with affection.

7. Every Human Person a Magnificent Creation of God's Love

Fr. Louis had several admirable qualities. Whenever required, he would go out of his way to render valuable counsel on matters concerning the growth of the Province. He never failed to appreciate whenever the members, both the priests as well as the scholastics did extraordinary good things. He always kept a track of their personal and intellectual growth. He saw everyone and everything around him as a magnificent creation of God's love. He was an angel because he believed something good in everything he saw.

8. Fr. Louis Was a Visionary for Tomorrow

Fr. Louis made decisions that would create a bright future. He knew the power of words and the power of silence. He never tried to succeed alone. He was a team player. In order to revive the community spirit that had been shaken and disturbed due to internal conflicts and polarizations, dialogical methods and community-building programmes were devised and implemented by him, especially in appointments, transfers and canonical visitations.

9. Zonal Gatherings in the Province

In order to strengthen community life in the province, the area of the province was divided into six zones with the following objectives[184]

1. To foster better communion among the members
2. To give a particular focus of mission in response to the needs of the geographical area

---

183 Haris, SDB. "**Leadership Secrets of Jesus**", from Video, DIBICA Digital Studio, Chennai, 2015.

184 Vadakumchery, Johnson, "**History of St Paul Province**", Department of Evangelization, Bhopal, 2018.

3. To prepare common plans for realizing the missionary focus and to cooperate in their implementation

The Zonal animators arrange bi-monthly recollection, Zonal gatherings, visiting members and sending reports of the events and gatherings to the provincial council. Annual joint gatherings of the Zonal animators and the provincial council are convened to evaluate the activities at the Zonal level. The Provincial team visits the Zones at least once a year for evaluation, planning and live-together with the members. Besides, the mode of conducting these meetings, as well as the roles and functions of the Zonal animators etc. are governed by the Provincial Administration. Moreover, at the province level the following three programmes are arranged:

1. Annual retreat, preferably during Dussehra/Deepavali holidays
2. Periodic get-together of members doing different ministries such as – formators, educators, social workers, pastors for evaluation and consultation
3. Annual Province Day of three days

10. Annual Family Day

This was meant for a healthy mixing and mingling of diverse groups, young and old, superiors and community members, formators and educators, social workers and pastors and all in the community to forge them into a harmonious community. Its dates would be announced one year in advance, usually in the month of May, looking at the convenience of both schools and formation houses, so that not only fathers but also scholastics and senior aspirants as well as juniors after their first vows will be able to take part in it. First day is set apart for the meeting of the brothers under the formation coordinator with special programmes of group dynamics etc. At some sessions the provincial team use to interact with them for mutual familiarization and better communication etc.

11. A Man with Multifaceted Personality

Fr. Louis was a man with a multifaceted personality, infectious smile, compassion and true integrity, who touched the hearts of his students as well as the members of the Province. He was always vocal and clear in what he thought. He stood up for what he believed was right and correct, never hesitating from expressing his opinion when and where it mattered – a quality I admired in the life of Fr. Louis! He was a charismatic leader who used his experience and competence to take CMI congregation as well as St. Paul Province Bhopal to its rightful place. He was extremely industrious that in spite of his ill health, he went on performing his *dharma* (duty) as a theology professor till the last day of his life on earth. He lived his life wholeheartedly and fully that fear of death never entered in his heart.

Fr. Louis lived a life trusting in the Lord. He had experienced the Lord's care in all his life, especially during difficult times. As an obedient CMI, he accepted the superiors' directions. He experienced the special care of the Lord on several occasions. Therefore, in his Golden Jubilee memento, he quoted the Psalm with these words: "The Lord is my Shepherd, I have everything I need". One could see in him the satisfaction of a life fully lived. He had no complaints. He was very happy in all situations. He remained steadfast in want and plenty, as a *sthitaprajna.*

12. Fr. Louis, a Great Soul Baptized by the Holy Spirit

It is virtuous to remember great souls. It helps us to get purified and enriched. We are ignorant about many things of Fr. Louis. The more we know the person, the more we love him. The more we love the person, our lives are transformed. As time passes, we tend to forget even our own roots. We even don't bother to reflect on our lives. It is when we try to examine our lives in the context of great souls like Fr. Louis, that we realize the depth of our own ignorance. "*Indeed he is a saint baptized by fire and spirit.*"[185] We have around us a lot of stars who amaze us and motivate us to reflect. The life and message of Fr. Louis Malieckal attract us as one such bright star since he brought unity and solidarity in the religious communities in which he lived. His memories and contributions are not to be treated as transient; rather they should be preserved in our minds forever. We are challenged to emulate the good qualities from the life of Fr. Louis.

There are three types of people; the first category lives out of their convictions and principles, the second is led by traditions, past history, dogmas, rules and regulations and the third category is sensitive, driven by feelings, by circumstances and by environment.[186] Fr. Louis belonged to the first category of people. He can be named as a ***self-actualized person*** as it is said in the motivational theory of famous humanist psychologist Abraham Maslow.[187] It is difficult to accept that he is no more. His legacy will undoubtedly live on. He touched so many lives, in such a profound ways that the coming generation will chant his memorable glories and anthems. Let us try to emulate the values and vision shown by Fr. Louis.

---

185 Asha Menon, "A Saint Baptized by Fire", article in "The Life and Legacy of St. Kuriakose Elias Chavara" ibid, page, 122

186 S. Covey, Stephen, "The Seven Habits of Highly Influential People, Simon & Schuster, London, 1992, page, 206.

187 Maslow, Abraham, "A Theory of Human Motivation", from the original paper presented by Maslow in 1943.

15

A Proponent of Participatory Administration

Jacob Peenikaparambil

Fr. Louis Malieckal was a man of multifaceted personality and his contribution to the society and the Church has been manifold. Although, he spent most of his life as a teacher in the seminary and a formator, he proved himself to be an excellent administrator when he was given the responsibility of the provincial of CMI St. Paul Province Bhopal. As the provincial of CMI St. Paul Province, Bhopal twice from 1999 to 2005, he focused primarily on building up the province community by strengthening the bond among the members. Another focus area of his administration was the human resource development of the members. Institutional expansion of the province was only secondary for him.

I had the opportunity to be in the provincial team as one of the councillors from 2002 to 2005 and I cherish the opportunity to be a team member of Fr. Louis Malieckal. It was a matter of great joy and satisfaction to work with him because he had adopted a participatory style of functioning. Since I had specialized in Project Management as a part of my MSW course and I could enhance my expertise in management as a coordinator of the development projects funded by Karl Kubel Foundation Germany, I shared with Fr. Louis my ideas for making the administration of the province more participatory, transparent and accountable. Fr. Louis was open to progressive ideas and suggestions. As a result, our team could make the provincial administration more professional by developing systems and processes that are participatory, transparent and accountable.

The General Synaxis 2002 had adopted two historical resolutions: Common pooling of financial resources of the province and setting apart 10% of the gross income at the General, Provincial and House levels for supporting the poor. Another important decision of the General Synaxis was the freedom given to the provinces to formulate Provincial Statutes. Although, the resolutions were welcomed by the members of the Congregation, their implementation was a tough job for the provincial administration. Because of the leadership of Fr. Louis Malieckal, the St. Paul Province Bhopal could implement these resolutions without much difficulty.

St. Paul Province, Bhopal was the first among all the CMI provinces to formulate the Provincial Statutes and to put in place a system for pooling the financial resources through the formulation and implementation of a Financial Policy. The Provincial Statutes of St. Province was taken as a model by many other provinces. The systems and processes for making the provincial administration participatory, transparent and accountable were inserted into the Provincial Statutes. This was made possible because of the initiative and determination of Fr. Louis as the provincial. The following are some of the administrative innovations under the leadership of Fr. Louis Malieckal.

1. Making the Provincial Departments Functional

Making the Provincial Departments (Pastoral Work and Evangelization, Social Apostolate, Education and Finance) functional with their budgets, separate bank accounts and periodic transfer of funds to the departments was one of the administrative reforms. Each department prepared a budget and presented it at the provincial council meeting in the month of March every year and the provincial council approved the budget after discussion and deliberation. The departments also presented an action plan along with the budgets.

After the approval of the budgets, money was transferred to the bank accounts of the concerned departments in quarterly instalments. The departments were asked to present quarterly statement of account to the finance department. The departments also presented a report, written or oral, at the bi-monthly meeting of the Provincial Council. In order to make the departments accountable, the Departments had to present a written annual report to the provincial council. The same report was presented at the annual province gathering.

2. Participatory Decision Making

All decisions concerning the province were taken by the provincial team. Only decisions concerning individual members were taken by the Provincial. The provincial council meetings were held at least once in two months. The dates of the Provincial Council meetings were decided at the beginning of the year and it was communicated to all members of the province so that they could send their applications to the Provincial Council well in advance.

As a part of the Provincial Council meeting, after the presentation of the minutes of the previous meeting, the councillors in charge of the departments presented a report of the activities of their concerned departments. This practice was introduced in view of making the department heads accountable as well as to share the progress of activities with the members of the provincial council.

If sufficient information was not available to take a decision on a particular issue, it was either postponed to the next meeting in view of gathering more information or a committee was appointed by the Provincial Council to make a detailed study of the issue and present a report to the provincial council.

His leadership was not like someone with power, but someone with authority. Fr. Louis himself makes the difference between power and authority. He had often pointed out that power is what one is bestowed with while one is chosen for a position/post in the community. for example when one is chosen as a superior/provincial/rector. The constitutions and the rules of the institution give you certain power to deal with that particular situation. But, this power goes away as the office time comes to an end. However, authority on the contrary is the inner strength of a God-centered life shining through a life of integrity and authenticity, which will remain with the person irrespective of whether one is superior, provincial rector or not. Fr. Louis was endowed with this authority. He had fostered it with a God-centered life. He had this inner strength from his life of authenticity and integrity. Therefore, he could influence the people around him. Both students and staff listened to him and responded to him with respect and gratitude. Everyone looked up to him as a source of inspiration. Everyone was willing to accept his words and guidance. He was the source of inspiration, which he had developed by a disciplined life, coupled with his intimate relationship with his Lord and Shepherd. In short we can say he had really become an ideal leader, an ideal mentor and an authentic guru in the fullest sense of the word.

3. Financial Planning and Management

In order to make central pooling effective, the St. Paul Province, Bhopal introduced the practice of each house/unit of the province preparing the annual budget along with annual action and getting the approval of the provincial council before the end of March every year. The houses/units having surplus income, especially English Medium Schools, will have to show in their budget the contribution they would be making to the Province Finance Department. All English medium schools have to transfer the income from the KG school excluding the salary of staff members, to the Province Finance Department.

The provincial council appoints a committee of three or four members of the province to study the budgets and make recommendations to the provincial council regarding the changes needed in the budget at the time of the approval. Taking into account the recommendations of the Budget Committee, the provincial council makes the needed changes in the expenditure and the contribution to the province finance department from each unit. Sometime before the approval of the budget a dialogue is done by the provincial team with the members of the concerned unit/house.

Once the budget is approved the units have to send three monthly statement of account to the province finance department and the finance department gives the needed feedback to the units after studying the statement of the account. Thus the whole finance management system was made transparent and participatory. Prior to the introduction of this system the provincial and the councillor in charge of finance had a lot discretion in allotting funds to the different units and it often created discontentment among the members. After the introduction of the financial management system if any unit or house wanted to make any expenditure other than sanctioned in the approved budget, that unit has to make an application to the provincial team.

4. Annual Province Gathering

The annual province meet is a very important event in the calendar of the CMI St. Paul province, Bhopal. It is of three days programme. This practice was started at the initiative of Fr. Louis when he was the provincial. The members of the province are grateful to Fr. Louis for initiating this practice, especially the provincial team presenting the annual report and the annual statement of account before the members of the province.

The first day of the province gathering is the get-together of the brothers. It is planned by the Formation Coordinator. The members of the provincial council also participate in this get-together. The second day is meant for celebrations in view of building up the province community. The aspirants also join the celebrations. This gathering provides an opportunity to meet and interact with most of the members of the province. The silver jubilee of first profession and of the ordination and *Shashtipoorthi* of the fathers are celebrated during this occasion. In the evening cultural programmes are organized. All members of the province, especially those who are in India, are expected to take part in the province gathering.

The third day is the most important day of the province gathering. This day is set apart for a serious meeting that makes the provincial team accountable to the members of the province and it consists of the following activities.

1) Presentation of an overview of the developments/progress in the province, including the implementation of various activities, through the presentation of reports by Fr. Provincial and the Councillors. The

zonal animators, superiors/directors also share the developments in their respective areas during the year.

2) Presentation of the consolidated statement of account of the province by the Provincial Finance Department. The members of the province come to know the sources of Income and the pattern of expenditure of the province during the year. They also come to know how much was the total income of the province during the year, what was the total expenditure and what is the balance. The members of the province have the opportunity to ask clarifications and even to question the provincial team. Financial transparency is one of the ways to prevent corrupt practices in any organization. Fr. Louis, being a person of integrity, did not want any suspicion on the part of the members of the province regarding the financial transactions in the province.
3) Presentation of the action plan of the province for the coming year and the budget for the coming year. Because of this practice the members of the province come to know what the provincial council is planning for the coming year. The members have the freedom to express their agreement and disagreement with the activities planned by the provincial team.
4) Annual General Body Meeting of the two societies of the province, CMI Seva Sangh and St. Paul Society, is also held on this day.

In many religious congregations the ordinary members do not know anything about the finance of their respective provinces. There is no practice of publishing the consolidated statement of account of the provinces. Nowadays we hear about financial irregularities and manipulations in some dioceses and religious congregations. Financial transparency is an indicator of spirituality. All provinces of religious congregations and dioceses should make public their audited statement of account. After all, this document is made available to the Registrar of Societies and Income Tax Department. Why not it be shared with the public? The dioceses and religious congregations exist to serve the people. By the very fact they enjoy income tax exemption, they are bound to be accountable to the public.

5. Registration of a Separate Society for Social Work

As I was in charge of Social Work Department, I made a suggestion to form a separate society for social work in the province in view of availing government projects. In order to apply for government projects an organization has to submit along with the application the annual report and audited statement of account of the organization for the last three years. If the organization has religious objectives it is difficult to get the projects sanctioned. Therefore, sending application for government projects on behalf of CMI Seva Sangh and St. Paul Society was not feasible. That is why the proposal to form a separate society was mooted. Fr. Louis generously accepted the proposal and it was approved by the provincial council. Thus, came into existence Sanjeevani Service Society. Fr. Louis was generous enough to make the Councillor in charge of Social Apostolate as the President of the Sanjeevani Service Society. Provincial is expected to be the President of all registered societies/Trusts in the province. Sharing authority is an important dimension of participatory administration and that is what Fr. Louis adopted during his tenure as the provincial.

After the registration of Sanjeevani Service Society, the assets of Sanjeevani Usri, Narsinghpur district, was transferred from CMI Seva Sangh to the new society through the legal process. Sanjeevani Service Society applied for Foreign Contribution Registration and it got FCRA registration within six months. Thereafter the 10% of the gross income of the province is transferred to Sanjeevani Service Society in quarterly instalments. The General Auditors from time to time have appreciated the systematic way the 10% of the gross income of the province is used for social work. The province also can be proud that it has a credible organization to receive funds from the government and the other donor agencies. This was made possible because of the liberal attitude and broad vision of Fr. Louis Malieckal.

6. Conclusion

There is a saying in Hindi, "*Manush janmse nahi, karmse mahan hotahai.*" A person becomes great not by birth, but by his actions. Every human being is sent into the world for fulfilling a specific task for making a significant contribution to humanity. A person who identifies his unique role and tries his best to fulfil that role leaves a legacy. Participatory administration by giving freedom and autonomy to the team members along with accountability is a significant dimension of the legacy of Fr. Louis Malieckal. Fr. Louis was a man who firmly believed that authority is given to a person to fulfil responsibility. A person who is aware that authority and power are meant for fulfilling responsibility will not succumb to the temptation of abusing or misusing power and authority. Today the Church in India is facing various external and internal challenges. Allegations of abuse of power by those in leadership positions are damaging the image of the Church and its credibility is adversely affected. Let the Church leaders take inspiration from persons like Fr. Louis Maliekal and focus on fulfilling their responsibility instead of going after power. Let them learn from Fr. Louis how to make themselves accountable to the community, being aware of the fact that they are not owners but custodians and stewards. People of God are the real owners.

16

An Ambassador of Peace and Reconciliation

Dr. Johnson Vadakumchery

The present article is mainly based on the biographical notes of Fr. Louis Malieckal. He had given them to the present writer as a part of the data collection for writing the history of St. Paul Province Bhopal. In answer to the questionnaire on personal data, he had given elaborate details about his own work in North India as a member of the Province. Wherever quotes are given without any citation, they are excerpts from this manuscript. The names of persons and places are omitted. There are several occasions in which he had specifically mentioned the theme of discernment and how he was committed to its fulfilment.

1. Christian Discernment

The basic notion of Christian discernment is that it is guided by the Holy Spirit to arrive at the best decision leading to future action. Spiritual discernment is a calling on the Holy Spirit to lead or give direction on a matter. It is how the Spirit shows the church or its people what God wants them to do and be. The Greek word for the gift of discernment is *Diakrisis*. The word describes being able to distinguish, discern, judge or appraise a person, statement, situation or environment. In the New Testament it describes the ability to distinguish between spirits as in 1 Corinthians 12:10 and to discern good and evil as in Hebrews 5:14. True discernment means not only to distinguishing the right from the wrong; it means distinguishing the primary from the secondary, the essential from the indifferent and the permanent from the transient. And yes, it means distinguishing between the good and the better, and even between the better and the best. Discernment is the duty of every Christian as described in First Thessalonians 5:21-22 "But examine everything carefully; hold fast to that which is good; abstain from every form of evil". That is why the Psalmist prays, "Teach me good judgment and knowledge" (Ps.119:66). Discernment demands openness and ability to listen. Openness to receive the Word and the words of others is a pre-requisite to real discernment. It is through humility that one received the message of God. Fr. Louis had such an openness at all levels that he would listen to others very keenly which brought about an understanding heart. That helped him to win the hearts of people, seminarians and other members of the team wherever he worked.

2. Post Vat II

Fr. Louis was chosen to be a professor of Mathematics in Christ College Bengaluru. Meanwhile the winds of change that were unleashed at the *Church in India Seminar* held in Dharmaram College from 15-25 May 1969 thoroughly brought about changes in all walks of life in the Church.

There was a core group of few priests and seminarians opted for Indian liturgy, cultural adaptation of simple lifestyle and remaining in a small hut with minimum facilities of common people. Cardinal Parekkattil had encouraged the Indian liturgical innovations. Fr. Louis joined with the Indian liturgical team. He composed some songs and *bhajans* of Indian taste and culture. Seeing his interest in Indian liturgy, the major superiors sent him to Louvain for higher studies in Liturgy. He took it as a matter of providence and tried to do justice to his studies. His keen interest in evolving an Indian liturgy was evident in his choice of the doctoral thesis. The book was titled, *Yajna* and Eucharist: an Inter-religious approach to the theology of sacrifice.

3. A Great Personal Crisis

He had to face a great crisis in his personal life. He was sent for higher studies with a view to teach liturgy in the common study house. But, as he has completed his doctoral studies there was a sea-change in the academic atmosphere. He was totally shocked to know that ultra-radical orientalists have taken over the liturgical reins. Hence, he was sent to an upcoming seminary situated in a remote rural village Ashta. His own reflection about the fish out of water crisis is described as follows: "My story of the CMI presence in the north starts effectively with my life and activities at the Khrist Premalaya Regional Theologate (KPRT), Ashta. This phase of my life started apparently because I 'failed' or was judged dangerous to be part of the study house's rising spirit of oriental liturgism. However, my life did not end there as a 'failure', but as great success, mainly because I was able to discern God's Providence working all through and committed myself fully to its realization".

When he got the appointment to Ashta rural village from the European city of Louvain, like the disciples after Pentecost he re-read his own life and found how God was preparing him for His own work. "My option to study Sanskrit language in my school days and that of Hindi in the college, and later my Superiors' decision to send me for higher study in theology etc., all were God's preparations for me to be called for taking up the KPRT, Ashta mission, though this was not at all in my own conscious mind. Therefore, when I was asked all on a sudden at the conclusion of theology study by the then Prior General to become part of the Ashta mission, I pro-acted and obeyed the instruction, though it was a 'shock' at its face value and had even been advised by my 'friends' not to conform to the pressure from above. In this way as I began my journey to Ashta from Louvain, Belgium, a kind of 'betrayal-feeling' at the hands of higher authorities was also accompanying me and it got aggravated on my landing in Ashta".

4. Challenge of Contextual Theology

In 1983 Fr. Louis was appointed by the then Prior General as core-team member of the budding MP Regional Theologate, Ashta. This Theologate was a pioneering venture in the field of priestly formation as decided by the then undivided M. P. bishops conference led by the metropolitan archbishop Eugene D'Souza, after a series of thinking, consultations and decision-making at different levels in the spirit of the II Vatican Council's call for contextualized priestly formation. The buildings were akin to the villagers explicitly showing simplicity. The construction was restricted to the ground floor structures. The curriculum contained additional courses on social analysis, scientific research methodology, cultural anthropology, exposure and living with the villagers and contextualised action-reflection-action.

5. Metanoia

Fr. Louis was exposed to the down to earth realities of rural life in North India for the first time in Ashta. The new environment has made radical changes in thinking, living and action. Unlike Louvain, the facilities were very much limited in the rural area. The caste complexities, segregation of people, ambitionless life of villagers were quite new for him. He was following more or less a *brahminic* tradition; the challenge was to be open to the life of a dalit or tribal. His doctoral study was on *yanja* and Eucharist. But, here he was amidst the common people struggling to eke out a living. Ashta has challenged him to sacrifice himself to turn over a new leaf of life. It was a radical transformation from that of a Brahmin to an underprivileged in the society; from *brahminic* presuppositions to that of an indigenous person. No wonder that at the initial stage Fr. Louis felt like a fish out of water. In his own words, "When I had joined the initial team of the seminary in Ashta in 1983, a few months after its formal launching in Bhopal, I found myself in a totally disappointing and hopeless situation for the following reasons: First of all there was the lack of necessary infra-structure facilities; secondly there was lack of sufficient number of members on the staff; thirdly there was lack of a sizable number of students on the rolls. For me a kind of 'cultural shock', because I had landed there straight from Europe after my doctoral studies, obeying the order of my religious superior, without any preparations fitting to the context.

Consequently, it took several months for me to come to terms with the 'reality of this village seminary'. The process began by asking myself a few questions like: What could be the purpose of starting this seminary in this unknown country-side, far away from the city of Bhopal? What must be the vision behind this humble seminary housed by a cluster of simple buildings in the midst of number of small villages near a humble township like Ashta? What is the task assigned to me by Providence in this particular context?

And the following 11 years (1983-94), until the CMI congregation handed over charge of the seminary in April 1994 to the Pallotine fathers, my whole life was focused on studying the vision and objectives on the one hand, and chalking out and implementing the necessary action plan towards that vision of a new style of priestly formation on the other, as dreamed by the M. P. bishops in the spirit of the Council. And I am happy to note that my committed efforts with the cooperation of the team members produced good results. The name of 'Ashta seminary' led by the CMIs offered a paradigm shift in the field of formation and it gradually got wide currency in the whole of North India, especially in the undivided MP state. The positive CMI-influence on the students was mainly due to the unity, simplicity and integrity of the staff-members and their solidarity with the formees as well as the people of the locality."

6. Openness to the Spirit

When Fr. Louis was appointed Rector in 1986, the resident staff members were just four. At a time he had to handle many responsibilities. Hence, he was strict to students; often made close observations and made spot corrections. Soon realized that this was being taken negatively by the students; a kind of unrest and tension began to mount among them. "Gradually I felt that something was lacking somewhere in the community, that my approach at least at the theology stage of formation would not hold water. It was then that I came to know a little more about the late Pope John XXIII and his way of handling similar situations: In one of his allocutions/audiences to Rectors/Major Superiors/ Formators, he seems to have observed in this way: You shall see all things that happen in the community; shall look at closely some of them; but correct only a few key mistakes. I liked this trilogy: See everything; look at some of them, and correct only a few as a general principle of my approach to formation.

And I have been practicing it ever since, all through my offices of authority and have found it very effective both in keeping peace of mind, and peace and progress in the community.

By imposing order and discipline in the community, no inner transformation and growth of the members would take place. Externally everything may appear fine and smooth sailing to the satisfaction of the Superior / Rector / Formator concerned. But, in reality the spirit within would be getting rotten; and deformation, instead of transformation would be the end result. The only way to ensure inner growth and transformation is to infuse trust and confidence in the members about the person, words and actions of the Superior / Formator. This of course requires self-emptying and sacrifice on the part of the Superior / Formator, coupled with integrity and transparency in all that he does. He would thus become a person of 'authority' for the members who would look up to him as a source of inspiration, leading to willing and faithful acceptance of his words and deeds."

Action-Reflection-Action methodology was followed in the seminary at the theological level. The students were sent to the villages for visits or living with them for a considerable time involving in the village life. Then they were helped to reflect upon the people. Thus the interaction with the people became matter of theologization, prayer and help. This demanded spontaneity, ability to reflect and relate them with the plan of God.

7. Sarv Dharma Samiti

As an out-reach to the common people a Centre for Religious Dialogue, *Sarv-dharama-samiti*, was established as early 1988, getting the cooperation of the religious heads of Hinduism, Jainism, Sikhhism, Islam and Christianity in Ashta. The seminarians were fully involved in the organization of programmes. It was the need of the times as there used to be communal disharmony and even violence during major festivals of Hindus and Muslims. Hence, this centre has produced very good results of religious harmony, mutual appreciation and acceptance. On the occasion of the 15 anniversary of the centre Fr. Louis was honoured by the Ashta public. He was also felicitated for this at the 25 year of the starting of the seminary.

In the pastoral field the seminarians were very active. A book on homilies in Hindi, *Prempravachan*, with the cooperation of the deacons was published from the seminary. It was the first of its kind in Hindi belt. Publication of these volumes certainly contributed towards boosting the reputation of the CMIs especially among the Hindi-speaking Catholics.

This positive 'Ashta CMI-image' played a major role in boosting the CMI mission image in the North among the dioceses and religious congregations whose candidates were students of Ashta under the CMIs during the years 1980s and 1990s.

8. Launching of Samanvaya Theologate

Ashta Theologate was a common study house for all the diocesan candidates of undivided Madhya Pradesh. All the Bishops of Madhya Pradesh were involved in it. Liturgical celebrations were in both the rites Latin and Syro-malabar. After a few years, the Bishop of Satna started a separate theologate for Syro-Malabar candidates without taking other Bishops into confidence. May be he himself was not sure about its future. Immediately it precipated a division based on rites. Eventually it became imperative that Ashta may remain a Latin seminary and the candidates were admitted accordingly. The Archbishop was in search of a Congregation that would replace the CMIs. Finally it was decided to entrust the administration to the Pallotine fathers. The course of development helped the mature launching of Samanvaya Theologate with the expertise of the CMI staff there. Though one may see the clash of rites, It was a providential movement to start a mission theologate.

"Whatever be the reasons, from the human point of view, that led to the withdrawal of the CMIs from Ashta Seminary, it was a blessing in disguise and in accordance with the plan of God as I see it, because, had it not been so, I wonder whether the CMI Samanvaya venture would have taken shape at all." The idea of a CMI mission theologate was in the air for a long time. Discussions and seminars, write ups were conducted at different levels of administration. A follow-up for the mission philosophate, Darsana, was necessary. The Ashta experience of the CMI staff catalysed the process. It took off at the right and acceptable time. When the question of withdrawal within a fixed time frame was finally decided by the Prior General, steps for launching the Mission Theologate began to gather momentum. The Prior General assigned Fr. Louis the duty of handing over charge of Ashta seminary to the Pallotine fathers with all its assets and liabilities. It was done through a fully transparent statement of accounts before April 1994. He was also asked to take immediate steps to open the proposed mission seminary in July the same year.

9. Ministry out of Sagar

The Generalate had assigned to Sagar mission the neighbouring Latin dioceses of Bhopal, Indore , Jabalpur and Jhansi as Extended Territories where the CMI community could extend its mission in course of time. Accordingly, towards the close of tenure of Bp. Clemens in 1987 the community seriously considered the matter and started its first mission school in 1988 in the suburb of the city of Bhopal, in the sector called Anand Nagar. Later this move turned out to be a blessing in disguise to launch new ministries like Navchetna communication centre. The media centre was started functioning, first at St. Paul School, before it was shifted in the early 1990's to the present site near Lalghatti, Bhopal. Before long it was accepted by the M. P. Bishops as the Regional

Communication Centre as it started doing commendable services in the three areas of performing arts, production of cassettes and CDs and publishing the student magazine “Heights”. Naturally this new avenue of mission helped to diffuse much of the tension connected with the Silwani issue.

In the early 1990’s the CMI community before the crisis in the mission gathered to a head, had moved further to the second ‘Extended Territory’, namely the diocese of Jabalpur, taking charge of strengthening the already existing Christian ashram called Sccidananda Ashram, in the town of Narsinghpur. Later, it turned out to be another providential position to carry on the mission in a meaningful way in the midst of the Silwani crisis and after. The presence in the ashram of a few revered members and the functioning of it to the satisfaction of the Bishop of Jabalpur helped the community to start other ventures in the diocese of Jabalpur by opening a social service centre by the name Sanjeevani at the village Usri in the year 1992 and a school named Chavara Vidya Peeth in the town of Kheri in the year 1995. There is no doubt these three ventures – ashram life, social service and education mission, taken up by the community in the 1990’s, far away from the home context of Sagar, where it was struggling to survive meaningfully during these years, certainly was a blessing in disguise to soothe the tension - ridden situation.

10. A Crisis Manager

Fr. Louis was elected Provincial at a very crucial time of crisis. He had to see to the members of the province on the one hand, on the other he had to balance the relations with the Bishop of Sagar who had to implement the Instructions from Rome by recalling the religious. At this crucial juncture, he considered the Auditor’s recommendations as a providentially given road map for his ministry. He was elected Provincial for a second term to continue the revival and revitalization of the community.

Towards the close of the second millennium, a Mission Audit 1999 was conducted by Dr. Sebasti Raj SJ covering all aspects of religious and mission work. His concluding remarks were as follows: “The CMI St. Paul Province has seen a considerable amount of growth in its number, resources and in its apostolate since its creation as a separate province and has established its identity and credibility. This mission audit has brought out the strength and the shortcomings of the province and its members in all aspects - formation, religious life, apostolate and administration. It has proposed the desirable thrust for the province and has also presented some concrete recommendations that will enable the province to consolidate the areas of its strength and take corrective measures to eradicate its shortcomings. It is hoped that these recommendations will be taken in the right spirit and implemented enthusiastically and seriously. It is also hoped that through these efforts, the entire province will experience a new life of renewal and re-dedication, which is the call of history at the threshold of the third millennium." (Sebasti L. Raj, SJ, *Mission Audit 1999*, Unpublished No. 84, p. 96).

11. Six Years of Revival and Revitalization 1999-2005

"As may be seen in the above concluding words of the Mission Auditor, he had proposed several recommendations covering all aspects of the mission: formation, religious life apostolate and administration which will enable the province to consolidate the areas of its strength and to take corrective measures to remove its shortcomings. Now, what was left for the required revival was mainly, if not only, to implement them, of course with a 'human face'. And that is what the next provincial team did during the two terms from 1999 to 2002 and 2002 to 2005.

During the first term of three years (1999-2002) the focus was on human resource management (HRM), namely properly making use of the strengths and talents as well as taking care of the needs and weaknesses of all members – fathers and those under formation. The first step taken was to make peace with those members who seemed to be unsure of their place in the province. It was not a question of appeasement of disgruntled elements, but of finding suitable avenues of work to their taste in which they could make maximum contribution to the mission in the given circumstance of the province.

Similarly, the Provincial team made it a point to meet the Bishop of Sagar personally and to discuss matters concerning future course of action in the diocese and particularly in RDSS in the light of the Instructions from Rome. Although he was not enthusiastic about it, that step was necessary in order to keep the already strained relationship in a workable condition.

In order to revive community spirit that had been shaken and disturbed due to internal politics and polarizations, dialogical methods and community-building programmes were devised and implemented, especially in appointments, transfers and canonical visitations. The entire province was divided into different zones with the following objectives: Zonal Centres were formed with a Zonal Animator to foster better communion among the members, to evolve a particular focus of mission in response to the needs of the geographical area and to prepare common plans for realizing the particular focus. At the province level the following three programmes were arranged. Annual retreat preferably during Dussehra / Deepavali holidays, Systematic and periodic get-together of different sectors of the province – formators, educators, social workers, pastors for evaluation and consultation, Annual Province Day of three days".

12. Annual Province Day

An annual province gathering was designed with suitable programmes of evaluation and relaxation, including a financial statement of accounts for discussion and suggestions. This was meant for a healthy mixing and mingling of diverse groups, young and old, superiors and members, formators, formees, educators, social workers, pastors and in general activists and passivists to forge into a harmonious community. The dates of the gathering were announced one year in advance and usually in the month of May and looking at the convenience of both schools and formation houses so that not only fathers but also scholastics and senior aspirants as well as juniors after their first vows will be able to take part in it. First day is set apart for the meeting of the brothers under the formation coordinator with special programmes of group dynamics. At some sessions of it the provincial team will be interacting with them for mutual familiarization and better communication. Second day is for a live-in of fathers and brothers mainly for better communication, integration and also relaxation and third day is only for the fathers for presentation of the activities of the registered societies and trust for the year, ending with a business meeting of the various societies. Since the meeting is very often towards the end of the month of May, usually the audited statements of accounts of all the registered bodies will also be presented and discussed. All these are meant to promote transparency, cordiality and hence mutual acceptance of the whole province as one unit.

In the governance of the province, whereas the personnel-centered approach of the previous term still continued to some extent in view of reaching the desired level of unity and harmony on the one hand, the team also took serious steps for increased institutional presence and financial discipline of the province on the other.

13. Approved Statutes of the Province

The General Synaxis 34 of 1996 had already initiated the idea of having provincial directory for individual provinces. It was meant to adapt the religious and apostolic life to the needs and circumstances of the mission region concerned. Accordingly, St. Paul province had prepared a draft of the Provincial Directory and began using it in 2002. But, it was in 2003 that it was formally revised, got approved by the General Council. Fr. Louis as Provincial promulgated the Statutes in the province for the faithful observance of all the members of the province. In the formulation and later in the revision of these statutes Frs. George Thanchan and Johnson Vadakumchery contributed considerably. Change of its title from directory to statutes and relevant principles behind its use are according to Resolutions nos. 40-42 of the General Synaxis 35.

Provincial Statutes of St. Paul Province, Bhopal soon became a model for many provinces, especially of the mission context and was therefore in great demand for some time. It is a matter of experience that overall discipline of a religious community depends very much on the level of financial discipline obtaining in it. Keeping this point in mind, the provincial team introduced necessary means of regulating the creation and distribution of finances. Thus proper systems of "central pooling" of finances from income-generating institutions with strict budgetary control of annual income and expenditure of all institutions as well as of persons were incorporated into the management.

The Annual Province Gathering was introduced as a part of renewing the community spirit and cordiality. This was an occasion to evaluate the functioning of these matters concerning financial discipline. The Provincial statutes numbers 142-43 state, "Every year preferably in the month of May or middle of June, a meeting of the members of the province shall be convened. There shall be effective interaction between the members and provincial administration. A comprehensive report of the affairs of the province, a consolidated annual statement of accounts of the province and an action plan for the coming year shall be presented at the meeting. There shall be sufficient time for the members to ask clarifications and to give their views and suggestions. In order to prepare the comprehensive report of the province, each unit shall make available to the provincial council a brief report of the apostolic activities undertaken. The council shall make available to the units a format for preparing their reports."

Another set up included in the Provincial statutes for the same purpose of maintaining discipline in the administrative system is called Planning Commission, consisting of seven members elected by the Provincial chapter for a six year term, three of them continuing for the whole six years. Its roles and functions are stipulated in the Statutes number 162-63.

In course of time the administration took up several measures of expansion and consolidation of the community. Some of them were the following: Strategic Plans were prepared both for the Province in general and for each unit. In that way the planning, monitoring and execution and evaluations were facilitated. Appointment of a Province-Level Formation Coordinator to help the Provincial to look into various aspects of formation of the candidates. Signing of a contract between the Province and the bishop of Port-Elizabeth South Africa. Accepting the invitation of Most Rev. Archbishop Abraham Viruthakulangara of Nagpur, and after getting the no-objection letter from the Provincial of Mar Thoma Province, Chanda, St. Paul Province Bhopal made a maiden entry on to the Chhindwara district by taking charge of the Barkui parish. During the second term of office Fr. Louis as Provincial (2002-2005), carried out the revival and revitalization programmes more intensively and initiated some new ventures for the growth of the province. The following were the main activities:

The shifting of the Provincial house from Padaria to Govind Garden Bhopal was a providential blessing. Padaria was at a remote area from the city and there were no communication facilities of phone, regular supply of electricity or any plying of vehicles. When several attempts of a search for land failed, a house was ready for sale at Govind Garden. It was a God-given opportunity as it was not far from failway and bus stand as well as on a main road of travel by most of the members working in Silwani or Sagar. At first it was an annexe of the Provincial house and later it was developed into a provincial house. The St. Paul school campus was extended by purchasing the adjacent plot of land; for the stay and medical treatment of members Sagar Bhavan Thrissur had an additional building with a beautiful chapel. At Kareli and Kheri houses were constructed for the OSF, CMC Sisters who were working in the schools. Chavara Bhavan Kheri was constructed for the residence of CMI fathers.

"Here I would like to mention one principle of administration, I learned from experience: "Bend without breaking". This is not a question of compromising values or basic principles. Rather it means that we shall not be adamant and inflexible in front of opposing views and opinions, leading to a break up of relationship. It is this positive attitude of tolerance and submission to Providence that paved the way for the phenomenal growth of the province."

14. Harbinger of Reconciliation in Sagar Crisis

Though CMIs have started the Sagar Mission, they had to face challenges from the second Bishop who had very specific understanding of authority in the church. "I came to know during my life in Ashta that the Sagar Bishop of the times was a person of fixed views and so likely to be a man of prejudices. Therefore, during my first tem of office as Provincial (1999-2002), I tried my best to keep a dialogical approach to him. I have sat hours before him more than once and listened to his complaints about the CMI fathers of the diocese and about the status quo of RDSS, Silwani. I hoped that this friendly approach would ease the tension and more positive relationship between him and the province could be created. However this did not take place, although it helped to keep a certain balance without allowing the relationship to deteriorate. Therefore in my second term (2002-2005), I had no sympathy for him, but questioned him calmly without being charged with emotions with regard to his attitude and behavior on several occasions.

When I look back on the growth of St. Paul Province, Bhopal, my tenure of the office of provincial may be seen as one of restoration of peace and a process of building confidence of the members in their self-worth and resourcefulness."

15. A Messenger of Reconciliation

There were some conflicts in the archdiocese of Bhopal as a segment of the clergy were against the new administration. Court cases were filed and there was growing ill-will among clergy. Various attempts were made but there was no tangible reconciliation. It was at this juncture Fr. Louis could arrange for batch-wise retreat in Yesu Ashram Padaria in which all priests took active part. The deal was clinched but for a little resistance from one section. However, most of the misunderstanding and accusations were shared and rectified through these graceful sessions. It was a providential intervention that brought about peace and harmony in the diocese once again.

When we look into the entire life history of the person of Fr. Louis, we can see that he was a person of great discernment. He himself has undergone the kenosis through his openness to others. He has also tried to be a messenger of peace and reconciliation by involving to mediate in various crisis ridden instances and proved his mettle for the love of the Church and people of God. His legacy involves a staunch belief in the providence of God, discerning it and committing to fulfil it faithfully. Through the eyes of faith he read the signs of the times and contributed to the building up and nurturing of an Indian Church bereft of its western garb.

PART V

UNPUBLISHED ARTICLES OF FR. LOUIS MALIECKAL

17

From Dharmaram to Khrist Premalay Ashta MP Story of the CMI Legacy of Major Seminary Formation

Fr. Louis Malieckal

Introduction

On the occasion of the Diamond Jubilee of Dharmaram College, as one of the earliest students, belonging to the 2nd/ 3rd batch (1958/59), I am delighted to present this short write-up on my Alma-Mater focusing on its legacy in the field of religious-priestly formation. I shall begin making a brief review of the road it travelled from the Malpanate system of the Founding Fathers through Pallipuram-Mannanam-Chethipuzha to Bangalore. I shall then move on to KPRT, Ashta focussing on its birth and growth until our withdrawal, rather unexpectedly.

1. Priestly Formation in Kerala from the Time of St. Chavara

The system of local/parish level training of candidates to priesthood continued for a long time , till about 1854, when Vicar Apostolic Bernadine Baccinelli suppressed the local/parish level malpanates and established instead four seminaries at Mannanam (1833), Vazhakulam (1866), Pulincunnu (1868) and Elthuruth (1872), all attached to the emerging T.O.C.D (later C.M.I) monasteries. Later they were correlated with the newly started common major seminary at Puthenpally for all Kerala under the direct supervision of the vicar apostolic and administered by the missionaries.[188]

188 Cf. Mathias Mundadan, *Blessed Kriakose Elias Chavara*, Dharmaram Publ., Bangalore, 2008, p. 245.

From the above, it can be seen that at the time when Chavara studied for priesthood, the malpanate system was much in vogue and Fr. Thomas Palackal was his malpan, who began teaching since 1818 at Pallipuram with six students, and young Kuriakose was one among them.[189] Fr. Palackal, before becoming malpan at Pallipuram, was long secretary to the vicar apostolic of Verapoly from 1808 t0 1816, and also ever since consulter to the vicars apostolic. In both these capacities he gained the esteem and love of his superiors and associates alike. Hence, as malpan of the seminary he commanded respect and affection of his disciples like St. Chavara. It was with great thirst for knowledge and with an open universal outlook, that he formed the priest candidates, studying under his care.

1.1. St. Chavara as Malpan and Rector

Our saint had been playing an important role in the formation of the seminarians as Professor even before the demise of Fr. Palackal. Even as Deacon in the Pallipuram seminary, Chavara had some experience of teaching and managing the seminary affairs, because Fr. Palackal (Rector) used to entrust the charge of the seminary in his absence to young Kurakose, including the task of giving some lessons to his classmates, as attested by Fr. Philip Koyipallil.[190] And after the death of his Guru, Malpan Palackal, Msgr. Francis Xavier, Vicar Apostolic of Varapuzha, gave Chavara in 1844 the patent letter constituting him as Malpan, and also as Examiner of the priests of the Syrian rite of the Vicariate to give them approval for hearing confession and for preaching in the churches.[191]

From the history of formation of priest-candidates in Kerala at least from the time of the CMI Founding Fathers, as has been explained above, it is well known that the CMI congregation holds a heritage of training candidates to priesthood, both diocesan and religious. And this formation has always been context—friendly and culture-oriented.

2. Contextualized Priestly Formation: Legacy of the Founders Re-visited

When the almost 200 year-long history of priestly formation in the CMI congregation is carefully gone through,[192] it can be seen that at all stages of its onward movement, it has always been context-friendly and culture-bound, as we have already noted. The malpanate style of training the candidates under the well-known Malpan Fr. Palackal at Pallipuram (1818) was according to

189 Ibid. P. 57

190 Cf. *Short Biography of Rev. Fr. Kuriakose Elias Chavara....*,Pulincunnu, 1929, p. 6

191 Cf. *Collected Works of Chavara* (CWC), Vol. I, p. 46.

192 The period of 200 years is calculated from 1818 (Pallipuram seminary) to the present day.

the general Gurukula pattern of training the seekers (sadhakas) in the whole gamut of Vedic Hindu tradition. The first Syro-Malabar common seminary established in 1833 at the monastery Mannanam inherited this style of formation and carried it forward through Fr. Porukara and St. Chavara. But, soon followed the sad event of the death of Malpan Porukara in 1846, and then Chavara was left alone to bear the huge responsibility of carrying forward a number of unfinished dream-projects and programmes .

The tradition established at Pallipuram by the great Malpan Fr. Palackal which was continued at Mannanam and other seminaries attached to the monasteries by his colleagues and trusted disciples like Chavara, marked a new paradigm shift in the theological education among the St. Thomas Christians. These centres of sacred learning were accepted by the authorities as competent to produce excellent results, replacing the many local seminaries.

An indigenous printing press, an indigenous monastery (religious community life) and an indigenous Church authority, were three streams of a holistic process of incarnating an indigenous Church in Kerala envisaged by St. Chavara. He saw that, in order to deeply influence and win the respect of the people, the priests must have good knowledge and spiritual insight. Only then would they be able to integrate Christian theology into the Indian context. He must have been aware that in Kerala, the proud inheritor of Adi Sankara's footprints, timid preaching by untrained priests would not create a social, cultural and spiritual synergy. Rather, he thought of a set of trained scholarly priests, who were competent in blending Christian theology with the traditional Indian spiritual outlook. Thus we find, the priests who were trained in the Mannanam seminary were Chavara's trusted lieutenants in fighting against the Roccos schism which almost eclipsed the Church in 1861.

2.1. CMI Contextualized Priestly Formation: From Chethipuzha to Bangalore

For some time after 1887, the CMIs made use of one or another monastery to cater to the educational requirements of its candidates, but finally both philosophy and theology courses were given at Chethipuzha, till in 1957 the scholasticate was transplanted to Dharmaram Bangalore. The growth of this central study house of the CMIs Dharmaram College from its rather modest beginning in 1957 has been phenomenal during the past more than fifty years as it is going to celebrate its 60th year (Diamond Jubilee) in the next year 2017. Several thousands of young men to priesthood (CMIs, Non CMI religious and diocesans), having completed their priestly studies and formation, have crossed the portals of this institute to serve the Church in various capacities and in her different needs. Thus St. Chavara's vision of systematic formation of priests for the Church has been fulfilled to a great extent.

Moreover, shifting of the location from Kerala to Bangalore - a multi-cultural metropolitan city outside Kerala, as well as the change of name of the institute as Dharmaram ("Garden of Virtues") was a significant step in realizing further the vision of St. Chavara through context-friendly actions in order to suit the emerging requirements of mission outside Kerala, viz in India at large and abroad eventually.

It may be noted that the opening of a secular college (Christ College which is now Christ University) in the year 1969/70 close to Dharmaram College was intended by the CMI visionaries like the late Bishop Jonas Thaliath to integrate secular studies with theological education of the priest-candidates in the light of the Council's directives on renewal and updating of Church institutions in general and priestly training in particular.[193]

3. Favourable North India Church-Context to Start KPRT, Ashta

Thus CBCI produced a provisional draft with the title *Programme of Priestly Formation in India* (PPFI) in the year 1971, which was prepared in the light of the Council's teaching on the issue and following the recommendations of the *Ratio Fundamentalis* issued by the Congregation of Catholic Education in 1969. The document PPFI was further revised and updated to suit the context of the Hindi-Belt in the next meetings of the Bishops in Ranchi in 1979 and in Patna in 1980. The final draft contained several recommendations proposed by the Rectors of the Hindi-region emphasizing "missionary formation" of priest-candidates of the major seminaries. It is largely in the light of these recommendations that Khrist Premalaya Regional Theologate (KPRT), Ashta was started in the year 1982/83.

3.1. The Enterprise of Establishing KPRT, Ashta, M.P.

When the M. P. bishops decided to start a Regional Theologate under the name Khrist Premalaya (KPRT) in the spirit of the Council and the particular vision articulated by the regional consultation called Priestly Formation in North India (PFNI), the question of who could be entrusted with the task of effectively running the seminary appeared to them unanswerable for quite some time. Archbishop Eugene D'Souza of Bhopal, after having failed to elicit any positive response from other religious orders/congregations working in

193 Soon after the Council's closure in 1965, the CBCI organized the well-known **All-India Seminar on Church in India To Day** in the year 1969 in Bangalore of which the main venue was Dharmaram College. High on its agenda was the issue of transforming the post-colonial Church in India into an Indian Church. Since the kind of Church-renewal envisaged by the Council depended in large measure on the quality of priests who would serve the Christian community at various levels in the Church, there have been steps taken officially in the Church, since 1970 for the renewal of Church structures and institutions bearing directly or indirectly on priestly formation and theological education at large.

M.P. and elsewhere in North India, sought the help of the CMIs to take up the task of running the proposed regional major seminary in the context of the undivided M.P. state, responding to the clarion call of Vatican II. It was the year 1982/83, when Dharmaram College, 25 years after its establishment in 1957 had grown mature enough in the field of theological education and priestly formation in tune with the vision of the Council. Naturally the Prior General Fr. Thomas Aykara of the CMIs must have looked hopefully towards Dharmaram College before taking a decision in this regard with the consent of his team of Counsellors. Finally he "as a successful religious leader"[194] took the bold step of committing to the challenge thrown up by the Archbishop Eugene. Surely in doing so, he must have tried to foresee the consequences and implications of the steps forward in terms of the required CMI personnel, competent and resourceful in matters of academics, formation and administration of this new Major Seminary for the whole of the undivided Madhya Pradesh Church.

3.2. Dharmaram and Khrist Premalay: Story of Their Connectivity and Influence

After its formal opening in July 1982 in Arera colony Bhopal with just six students and three CMI staff-members,[195] KPRT was shifted within 10 months to the rural context of the township called Ashta in the spirit of the original vision of the seminary and was housed in the existing simple structures of country-tiled roofing in the midst of a cluster of villages, when this writer joined the group in May 1983, making the strength of the staff four.[196] From the letter of Fr. Aykara, referred to here, we may be able to guess the contribution of Dharmaram at the initial stage of KPRT's emergence as a Regional Theologate. The core team consisting of Frs. Eustace, Raymond and Prasad were experienced alumni of Dharmaram, especially Fr. Eustace who has been Rector of Dharmaram. While this trio was resident staff, a certain number of visiting staff from Dharmaram would support them going there to take classes

194 See my article "Profile of a Successful Religious Leader", in Thomas Kollamparampil etal Eds. *Power of Positive Presence (Festschrift in Honour of Prof. Dr. Thomas Aykara CMI)*, Dharmaram Publications: Bangalore pp. 111-128.

195 Fr. Eustace Thottan CMI (Rector), Fr. Raymond Mancheril, CMI (Administrator) and Fr. Prasad Puthukulangara, CMI (Spiritual Director) were the original staff-members.

196 Let me quote here some relevant portion of the letter, which Fr. Aykara wrote to me to Lovain, where my study was being completed, assigning me to KPRT. "........As you know perhaps, since 1982 we have taken up the core administration of M.P. Regional Theologate in Bhopal. We have sent a team of three permanent fathers: Eustace (Rector), Raymond and Prasad and other visiting professors from Dharmaram. M.P. Bishops are extremely pleased with their performance. Taking into account the shortage of resident professors I am assigning you to this community as Professor of Theology. Hope, you will have no objection. You will also teach at Dharmaram as visiting Professor......." (Ref. No. PG 265/83 d. 5th May 1983).

as and when required. At the same time the number three of the resident staff was certainly inadequate to run the seminary in its full swing. Hence Fr. Prior General was surely on the lookout for finding some more CMI staff members to add to the core team. That is why he, knowing well this writer's academic background and other areas of interest, straightaway added him on to this core staff, making a thoughtful as well as 'tactful' comment, "Hope, you will have no objection" in the letter of appointment sent to Louvain.

Thus the pioneering team at Ashta consisted of six students and four staff members including this writer. What sustained the team in that challenging situation in terms of the minimum conveniences and comforts of living, transportation, communication facilities, and health-care necessities, was the following enlightened comment, among other things, of one Hindu friend Dr. Raghuvamsh, Professor of Varanasi Hindu University, as recorded in the annals of KPRT:

> The Indian priests have not succeeded in identifying themselves with their wider Indian society. Because of their traditional life-style, they generally appear to belong to the well-to-do class. Till now on the cultural level too, they have been cut off from the Indian society even from the well-to-do class. Generally owing to their western life-style, eating habit and dress, priests are cut off outwardly, and because of their lack of acquaintance with the Indian culture, they are cut off inwardly too from the main cultural stream.[197]

For the next twelve years, until the CMIs withdraw from the scene in 1994 as desired by the higher authorities, transferring the responsibility to the in-coming religious congregation of the Pallotine fathers, there have been changes in the core team.[198] However we worked as a well-knit team of staff as well as students committed to 'doing theology' in the general vision of the Council, outlined in the Charter of Priestly Formation for India, and in particular according to the mission and directives presented in the PFNI. It may be noted that CMIs were not directly involved in discovering and formulating the vision and mission of this new Theologate in the spirit of the Council. It was very much the work of the Bishops of MP and major seminary formation personnel of North India. However we had to face squarely the question of their

197 P FNI, p.79.

198 Of the four members of the pioneering team at Ashta, three except this writer were transferred after three years, and new members appointed. At the end of a six-year period the contract with the M.P. Bishops was renewed for another six years more together with some other changes in the core team staff. Other staff-members of the core team, who joined later from time to time, were Frs. Simon Tharakan, Sebastian Perepadan, Paul Savio Puthussery, James Naduvilekutt and George Kaniarakath among others. However this writer had to continue till the end, twice being Rector from 1986 to 1994 for two terms of four years each.

implementation with appropriate methods and suitable programmes of action so that the goal of "formation for mission to be in mission" could be realized. I am happy to record here that we have been able to fulfil this "mission" in a remarkable way in the words of Archbishop Emeritus Paschal Topno:

> The vision of the bishops of Madhya Pradesh after Vatican II was realized by Fr. Louis and his devoted team of CMI professors in what is known as the action-reflection programme of theological training based on the living experience of the seminarians in villages and other life-situations. The results of this theological education are very encouraging. Many priests coming out of this Theologate personally opt for working in rural areas or among Dalits, tribals and slum dwellers. They develop a missionary spirit and love for the poor and the marginalized. Certainly Fr. Malieckal as the first Rector of Samanvaya has also inculcated the same spirit in this great institution.......[199]

4. Concluding Remarks

The story of the establishment of Khrist Premalay Regional Theologate, MP in the Silver Jubilee year 1982 of Dharmaram College (1957-82) by the Bishops of the undivided MP, entrusting its full administration with the CMIs for the next 12 years, and our withdrawal from it in 1994, in spite of our very successful administration, as attested by none other than a retired Ecclesiastical Head of that Church, as noted above, might be a point of reflection and research for the posterity, situating it especially in the Diamond Jubilee Year 2017 of the same CMI institution Dharmaram College.

---

199 Most Rev. Paschal Topno, S.J. "A Tribute to Fr. Louis Malieckal, CMI", in Davis Varayilan Ed. *Theology on Wheels: A Movement for Contextualized Theological Education* (Festschrift in Honour Dr. Louis Malieckal, CMI), ISPCK: Delhi, 2011, p. 328.

18

Contextualized Theological Education and Mission in India Since the Council Contribution of Samanvaya Theology College, Bhopal

Fr. Louis Malieckal

Introduction

Ever since the Council of Vatican II, with its forward-looking directives on priestly formation, in tune with its declared goal of *aggiornamento* "renewal & up-dating" of the Church and its institutions, traditions and practices, there have been several studies on the question of 'theological education in India'[200] reflecting on the various aspects of the question. If *aggiornamento* was the declared objective of the Council including the content and method of priestly formation and theological education, we need to cast at least a quick glance at the situation before the Council: The period of pre-Vatican formation and theological education can be divided into two and called pre-Tridentine and post-Tridentine periods. The first one can be suitably expressed in terms of the phraseterm "apprenticeship–model", namely, the seminarian will learn what may be called a 'catechism' theology under the sole guidance of the local parish priest in carrying out his priestly duty, understood at that time mostly in terms of cultic performances. In the 13th century this situation had given rise to the presence of "ignorant and unformed" priests.[201] The second one may be

200 The pertinent books and articles will be mentioned below in the course of our discussion.

201 In 1215 the IV Lateran General Council decreed punishments for bishops who ordained such priests. See Tanner N. Ed. **Decrees of the Ecumenical Councils**, vol. I (Nicaea-

called "bank deposit" model in which the theological education is just dumping information data into the minds of students who have no time or interest to assimilate them. Naturally such education will not challenge the students nor raise critical questions and consciousness in them, which is necessary to bring about social changes.[202] The thrust of the Tridentine decree on formation was to make sure the availability of a law-abiding and obedient group of clerics to do the bidding of the official Church.[203]

Against this back ground it can be seen that a number of the 16 documents of Vat. II reflect in their particular contexts of discussion on the need of well-formed clergy.[204] It is in the two major decrees *Optatam Totius* (OT) *and Presbyterium Ordinis* (PO) that we get the Council's specific proposals for up-dating priestly formation and theological education of the seminarians. In the light of these proposals and directives of the Council new trends in theological education began to take shape in the post-Vatican II renewal context of India.

In this paper therefore our presentation will be as follows: First we shall examine what the Council has said about theological education and priestly formation mainly through its two documents OT and PO. Then we shall see the impact of the Council teaching during the past five decades with regard to both the content and method of formation and education in the theological faculties and seminaries in India, and then we shall point out the contributions of the CMI Samanvaya Theology College during the past 20 years in the area of contextualized theological training and priestly formation. Finally we shall consider the importance of a theology in context for authentic mission of Jesus Christ in India.

Lateran V), Sheed & Ward and Georgetown Uni. Press, 1990, p. 248.

202 Paulo Freire distinguishes two types of education – banking type and problem-solving type. See his book, **Pedagogy of the Oppressed**, 45-50.

203 See canon 14 of Trent in Tanner N. Ed. op. cit. vol. II, p. 749.

204 Apart from the two major documents on priestly training , namely ***Optatam Totius***, (OT) Decree on the Training of Priests and ***Presbyterium Ordinis***, (PO) Decree on the Ministry and life of Priests, which we shall examine separately, there are occasional references in the following: ***Christus Dominus***, Decree on the Pastoral Office of Bishops in the Church, especially article 16 where we read "They (bishops) should therefore give their support to courses of study and arrange special conferences in which priests from tiem to time can meet together for undertaking a longer period of spiritual exercises for the renewal of their spiritual life and also for acquiring a deeper knowledge of ecclesiastical studies, especially sacred scripture and theology, the more important social questions and new approaches to pastoral ministry." ***And Ad Gentes,*** Decree on the Church's Missionary Activity, in which no.16 underlines the need of priests in mission countries and no. 20 the need for having renewal courses to up-date priestly formation.

1. What the Council has Said on Priestly Training and Theological Education

In this section we shall consider mainly the important texts from the documents concerned, accompanied by a running commentary to highlight the question at issue. Taking note of the context of pluralism in the world-vision of the 20th century in general, which was quite different from that of the period between I and II Vatican,[205] the Council directed local Churches and Rites spread out through different nations to work out separate programmes of priestly theological education and formation suited to their contexts. Let us listen to the Council Fathers:

> In such a great variety of peoples and regions only general laws can be laid down; so in each nation and rite a special 'programme of priestly formation' is to be initiated and determined by the Episcopal Conferences. The said programme is to be revised at suitable intervals and approved by the Apostolic See; thereby the general rules may be adapted to the special circumstances of time and place; so priestly formation may always match the pastoral needs of those regions in which their ministry is to be exercised. (OT 1)

In the following few sections of this documents the Council offers directives and remarks on how to foster priestly vocations, make changes in the courses taught in major seminaries, revise the curriculum of ecclesiastical studies, give more care to spiritual formation, and to pay special care for pastoral training and on-going formation. Thus the document says that in major seminaries "training of the students should have as its object to make them true shepherds of souls after the example of Lord Jesus Christ." (OT 4). The document then speaks about the need of training in the threefold ministry of the Word, sacrament and shepherd. For this the Council lays stress also on the importance of "competent educators" and "professors" who should be "chosen from the best and should receive a careful preparation in sound doctrine, suitable pastoral experience and special training in spirituality and teaching methods." (OT 5). After emphasizing spiritual and pastoral training, the Council asks that the ecclesiastical studies be revised. However the Council insists, "Before seminarians commence their specifically ecclesiastical studies, they should already have received that literary and scientific education which is a prerequisite to higher studies in their country." (OT 13)

---

205 Towards the end of the 19th century efforts were made to revise Thomism which was the only accepted category of thinking in the Church. Pope Leo XIII's encyclical ***Aeterni Patris*** (1879) bears witness to this fact. Thomism/Neothomism and its ontology had to deal with a fast-evolving world; its ability to respond adequately to existential questions was limited.

It is the document *Presbyterium Ordinis* which dwells specifically on the ministry of priests as participation in the bishop's office of service (PO 2), which in *Lumen Gentium* has been set forth as comprising threefold action of preaching the word of God, administering the sacraments, especially the Eucharist and governing or shepherding the people of God, the Church (LG 25-27; PO 4-6). In PO 19 focus is on the need of pastoral experience strengthened by sufficient knowledge of secular affairs in order to be animators and facilitators for the people in their daily problems and difficulties. Let us look into the relevant portions of this document:

> Moreover, if priests are to give adequate answers to the problems discussed by people at the present time, they should be well versed in the statements of the Church's *magisterium*.......They should also consult the best approved writers on the science of theology..Secular culture and even sacred science are advancing at an unprecedented rate in our time. Priests are therefore urged to adequate and continuous perfection of their knowledge of things divine and human. In this way they will prepare themselves to enter with greater advantage into dialogue with their contemporaries.
>
> To facilitate study and the more effective learning of methods of evangelization and the apostolate, every attention is to be given to providing priests with suitable helps.....In addition, bishops, either individually or in collaboration with others should consider more effective ways of arranging that their priests would be able to attend a course of study at certain times, especially for a few years after ordination....... Bishops should also be careful to see that some priests devote themselves to deeper study of the sacred sciences. This will ensure that there will never be any lack of suitable teachers for the education of the clerics....... (PO19).

2. Impact of the Council in India on Contextualized Theological Education

Soon after the Council the Church in India organized the well-known "All India Seminar on Church in India Today" in the year 1969 in Bangalore in which about 600 people participated, representing all sections of the people of God – lay people, including sisters, priests, and bishops. During the seminar many issues pertaining to the life and mission of the three Churches in India were discussed. High on the agenda was the issue concerning the transformation of a post-colonial Church into an Indian Church. It laid stress on spirituality, dialogue with other religions, evangelization and Indian culture, education, socio-cultural activities, communication media etc. But, at the seminar itself not much was said about priestly formation and theological education.[206]

206 Errol D'Lima, "Priestly Formation for Service to the World," in Jacob Kavungal et al. Eds. **Vatican II: A Gift and a Task**, St. Pauls Bandra, 2006, pp. 226-245, (235).

At the same time the implementation of the seminar's recommendations and resolutions in view of a renewal of the Church in the light of the Council would depend in large measure on the priests who served the Christian community at various levels in the Church. And it remained a moot point whether the traditional mode of training priests would equip them for the task ahead. Therefore since the year 1970 there have been several steps taken at official levels of the Church in India for renewal of Church structures and institutions concerning directly or indirectly priestly formation and theological education at large.

2.1. Priestly Formation in India: Steps Taken by CBCI and its Commissions

The Catholic Bishops' Conference of India (CBCI) produced a provisional draft with the title "Programme of Priestly Formation in India" (PPFI) in the year 1971, which was prepared by the '*Commissio Technica* for Seminaries set up by CBCI. **It may be seen as the first concrete and substantial outcome of the Council's theology concerning priestly formation.** This was prepared not only in the light of the Council's teaching on the issue but also following the recommendations of the *Ratio Fundamentalis* issued by the Congregation for Catholic Education in 1969. It begins the discussion of priestly formation by situating priestly vocation in the context of the Christian vocation in general.[207]

All vocations in the Church are manifestations of the riches of Christ and so have to be esteemed and fostered by the whole Church. Priestly vocation has to be seen against this wider background of the Christian vocation which is rooted in the sacrament of baptism, making every Christian an instrument of the realization of God's Kingdom. It is the work of the Holy Spirit who distributes his gifts to each one for the building up of the Body of Christ.

Therefore, it follows that the theology of Christian vocation needs to get sufficient importance in the curriculum of the seminaries and faculties of the formation institutes concerned.[208] It can be seen that in the vision of the above document the priesthood envisaged by the Council could be better described as a service to the people than as exercise of power (*potestas ordinis*) for confecting the sacraments., as Errol has rightly remarked in the said article.

a. Towards a Charter of Priestly Formation for India

Meanwhile the said 'Programme of Priestly Formation for India' was passing through a stage of experimentation, being tried in some seminaries at least in a limited way. Moreover, it was felt that there was need of regional consultation

---

207 Refer to ***Ratio Fundamentalis Institutionis Sacerdotalis***, January 6, 1970: AAS 62 (1970), 321-384; also see Errorl D'Lima, art.cit.in J. Kavungal etal Eds. Op. cit. p. 235.

208 See *Ratio* p. 1.

on the matter, especially for the North Indian Region, before a revision of the existing 'programme of priestly formation'. Thus the question of a study on priestly formation in the Hindi Region was raised during the CBCI meeting at Ranchi in 1979, which was discussed in more detail at the next meeting of the bishops in Patna in the year 1980. And the same year January Rectors of this region who had met at Allahabad seminary decided to undertake a serious study of 'missionary formation' in the seminaries and a memorandum of recommendations was submitted to the bishops of the Region. The bishops endorsing the memorandum passed the following resolution:

> The Bishops of the Hindi Region fully support the desire of their Seminary Rectors to make a serious and systematic study of seminary Formation in this region in all its aspects, especially as regards the Formation of priests for the pioneering work of evangelization in the Missionary context of North India, including the study of any new set up required.[209]

Encouraged by the bishops' positive response, the Rectors met again in March next year 1981 and formed a working committee to draw up guidelines for the preparation of a wider consultation. A comprehensive questionnaire was widely circulated to different sections of the people of God - bishops, priests, religious, including the lay people who were approached through its publication in various Hindi magazines. All the views sent in were collated and organized systematically, and thus the proposed regional consultation was held at **Navsadhana, Varanasi** from Feb. 23 to Mar.1,1982.The fruit of this consultation came out as a series of recommendations on contextualized seminary training and theological education for the various stages from vocation campaign to priestly ordination and beyond. As for what concerns us directly, namely the major seminary formation, there are recommendations both on content and methodology, that the syllabus lacks Indian realities, Indian philosophy and theology, liberation thrust and social teaching etc. As for methodology, the Consultation recommends 'action-reflection-action'(see-judge-act) method, breaking up crowded seminaries to study houses of smaller numbers, conducting the said 'action-reflection' programme as part of the curriculum etc. Let us look into these recommendations:

> 1 We recommend the starting of a new formation set up with a s mall number of suitable students and competent formators with the mandate of working out new and integrated courses by test-teaching. A feasibility study of this project is to be initiated.11a
>
> 2 ....Apart from the ministries performed during the academic year, every seminarian be engaged in a period of intensive ministry for at least one

209 *Priestly Formation in North India, (PFNI): Problems, Challenges Hopes, Navsadhana, Varanasi, 1982,* Inroduction, p. 3.

> month each year, outside the holiday period.....and that this be taken up immediately from the coming academic year as a regular part of the seminary curriculum.11b.

It is largely in the light of these recommendations that KPT (Krist Premalaya Theologate) Ashta, was entrusted to the CMI Congregation by the then undivided MP bishops conference in the year 1982/83 with just six seminarians and four staff-members including this writer.

Two years later at its Nagpur meeting in 1984 the CBCI decided to revise the 'Programme of Priestly Formation for India (PPFI)' and write it in the form of a Charter. The CBCI entrusted the task to its Commission for Clergy and Religious. The Commission held wide consultations at the national and regional levels, including a special sociological survey study under the title **Priests in Perspective.**[210] This ended with a National Consultation, held in Chennai (Madras) in 1987 on Oct. 20-25. The fruit of this consultation came out as a First Draft of the proposed Charter of Priestly Formation for India which was sent to all bishops and all those involved in priestly formation for their comments and suggestions. Finally at its Kottayam meeting in April, 1988 the CBCI approved the draft after due corrections as the **Charter of Priestly Formation for India (CPFI),** offering general guidelines for the spiritual, intellectual, psychological and pastoral training of the future priests, allowing at the same time for adaptations according to the contexts, needs and traditions of different Rites, Regions, dioceses and religious Houses of Formation.[211]

The Charter deals with, among other things, the following aspects of formation: personal growth, spiritual development, integration of personality, intellectual and pastoral formation, formation in small groups with a Master for each group, periodic evaluation by the seminarian himself, his peers and the staff, sufficient exposure to Indian realities, being close to the people and sharing their cares and concerns. Besides, integration of philosophy and theology as found in the Indian context is envisaged.[212]

---

210 11a PFNI, p. 13, section F. Long-range Objectives

11b Ibid., p.14 (Section B/e)

Paul V. Parathazham, ***Priests in Perspective; Preliminary Report of an All India Survey***, JDV, Pune, 1987.

211 Cfr. **Charter of Priestly Formation for India**, by CBCI Commission for Religious and Clergy, Delhi,1988, p.4.

212 See also Errol D'Lima, art.cit. in J.Kavungal etal,eds. Op. cit. p. 237.

3. More Recent Official Directives on Priestly Training and Education

One of the significant Church documents on seminary training and theological education since the Council that was issued in 1992 by Pope John Paul II as his apostolic exhortation was *Pastores Dabo Vobis (PDV)*, that treated of priestly formation in the circumstances of the present day.[213] This document takes into account what the Council had said about priesthood and priestly training, about other Church documents dealing with formation as well as the results of formative experiments carried out in certain seminaries and institutes of theological formation. While the document dwells on the different areas of priestly formation – human, spiritual, intellectual and pastoral, following the Council, **special emphasis is laid on human formation, saying that it is the basis of all priestly formation and adds:**

> So we see that the human formation of the priest shows its special importance when related to the receivers of the mission; in order that his ministry may be humanly as credible and acceptable as possible, it is important that the priest should mould his human Personality in such a way **that he becomes a bridge and not an obstacle for others in their meeting with Jesus Christ** the Redeemer of man.. (PDV 43 emphasis added).

Speaking about intellectual formation of the seminarian, special mention is made about his theological education. It observes that the relationship between *magisterium* and theological education should not be one of conflict, but of cooperation because ultimately both "have the same goal: preserving the People of God in the truth which sets free and thereby making them 'a light to nations.'"[214] Besides, PDV considers the seminary as an educational community, built around people involved in formation, and notes that" the unity of the educators not only helps the educational programme to be put into practice properly, but also and above all, it offers candidates for the priesthood a significant example and a practical introduction to that ecclesial communion which is a fundamental value of Christian living and pastoral ministry."[215] These and other criteria of priestly formation set down in PDV were matters of scrutiny by Rome during the apostolic visitation of seminaries in India in 1997-99. The results of this visitation may be found in its report: General Norms and Recommendations, which were taken note of by the CBCI in its meeting in Jalandhar in February 2002, and decided to revise the CPFI (1988), incorporating these recommendations. The Revised Charter of Priestly

213 This exhortation is based on the material in preparation for and in the Synod of Bishops on the theme "The Formation of Priests in Circumstances of the Present Day", held in 1990.

214 ibid. 55.

215 ibid. 66.

Formation (RCPF) was issued in 2004 by Archbishop Peter Fernando on behalf of the CBCI. It is a comprehensive document, covering all aspects of priestly formation at different stages; its concern for formation in the Indian context is spelt out in practical directives.[216]

The Council's thinking on theological education and the response to it expressed by the National Seminar of 1969 gave momentum to a series of research seminars, think-tanks, ashram-living, experiments in liturgical celebrations, seminary training, inculturation of gospel message and so on. In particular the Indian Theological Association was founded in the year 1976, which ever since has been supporting efforts at creating a contextualized theology for India. Besides, the FABC (Federation of Asian Bishops Conference) having taken shape under the inspiration of Vat. II, supported the emergence of a Theology of Religions in the context of the reality of religious pluralism in Asia, after the visit of Pope Paul VI in 1970. Similarly, it also has been supportive of the emerging Theology of Liberation in the particular socio-economic context of Asia

4. Immediate Background of the Samanvaya Theology College

Before the Council there was not only any kind of method of theologizing talked about, but what was available in that category was also confined to a few massive institutes called major seminaries, where hundreds of priest-candidates were undergoing a kind of theological education which had hardly any bearing on the life in the outside world, almost like the under-trials within the four-walls of a massive central jail. "At that time the centres of theological education in India, whether Faculties or Seminaries, sometimes nicknamed as 'theological cemetries', were much more remnants of a colonial past, guardians of the status quo than centres of creative theologizing."[217] There was a need to make a clear distinction between priestly formation and theological education in the wake of the conciliar thinking. Many began to feel that if our seminaries and theological Faculties could be thrown open to all and if lay people were encouraged to study theology, lay theologians would certainly emerge and revolutionary contributions to the different branches of theology could be expected from them. Against this back ground different models of theological education began to emerge.[218]

216 Errol D'Lima, art.cit.in J.Kavungal et al, Eds. Op. cit. p.237f.

217 Felix Wilfred Ed. *Theological Education in India To day: Statement, Papers, and the Proceedings of the Eighth Annual Meeting of Indian Theological Association*, Pariyaram, Kerala, ATC, Bangalore, p.vii.

218 In this field, first comes the Jesuit Model of Regional Theologate Centres (RTCs). In its Decree in Formation their General Congress 32 (GS32) spelt out the methodology of forming the future Jesuits and said "Formation should be well integrated, sufficiently systematic, adapted to the exigencies of our mission and conducted according to the norms

For the following 12 years, until the CMIs withdrew from the scene, as desired by the higher authorities, in the year 1994, we worked as a well-knit team of staff and students, committed to 'doing theology' suited to the general context of North India, especially Madhya Pradesh.[219]

4.1. Samanvaya Model of Contextualized Theological Training in the Making

During the late 1980s and the early 1990s the CMI Congregation became increasingly aware of the need and relevance of the kind of new theological education and formation of its priest-candidates due to various factors in the field – the successful KPT, Ashta experience, challenges of the mission context of North India in which hundreds of CMI priests, including half a dozen bishops began to be engaged in a big way, examples of other agencies like the Society of Jesus with their meaningful RTC theological formation.

A slow but intense deliberation, discernment and multi-stage preparation at least since 1989 preceded the launching of this Theological College, "SAMANVAY", at Jagdalpur in 1994, the same year of our withdrawal from Ashta. What is characteristic of its theological education is its vision, method of learning and teaching as well as life-style. Of course all these still remain as unfulfilled ideals but sought after with more or less diligence by the communities concerned.

---

of the Church.......to establish critical dialogue between theology and human culture, between faith and the real questions and problems which occupy the minds of the people among whom we are sent to exercise our apostolate." Thus they started several RTCs, some of them still function very well now, but some others had to be closed down for various reasons. For details see P. Arokiadoss, "Regional Theology Centres and Formation of Christian Leadership", Antony Kalliath Ed. *Christian Leadership: The Shifting Focus in Theological Education, (*Bangalore: Dharmaram Publications, 2001), 288f.

A second important entry into this field was M.P. Regional Theologate (KPT) of which reference was already made above. It was put up in the premises of a small township, called Ashta on the road between Bhopal and Indore, housed in the then simple structures with country-tiled roof, that were till then used as the diocesan minor seminary almost in the middle of a cluster small villages. What sustained the pioneer-staff members, including this writer, in this venture was the following enlightened comment, among other things, of Dr. Raghuvamsh, professor of Varanasi Hindu University, as recorded in the above-said Consultation volume "Priestly Formation in North Indi" as follows:

The Indian priests have not succeeded in identifying themselves with the wider Indian society. Because of their traditional life-style, they generally appear to belong to the well-to-do class, Till now, on the cultural level too, they were cut off from the Indian society even from the well-to-do class. Generally owing to western life-style eating habits and dress, priests are cut off outwardly, and because of their lack of acquaintance with ther India culture, they are cut off inwardly too from the Indian cultural strream (PFNI, p. 79).

219 For the vision, objectives and activities of KPT during these 12 years in particular see F. Wilfred Ed. Op. cit., pp.112-115.

The spirit of this theological experience and enterprise may be said to have been captured by the term "***Samanvayam***" (Integration/harmony/wholeness). *Samanvayena sakshatkarah,* says Bhagavat Gita. Only through an experience of wholeness and harmony within oneself and with creation can one attain God-realization. And theological education must lead a person to a holistic and harmonious experience of personal integration in which knowing, loving and doing (*jnana-bhakti-karma*) are united. The theological programmes and life-activities of Samanvaya are accordingly organized in view of attaining this goal. Hence the shifting of location of formation, starting with Jagdalpur, through Rishkesh, and Bangalore to Bhopal with in the four years of theology, in order to familiarize the students well with the Tribal context (socio-economical marginalization), authentic Hindu religious context (religio-cultural pluralism), modern cosmopolitan city context Bangalore) and towards an experience of integration in the Bhopal Centre of Samanvaya.[220]

a. Samanvaya Programme During the Past Twenty Years

"Samanvaya" is basically a programme of theological formation, not institution-bound, but community-oriented, though academically it is an extension centre of Dharmaram Vidya Kshetram, (DVK) Bangalore.[221]

b. Special Features

We may briefly describe here some of the special features of samanvaya, which are necessary for contextualized theological formation.

i. Small Communities with Shared Responsibilities

The student-community for every year consists of 15 to 20 candidates. This pattern facilitates involvement and interaction of every member. It helps also personal growth through good participation in the community life and sharing of responsibilities. Some concrete measures are adopted in order to facilitates this process: Thus in the first year of theology, as they come from different backgrounds and experiences, through some group-dynamics programme genuine community atmosphere is created, and then they are properly introduced to the life-style and vision of Samanvaya through an orientation programme of about a week.

220 For a detailed presentation of these points see A. Kalliath Ed., op. cit. pp. 309-324 (article by Fr. S. Elavathingal, the present Rector of Samanvaya).

221 For the special features of Samanvaya noted in the following pages, I am indebted to a great extent to Fr. Sebastian Elevathingal's presentation in *Theology on Wheels,* Ed. By Davis Varayilan, Delhi: ISPCK, 2011, pp. 312-318.

ii. Student Initiatives in Community Life

Students are offered enough opportunities to unfold their ideas and plans in view of their future ministries and fields of mission. This is very important for personal growth and confidence-building. Personal initiatives with a sense of mission are always encouraged and guidance given to work out their plans and pursue them consistently with responsibility and accountability.

iii. Atmosphere of Freedom and Mutual Trust

As Pope Francis has rightly sounded, "Formation is a work of art, not a police action,"[222] and he adds, "problems are not solved simply by forbidding doing this or that. To avoid problems, young people try not to make mistakes, follow the rules smiling a lot, just waiting for the day to get out, after getting the certificate: 'Good, you have completed formation.' This is hypocrisy which is the worst result of clericalism, one of the worst evils."[223] Knowing this very well Samanvaya, ensures an atmosphere of trust and confidence in the minds of students instead of adopting corrective measures for occasional failures and mistakes. Of course, trust has to be constantly verified and justified by transparency and accountability. For that matter, it is everybody's task, including the staff to offer verifiable behaviour of trust and credibility for the edification of the community.

Year after year, as the students are promoted to the following stages of formation, the style of monitoring changes gradually so that in the final year they are capable of doing it by themselves. The role of the resident staff members is not simply teaching the subjects assigned, but also to accompany the students in their all-round formation.

iv. Simple Life-Style

Simplicity is the key to contentment and happiness in life, and happiness in community life is the measuring rod of a student's genuineness and authenticity as a Samanvayite. Therefore, students have ample occasions to sort out their problems, to express their opinions and to present their needs privately or in community. Structures of an institutionalized life style, likely to stifle creativity, spontaneity and openness are given only comparatively less importance, whereas freedom is allowed to experiment fresh and uninhibited life-styles.

222 "Wake up the World": Conversation with Pope Francis about the Religious Life, Eng. Trans. By Antonio Spadaro, S.J, on line accessed on 12 January 2015.

223 Ibid.

v. Contextual Exposure

Being a programme of contextualized theological formation, Samanvaya offers direct exposure of students to concrete life situations, and this is an essential aspect of the method of theological formation. This method gives importance to the ability of students to raise questions, emerging from the contextual experience, which is considered to be the starting point of Post-Vatican II 'doing theology'. Thus academic inputs are not to be limited to giving ready-made answers to possible questions, but must take into consideration the questions emerging from the contexts. Thus learning and teaching become participatory, following a 'question-answer' method.

Three Moments of Contextual Theological Inquiry Are:

A. **Encounter and Insertion; B. Experience and Reflection; C. Interpretation and Action.** This threefold inquiry is applied in a threefold typical context of Indian life and every year of theological formation is programmed in such a way that students get an experiential-theoretical and practical knowledge of these contexts. Change of place of every year has its advantages; it enables the students to encounter new contexts with fresh starting points and chances of making new contacts with missionaries and their varied mission approaches. Samanvaya Coordinating Centre and he two other Regional Centres have their specific theological thrusts in their programmes according to the particular context of the three Centres.

1. Tribal and Subaltern Context of Jagdalpur

The first year of theology is spent in this context with the central theological theme "God and the World". And most of the course programme this year is circumscribed by this theme. It is to help to develop a theological vision of the world as the primary locus of divine self-revelation and the medium of divine-human encounter and communication.

Theologizing in this context means interpreting this world and its experiences in the faith-perspective in such a way that the divine significance hidden in them is revealed, making the world meaningful on the one hand and making the Word of God actual and relevant to the world on the other. Such a theologizing would naturally lead to meaningful expressions and their effective communications, if done adapted to the language and idiom of the people concerned. For, in all religious cultures, stories, myths, symbols, rituals and celebrations are normal means of such communications.

In this rural context students are invited to experience the elemental nature, the freshness of the environment, to cultivate and transform the earth, thus to participate in the existential struggle of the rural poor and to realize the spiritual potential of the physical and material reality. Apart from their constantly being in touch with the subaltern groups by visiting and interacting with the villagers, a three-week-programme of rural life experience (action-reflection-action) is an inevitable part of this theological education.

2. The Religious-Cultural Context of Rishikesh

The second year of theology is spent here in this context, centred on the theological theme Christ and the Human, and as in the first year, here also most of the course programme will rally round this theme. The theological vision to be developed during this year is a deeper understanding of the person of Jesus Christ, who as the Way, the Truth and the Life addresses the human dilemma and answers the human search.

The method of learning is to expose oneself to the traditions and faith-expressions of other religions, mainly Hinduism, Sikhism and Buddhism, and try to understand them with an unprejudiced and open mind. By encountering other traditions, dialogically, the students are invited to develop a critical and creative approach to their own beliefs and faith expressions, by asking themselves how they would live their own Christian faith meaningfully and effectively in the context of these age-old spiritual traditions.

During this one year, apart from visiting the numerous ashrams, ashram inmates, sadhus and gurus, the students also are supposed to visits the ghats and take part in the artis, bhajans etc., they stay for a few days in some ashrams and make a pilgrimage to dhams and places like Badrinath, Joshinat, Hemkund etc.

Theological input sessions are conducted by experts on subjects related to the central theme; ashram experiences and pilgrimages are preceded and followed by preparatory / evaluator discussions.

3. Social-Pastoral Contexts of Bangalore-Bhopal

The third and fourth year theology is spent in about three semesters of which first semester is in Bangalore and the other two in Bhopal, ordinations being in the middle of the fourth year. The entire programme is circumscribed by the theme The Holy Spirit and the Church. During the first semester of the third year in Dharmaram Vidya Kshetram, Bangalore, the infra-structure, academic facilities and the large academic community of the campus are suitable to give the students an academic atmosphere in which they can consolidate their theological inputs and delineate their theological vision, which was in the process of developing in the past two years. Besides, Bangalore gives a number of possibilities of pastoral engagements, especially among the migrant Catholics of the city.

During the second semester the students move to Bhopal to complete the final phase of their theological education. During this phase they are given occasions to experience the working of the Spirit of God in ecclesiastical communities and in the social lives of the people at large. This is meant to develop an attitude for pastoral care in them. In the perspective of the general theme of this period, students are expected to gain experiential knowledge of the spiritual dynamism of the Church's growth through different kinds of pastoral and social engagements. These experiences are deemed o elicit in them questions on the meaning and relevance of the materials they learn in the class rooms. All these will help them to select a proper theme for their B.Th. dissertation, more practical than theoretical, contextual than speculative, which in the course of time add to the development of Indian Christian theologies.

4. Theology in Context and Mission in Samanvaya's Vision

In our foregoing discussion of contextualized theology and theological education the target-group was clerical or priestly candidates, precisely because of the fact that theological education, as it stands to day, is intimately connected to the theological formation of hundreds of seminarians across the country. At the same time this theological enterprise cannot be tied down to a particular group of the people of God; rather it has to be made more popular among Christians of all walks of life. For, 'Theology in Context' or contextualized theology means a faith-vision of the world realities that would help every Christian to live an authentic life in the world, but not of the world.

Moreover, the ultimate goal of contextualized theological education is fostering the 'Mission' of Jesus, which is entrusted to the Church at large. But, we have to understand the meaning of 'mission' in its Kingdom perspective in the following manner.

4.1. New Evangelization: An Asian/Indian Perspective

Towards the end of his Petrine ministry, the Pope Emeritus Benedict XVI had tried to emphasize the concept of new evangelization, introduced by his predecessors. From the history of the Church we know that Christianity's encounter with peoples of Non-Asian continents has resulted in numerical expansion of the Church in a big way for various reasons.[224] But, unlike in the

224 When Christianity emerged as a state religion in the Roman Empire in the 4th/5th century, "it became a '**dominant power block**', not only on the religious landscape, but also in the political spheres, economic realms and cultural milieu. The officials of the Church gradually emerged as the administrators of the land until a religious feudalism evolved in Europe. All this meant that **Christianity, a religion which did not have to reckon with other religions, developed an aggressive attitude towards others**." This attitude adopted successfully the rule "*cujus regio eus religio*" (follow the religion of the ruler of the region) to convert the 'barbarian religions' of the Northern tribes of the then Europe, mercilessly destroying their rituals, customs and worship centres so that before the end of the first millennium the whole of Europe became Christian. The same pattern of religious conquest was adopted later during the colonial period successfully with regard to the local religions

case of Non-Asian religions, the Church has not been very successful in its traditional approach to evangelize the Asian/Indian religions. We know that, the hallmark of Asian/Indian religious history is the multiplicity of religions and their dialogical existence for thousands of years, accepting this diversity and pluriformity as part and parcel of the Asian/Indian reality, and without imposing any religion's specific view of faith on others to create a monolithic religious community in the land. **This towering reality of religious pluralism in India can never be ignored by Indian Christianity** which is only a small community of less than 3 %. Here it is not a question of changing tactics or strategy of evangelization, but of **trying to deepen our understanding of the mystery of salvation offered by God to humanity, to the Asian/Indian people in particular.**

4.2. New Evangelization: As Mutual Evangelization

In this context the concept of 'new evangelization' may be understood as above. This arises certainly from the principle of inter-religious dialogue well accepted by us since the Council of Vatican II. But, genuine dialogue in the context of religious pluralism as in Asia/India is not a mere strategy for evangelization, but part and parcel of, or constitutive dimension of it. **It means, mutual acceptance and enrichment as well as challenge of the faith claims of the dialogue partners is taken for granted.** It means, while Asian/ Indian religions also claim to offer salvation to its followers, while we in fact encounter sanctity/enlightenment/transcendence in persons like Buddha, Krishna, Ramana Maharshi, Ma Amrtanandamayi and a host of others, how can we presume that these religions are excluded from God's saving plan? Does not this claim challenge the traditional Christian claim of 'exclusive salvation' and 'unique Saviour'? In fact John Paul II had recognized this major difficulty with regard to proclamation of Gospel in Asia/India. He writes.

> ......This is a great challenge for evangelization, since religious systems such as Buddhism or Hinduism have a clearly soteriological character. There is also an urgent need for [Asian] Synod on the occasion of the Great Jubilee in order to illustrate and explain more fully the truth that Christ is the one Mediator between God and man [sic] and the sole Redeemer of the world......[225]

Discussing this point Dr. Pushparajan, a well-known lay theologian in India, comments," Neither the Asian Synod nor its consequent document *Ecclesia in Asia* has convincingly explained fully how the truth that Christ

---

of Africa and Americas. (cf. Edmund Chia, fsc, Ed. DIALOGUE: Resource Manual for CATHOLICS IN ASIA, (FABC-OEIA publication), ISPCK, 2002, p.101. (Emphasis added).

225 *Tertio Millennio Adv*eniente, 38.

is the sole Saviour could be clearly distinguished from the founders of those religions. **So there is all the more reason for the forthcoming Synod to tackle it squarely.**"[226]

It may be noted that in such an understanding of religious dialogue we are not using dialogue as a method or means for proclamation, **rather we are proclaiming the Gospel dialogically to free, intelligent people who have their own God-experience.** When in 1974 FABC had its first meeting on the theme of evangelization, it saw evangelization as the dialogue of the Word of God with the realities of Asia – massive poverty, diverse cultures and multiple religions. The bishops seem to have taken seriously God's way of self-revelation to his own people: He does not impose, but waits patiently for a free response of his people. We have many such instances in the Bible. And Jesus also followed the same way of Yahweh, of Abba, Father. He proclaimed love and forgiveness, but did not force people. For example he was sad when the 'young man' turned away and he cried over Jerusalem. But, he did not make use of tactics of economic or political power; rather he offered himself in sacrifice for the Father's cause.[227]

4.3. New Evangelization : Affirming God's Universal Salvific Will

The traditional Pre-Vatican zeal for 'saving souls' from a wicked world and for 'snatching souls' from the clutches of the devil was due to a mistaken notion of salvation itself and a wrong interpretation of some Gospel texts. e. g. Lk. 14: 23, which reads "Go out into the roads and lanes, and **compel people to come in**, so that my house may be filled." The phrase, "compel to come in," was used to force the Latin American people for conversion.[228] But, Vat. II corrects this traditional mindset by a celebrated text of GS as follows:

> Since Christ died for everyone, and the ultimate calling of each of us comes from God and is therefore a universal one, **we are obliged to hold that the Holy Spirit offers every one the possibility of sharing in this Paschal Mystery in a manner known to God. (GS 22)**.

This perspective of 'God's universal salvific will', affirmed here is reflected in several other Council documents.[229] It is true, the Council did not say explicitly about the **salvific value of other religions** as such, but only about their devout followers, and Holy Spirit's action on them. However this provided an opening to other reflections on profound interreligious dialogue as belonging to 'God's salvific will.'

---

226 Art. Cited p. 32f.

227 Cf. M. Amaldoss, "Evangelization as Dialogue", in *Indian Theological Studies,* vol. XLVIII, no.1, March 2011, pp. 34-49.

228 Cf. M. Amamldoss, art.cit. p. 36.

229 Cf. AG 2; NA 1; DH 2-3.

4.4. New Evangelization: Other Faiths as Facilitators of Divine-Human Encounter.

Following the Council's explicit opening in salvation to the believers of other faiths, post-Vatican theological thinking on the role of religions as such to facilitate salvific divine-human encounter is steadily gaining ground. **We can find two complementary approaches in this regard** – the *a priori* approach of Euro-theologians and *a posteriori* approach of the Asian theologians. **Theologians like Karl Rahner follows a theoretical (a priori) approach**, and says that "If God is really reaching out to everyone with saving grace, God can do this only in a human and social way, given the social nature of human beings. This can happen only through the religions through which the humans-in-society reach out to God in their prayers and rituals."[230] **The Asian theologians like D. S. Amalorpavadas, from their practical experience with these religions (a posteriori),** hold that, "God is reaching out to them in and through these religions;"[231] that "the Scriptures of other religions may be considered inspired analogously and used by us in our own reflections and meditation."[232] And that "we could also participate in each other's worship under certain conditions."[233]

4.5. New Evangelization: As Work of a United Front of All Religions

All the six areas of concern of the Lineament,[234] are not only concerns for Christian proclamation, but also are challenges to any religions of the world. No religion alone can face them effectively. What is needed therefore is formation of a United Front of Religions for which mutual cooperation through genuine dialogue is a must. Earlier (colonial) evangelization was like a one-way traffic from the 'haves' to the 'have – nots' on polar terms, putting Jesus in opposition to their 'saviour-gods' like Buddha, Krishna and others. The past evangelizers' dichotomous view of the world and superiority complex about their culture and religion made them blind to the richness of the local cultures and high spiritual practices.

Now that the Church's attitude and approach to Asian/Indian religions has changed positively, **the so-called new evangelization has to be based on**

230 K. Rahner, Theological Investigations, vol. V (DLT: London, 1969), p. 128, quoted by Amaldoss, art. Cit. p. 38.

231 See Gaudencio Rosales etal. (eds.) For All the Peoples of Asia, Vol. 1 (Claretian: Manila, 1997), 14, quoted by Amaldoss, ibid.

232 D. S. Amalorpavadass, (ed) Research Seminar on Non-Biblical Scriptures (Bangalore:1974), quoted by Amaldoss, ibid.

233 Paul Puthanangady (ed), Sharing Worship (NBCLC: 1988) quoted by Amaldoss, ibid.

234 These are the six areas: Modern secularist culture, degraded society, consumerist and hedonist media, profit-oriented economy, scientism and technologism, and terrorism-fundamentalism (see para. no. 2.1, p.4).

the goal of realizing the unity of the divine economy of salvation in which all these religions are integral components.

This way of understanding the task of evangelization is very important, for,

> One of the fundamentals of Christian faith is that all humanity is one family with one history and one destiny......So, the new evangelization for us [Asians/Indians] living in religiously pluralistic context, consists not in announcing the good news as opposed to other religions......... Instead it will acknowledge the ontic unity of all humanity in one Father, and recognize their own individual personalities as children of the same Father.....**At the same time it will certainly extend invitation to all believers to recognize the new spiritual reality made available to them in Jesus** Christ....[235]

Apart from the Council's recognition of such an approach to evangelization,[236] **Pope John Paul II in his Encyclical Mission of the Redeemer (RM) affirms the centrality of the Holy Spirit in the work of human salvation, and thus he brings out the link between Christianity and other religions.**[237] According to Pope John Paul II the Church's relationship with other religions is dictated by a twofold respect: "Respect for man [sic] in his quest for answers to the deepest questions of his life, and respect for the action of the Spirit in man [sic]."[238] As Amaldoss has rightly said, this is a very crucial statement by the Pope. Namely, we have to respect the freedom of God and the freedom of the people, which cannot be limited by any social and historical structures. And the implications of this for evangelization are very important: Although, the Pope's intention in writing RM was to re-launch "*mission ad gentes*" he had to admit that it has to take new forms: Though we believe that Jesus Christ is the only mediator this does not exclude other "**participatory forms of mediation of different kinds and degrees**" (RM 5). **The other religions can facilitate salvific divine-human encounter in a mysterious way known to God.**[239]

5. Concluding Remarks

1. From the limited response of the Hindus and Muslims to Christian mission, in spite of hard works and struggles of the missionaries, it would appear that mission in India/Asia in the traditional sense is one of the most difficult and least successful in the world.

---

235 Pushparajan, art. cit. p. 38 (Emphasis added)

236 For example see NA 2:2; 2:3a; AG 11 etc.

237 See RM 28, 29.

238 RM 28

239 Amaldoss, art. Cit. p.. 9; see also RM 10 (Emphasis added).

2. But, success or failure of mission could be ascertained from two different perspectives, **namely quantitative and qualitative**. Mission in the traditional sense of preaching the Gospel to people, converting and baptizing them seems to be a failure to a considerable degree. **This is from a quantitative/institutional/numerical point of view**. However, mission, in terms of change of hearts and minds, and transformation of Indian social structures as well as acceptance of Christian/human values of life, we can say that most, if not all, strata of the society have been positively affected and influenced, of course in different degrees under the impact of Christian mission. **It is estimated that the less than 3% of the Christian community in India has made an overall impact of 24% on the Indian population. This is a qualitative result of evangelization.** In this 3rd millennium the effort of the Church in India/Asia implementing the call for the Pope's 'new evangelization' program has to be **to increase this qualitative dimension of Christian mission**. All our apostolic works – education, health care, social involvement of diverse kinds – have to imbibe the spirit of Jesus' low profile, but penetrative and effective way of announcing the good news, **More concretely,** we shall withdraw as far as possible from prestigious and competitive fields of service, and **invest more and more personnel and resources in frontier ministries**.[240] A major chunk of people deserving our ministry in this area are those displaced by the nation's faceless development thrust.
3. In India we do not have the Euro-American "eclipse of God". Our challenge is the all-pervading religiosity, co-existing with colossal mass-poverty. **For us, therefore new evangelization would be not so much conversion of the un-evangelized, as re-conversion of the evangelized, of the Christians themselves. In other words, mission in India does not concern the object, but the subject himself[241] who should have renewed enthusiasm and zeal to make Jesus Christ widely known, loved and followed,** to tell the story of this Jesus, in words as well as effective deeds of loving service in such a way that our people would feel attracted to the person of Jesus, desire to know him better, love him deeper and follow him closer.

240 Frontier ministry could mean services done to the most neglected and vulnerable people in the society, like migrants, refugees, orphans, destitute, old people, rejected by families, mentally and physically differently enabled, those affected by HIV/AIDS, street/shelter children etc.

241 Cf. Mar Gratian Mundadan, "Theological Education for Mission in Context", in Davis Varayilan Ed. Op. cit. pp. 31ff, quoted from Augustine Kanajamala, "Redemptoris Missio and Mission in India", in *Redemption and dialogue*, Ed. William Burrows, New York: Maryknoll, 1993, p. 204

As for Samanvaya's role so far in disseminating this ideal of mission among the Christians at large, we have to admit, may be little or not significant; but it tries to do it indirectly through the priests-students, being formed in the above-mentioned post-conciliar understanding of mission, until the opportune time, when non-clerical lay Christians also could be incorporated into this theological education for mission in context.